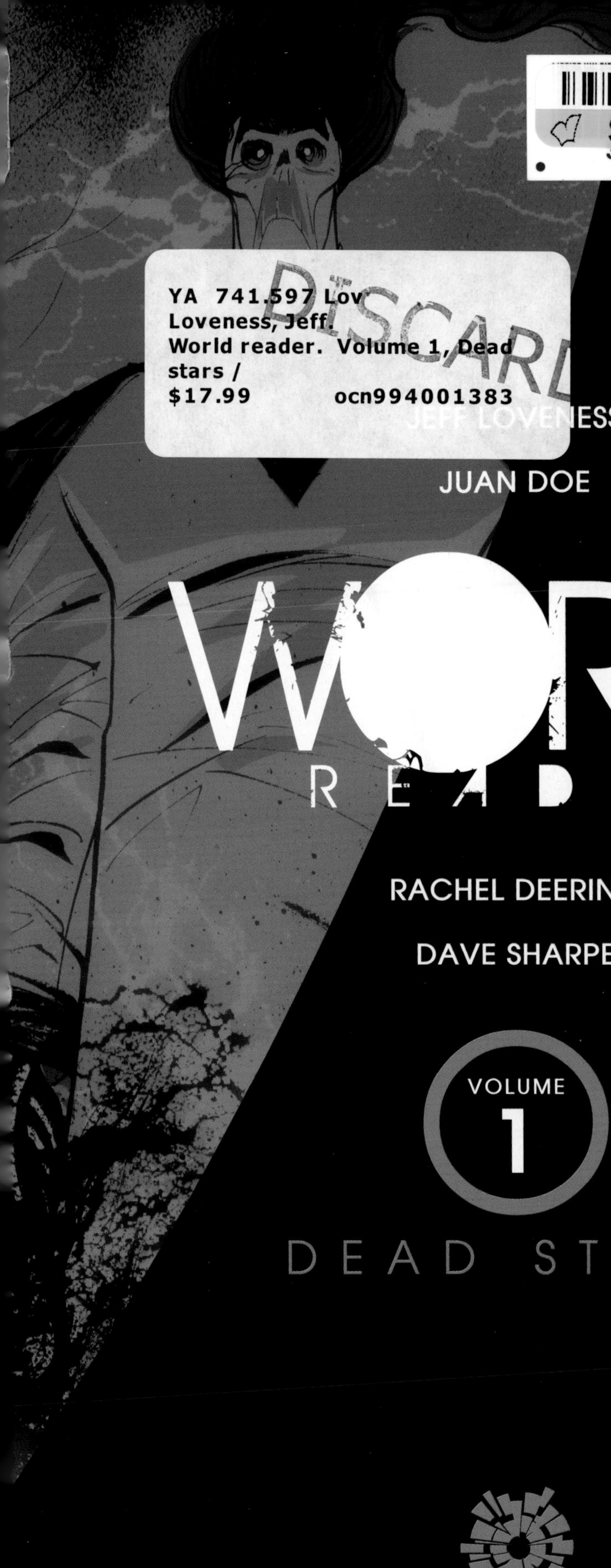

JEFF LOVENESS

JUAN DOE

WORLD READER™

RACHEL DEERING

DAVE SHARPE

VOLUME 1

DEAD STARS

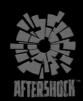

AFTERSHOCK™

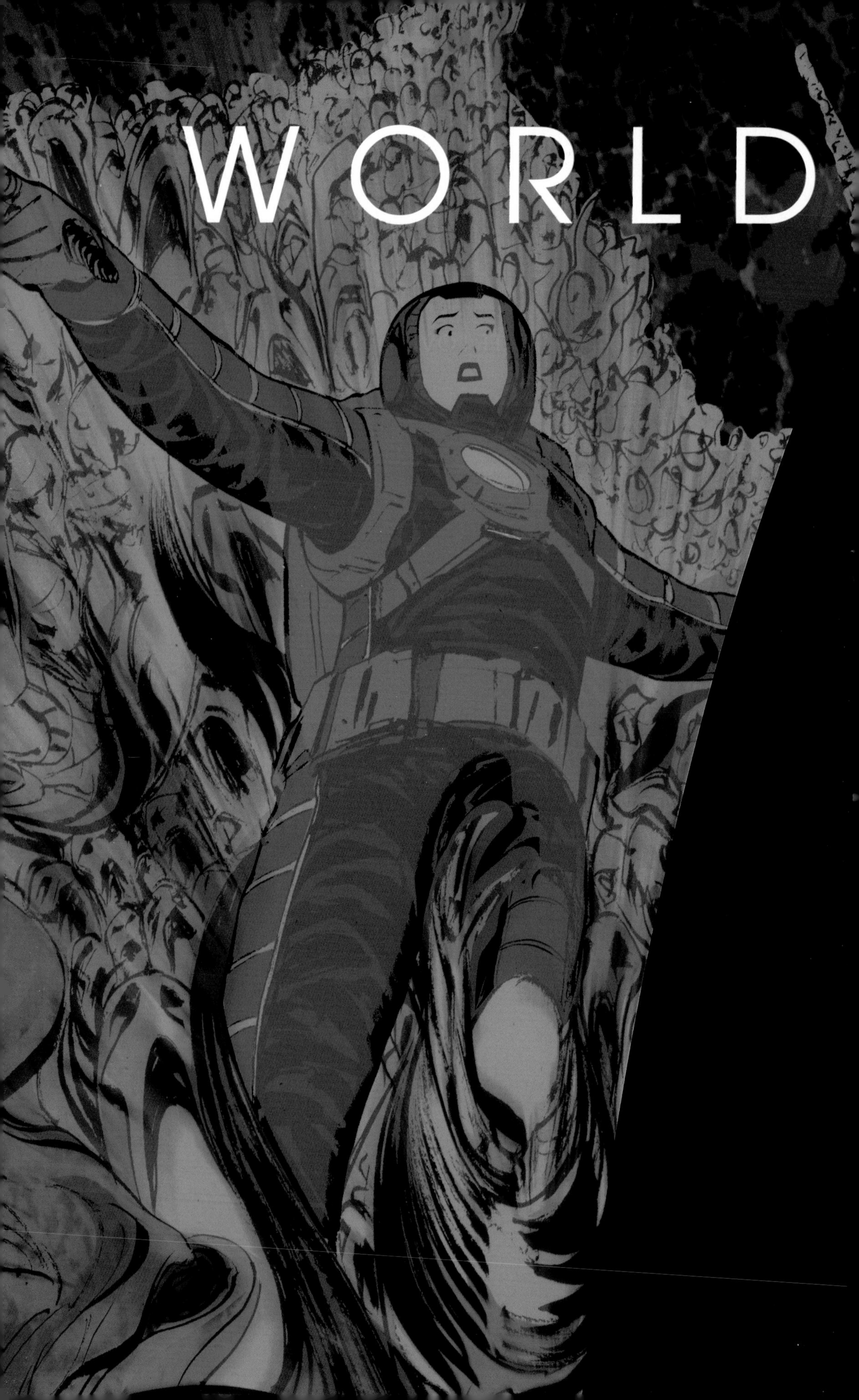
WORLD

READER
VOLUME 1
DEAD STARS

JEFF LOVENESS creator & writer

JUAN DOE artist

RACHEL DEERING (#1-3, 5) & **DAVE SHARPE** (#4 & 6) letterers

JUAN DOE front & original series covers

MIKE ROOTH & **ELIZABETH TORQUE** variant covers

JOHN J. HILL logo & book designer

MIKE MARTS editor

AFTERSHOCK™

MIKE MARTS - Editor-in-Chief • JOE PRUETT - Publisher/ Chief Creative Officer • LEE KRAMER - President
JAWAD QURESHI - SVP, Investor Relations • JON KRAMER - Chief Executive Officer • MIKE ZAGARI - SVP, Brand
JAY BEHLING - Chief Financial-Officer • STEPHAN NILSON - Publishing Operations Manager
LISA Y. WU - Retailer/Fan Relations Manager • ASHLEY WYATT - Publishing Assistant

AfterShock Trade Dress and Interior Design by JOHN J. HILL • AfterShock Logo Design by COMICRAFT
Original series production by CHARLES PRITCHETT • Proofreading by DOCTOR Z.
Publicity: contact AARON MARION (aaron@fifteenminutes.com) &
RYAN CROY (ryan@fifteenminutes.com) at 15 MINUTES
Special thanks to TEDDY LEO & LISA MOODY

AFTERSHOCKCOMICS.COM Follow us on social media 🐦 📷 f

INTRODUCTION

I've always had this story.

It was in a corner somewhere. An idea would arrive in the middle of the night or when I was in the shower. Sometimes I'd wake up with all of it. Sometimes I'd forget it. Sometimes I would scribble it in a notebook or tell a friend. Parts of it were in other stories, but I never quite got it all.

And finally, after a sad weekend where everything went wrong, I sat down and wrote it.

I've been a comedy writer for seven years now. I had never written anything like this. It was terrifying to do something so different than what I normally do. But then the terror became comforting, and that fear and comfort folded into the story. Because if there are other worlds out there, then there must be other people, like us. And maybe they're going through the same problems we are. Maybe they're looking up and feeling just as alone and uncertain about themselves. And even if we never meet, there's comfort in that. We're all reaching in the dark, but ultimately, we're reaching towards each other.

So, all that is to say, if you've got a story, and it's been bugging you for years, find a sad weekend for yourself, and write. Also, please get Juan Doe to draw it. He's gonna nail it. And also, here's an Audre Lorde poem that helped this story along the way. She's a much better writer than I am:

"And in the brief moment that is today
wild hope this dreamer jars
for I have heard in whispers talk
of life on other stars."

Now I need to find another story. I hope you like this one, and find many of your own.

1

"THE STARS BEFORE US"

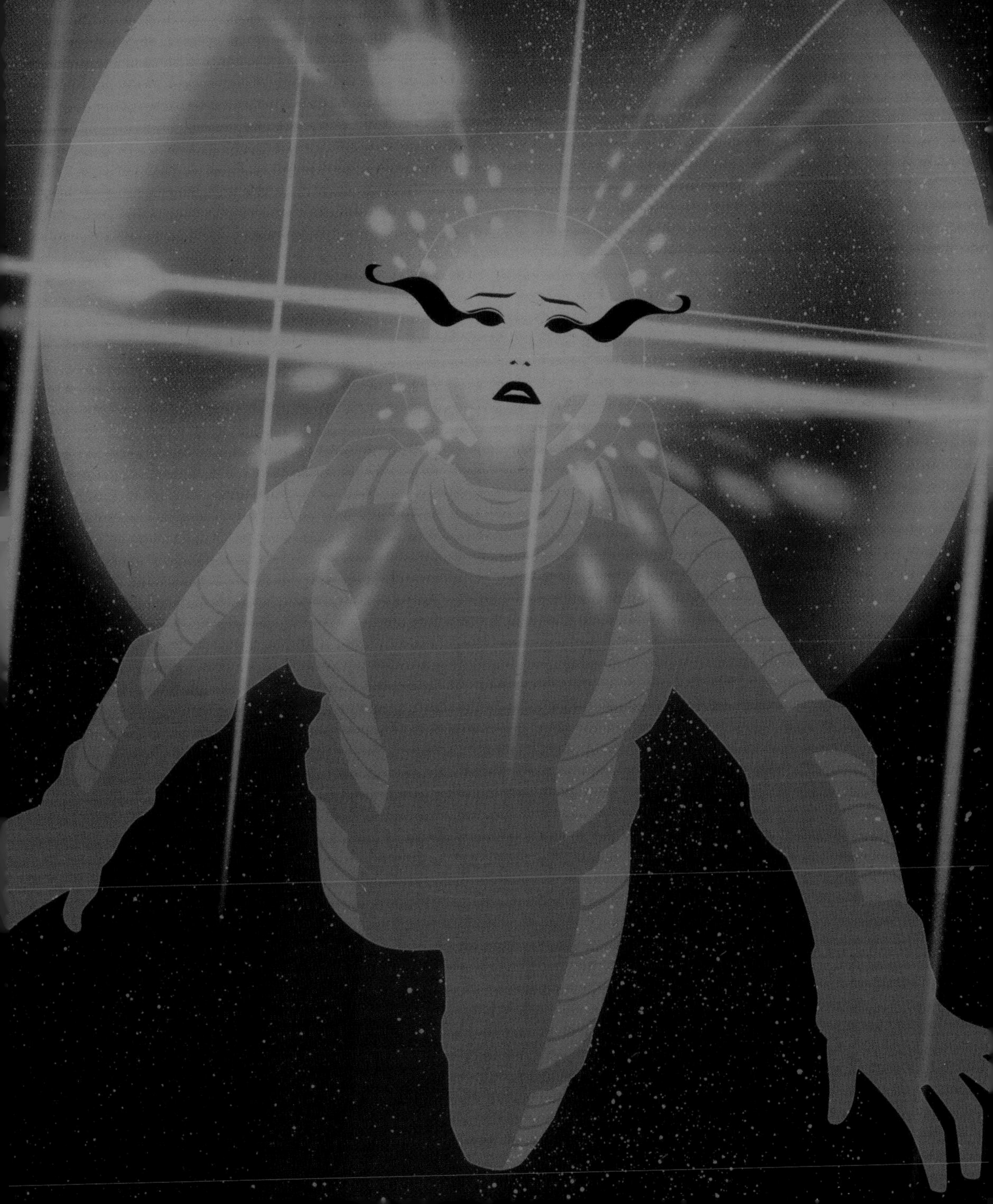

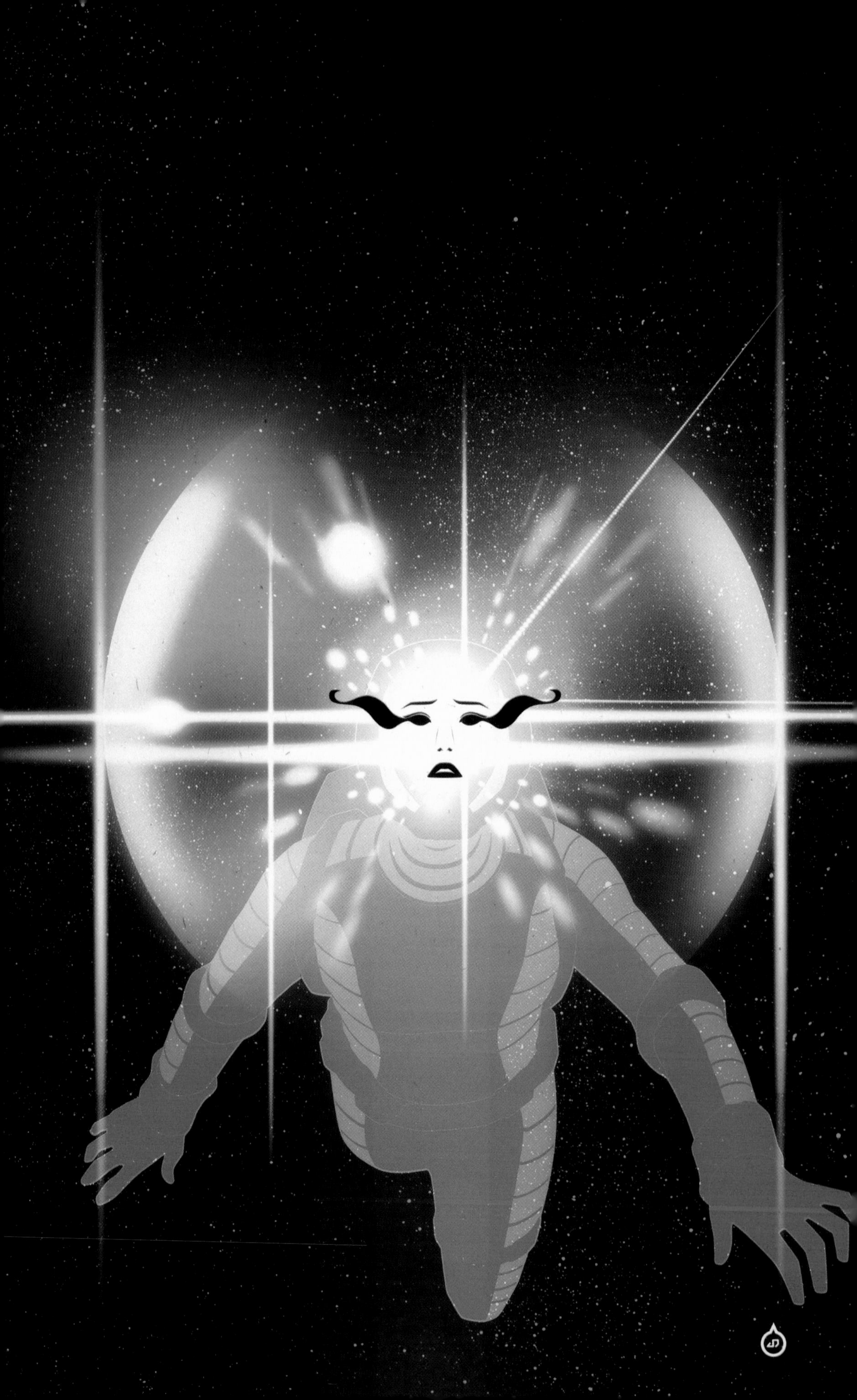

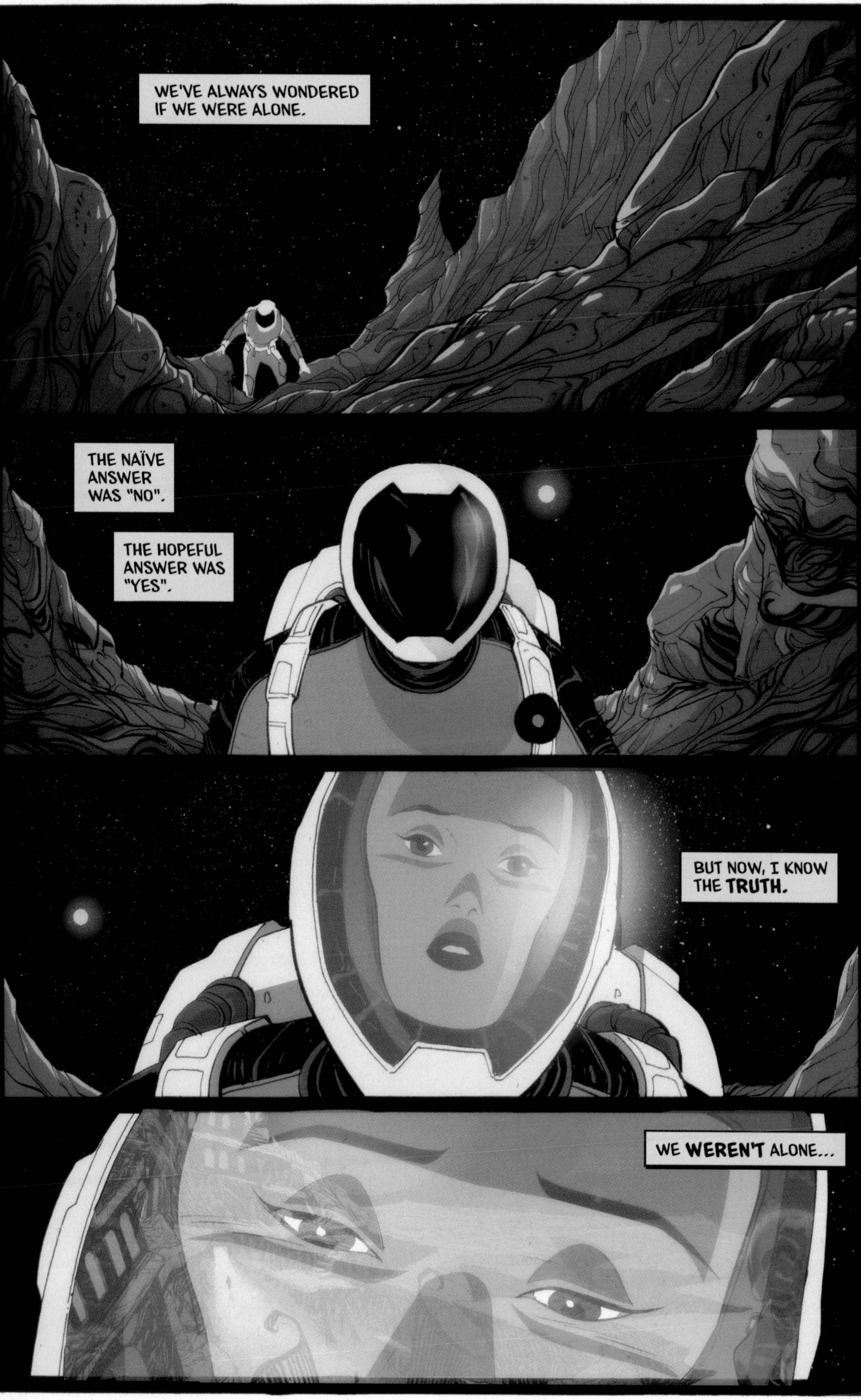
WE'VE ALWAYS WONDERED IF WE WERE ALONE.
THE NAÏVE ANSWER WAS "NO".
THE HOPEFUL ANSWER WAS "YES".
BUT NOW, I KNOW THE **TRUTH.**
WE **WEREN'T** ALONE...

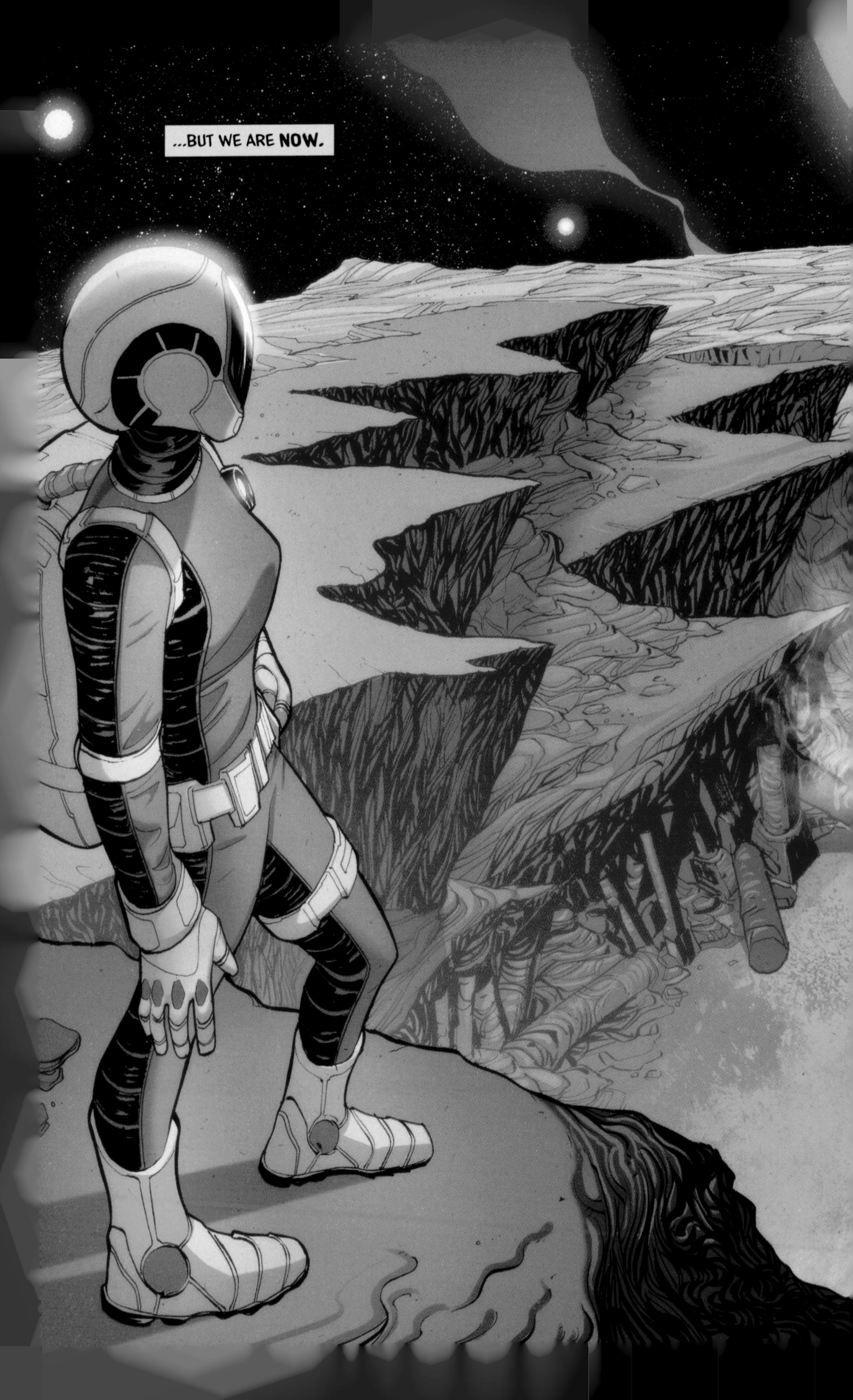
...BUT WE ARE NOW.

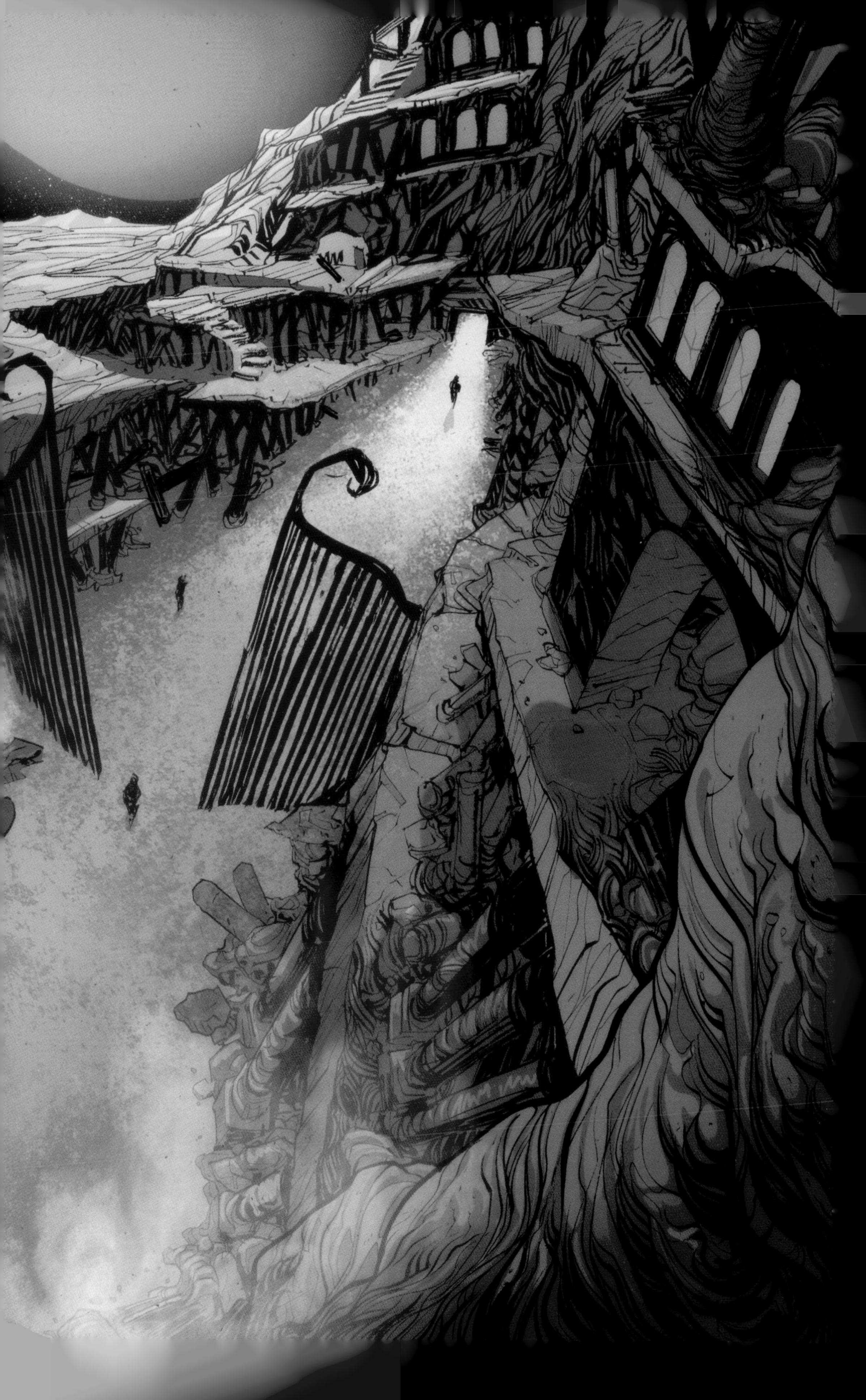

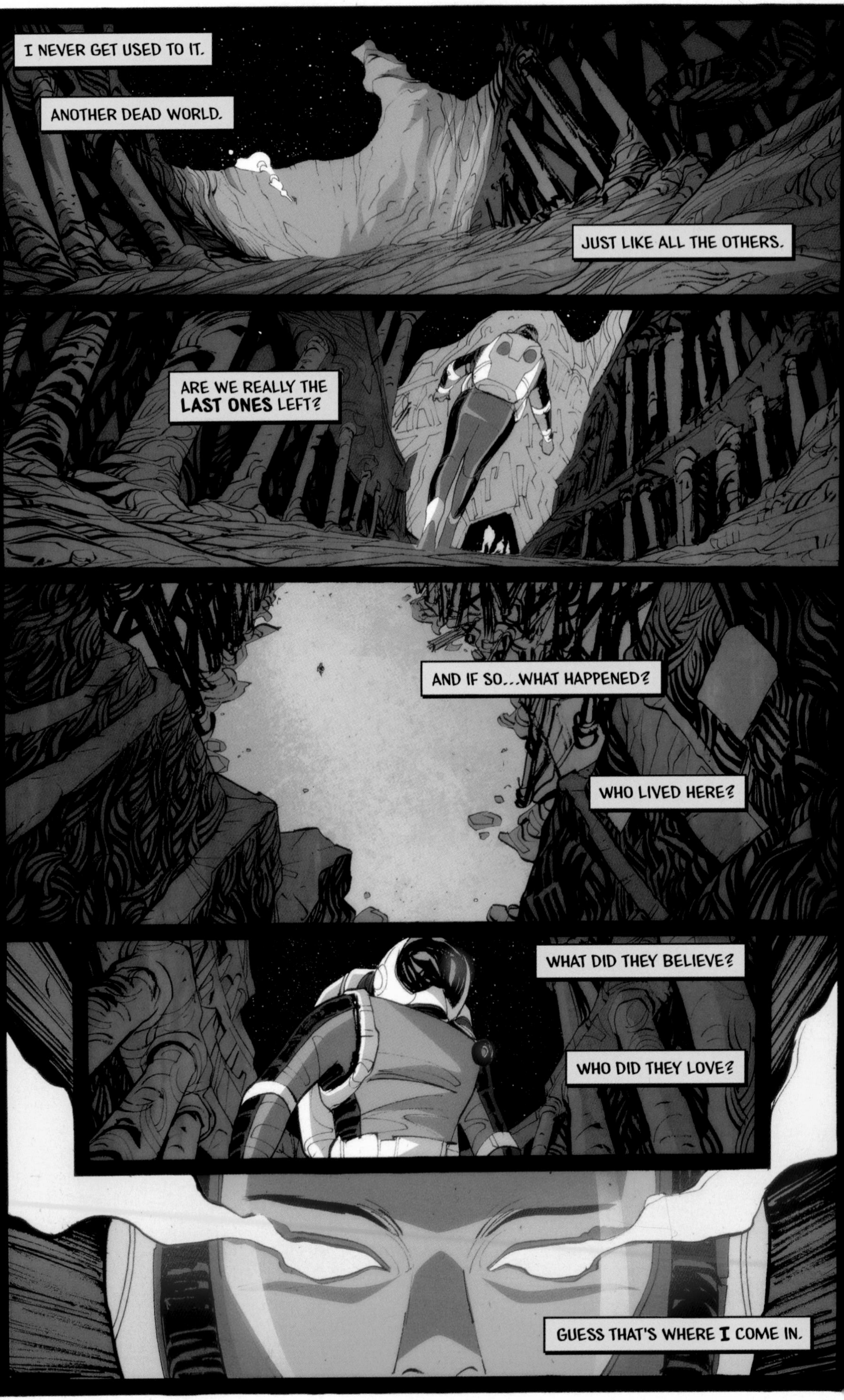
I NEVER GET USED TO IT.
ANOTHER DEAD WORLD.
JUST LIKE ALL THE OTHERS.
ARE WE REALLY THE LAST ONES LEFT?
AND IF SO...WHAT HAPPENED?
WHO LIVED HERE?
WHAT DID THEY BELIEVE?
WHO DID THEY LOVE?
GUESS THAT'S WHERE I COME IN.

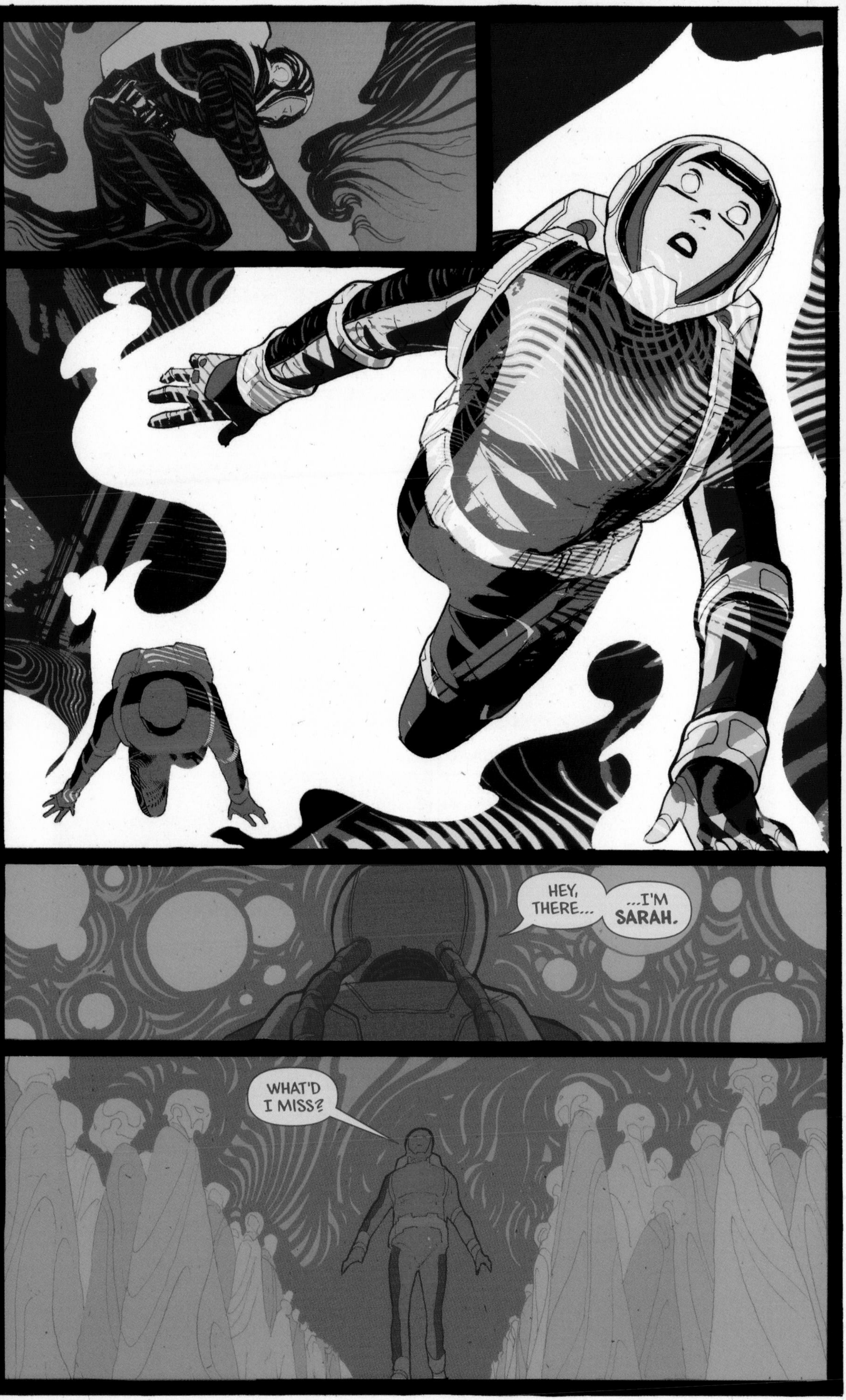
HEY, THERE...
...I'M SARAH.
WHAT'D I MISS?

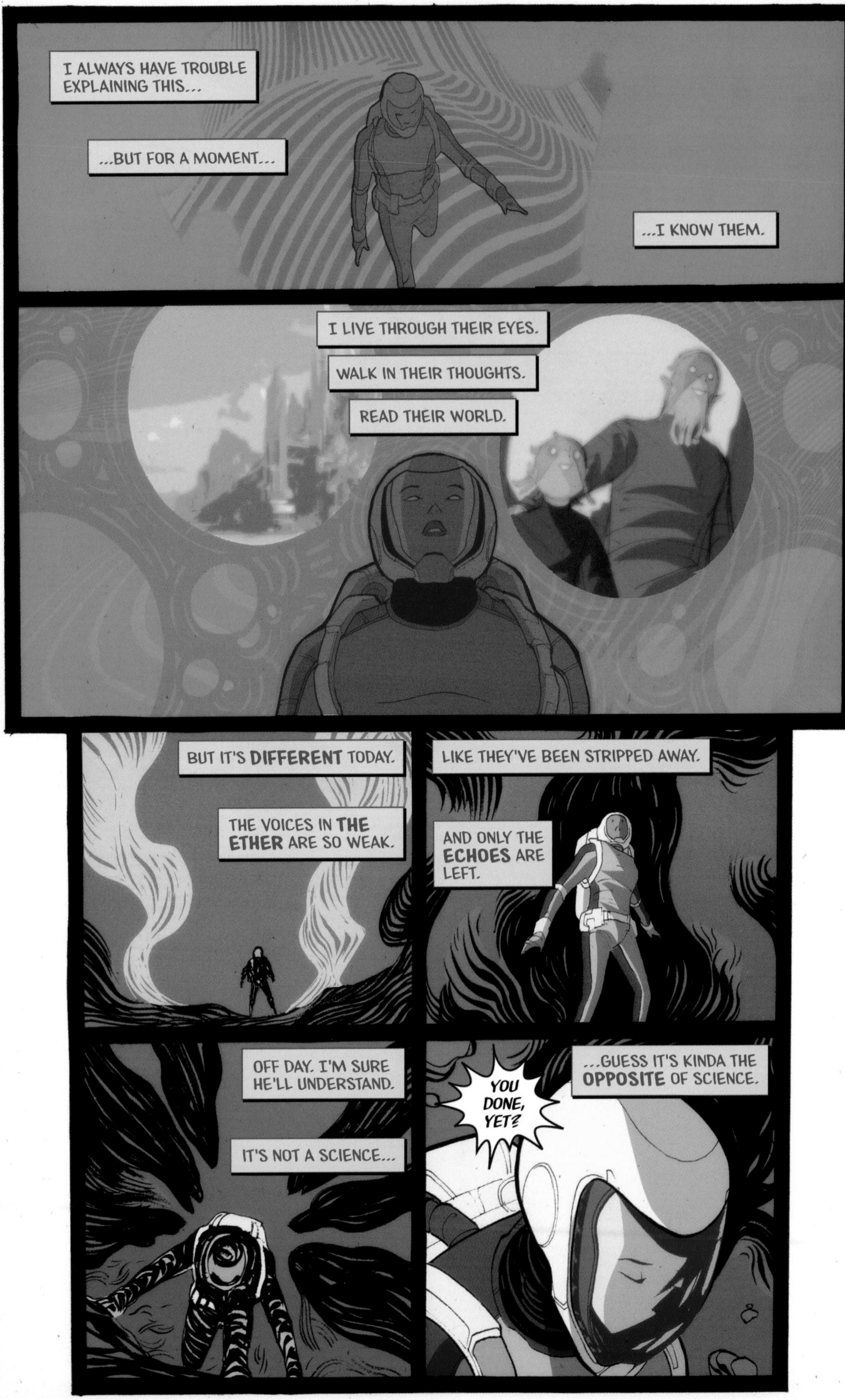
I ALWAYS HAVE TROUBLE EXPLAINING THIS...
...BUT FOR A MOMENT...
...I KNOW THEM.
I LIVE THROUGH THEIR EYES.
WALK IN THEIR THOUGHTS.
READ THEIR WORLD.
BUT IT'S DIFFERENT TODAY.
THE VOICES IN THE ETHER ARE SO WEAK.
LIKE THEY'VE BEEN STRIPPED AWAY.
AND ONLY THE ECHOES ARE LEFT.
OFF DAY. I'M SURE HE'LL UNDERSTAND.
IT'S NOT A SCIENCE...
YOU DONE, YET?
...GUESS IT'S KINDA THE OPPOSITE OF SCIENCE.

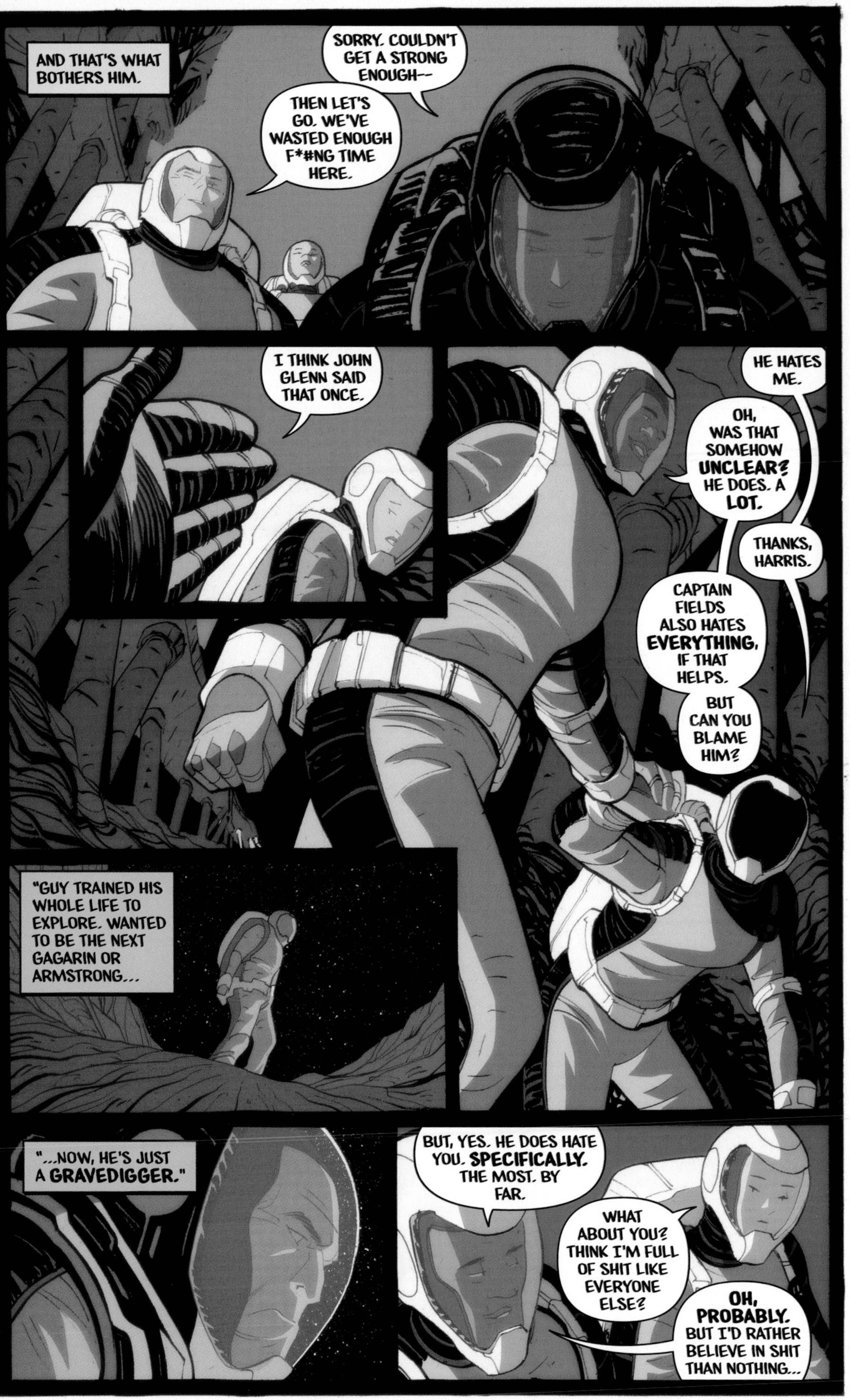
AND THAT'S WHAT BOTHERS HIM.
SORRY. COULDN'T GET A STRONG ENOUGH--
THEN LET'S GO. WE'VE WASTED ENOUGH F*#NG TIME HERE.
I THINK JOHN GLENN SAID THAT ONCE.
HE HATES ME.
OH, WAS THAT SOMEHOW UNCLEAR? HE DOES. A LOT.
THANKS, HARRIS.
CAPTAIN FIELDS ALSO HATES EVERYTHING, IF THAT HELPS.
BUT CAN YOU BLAME HIM?
"GUY TRAINED HIS WHOLE LIFE TO EXPLORE. WANTED TO BE THE NEXT GAGARIN OR ARMSTRONG...
"...NOW, HE'S JUST A GRAVEDIGGER."
BUT, YES. HE DOES HATE YOU. SPECIFICALLY. THE MOST. BY FAR.
WHAT ABOUT YOU? THINK I'M FULL OF SHIT LIKE EVERYONE ELSE?
OH, PROBABLY. BUT I'D RATHER BELIEVE IN SHIT THAN NOTHING...

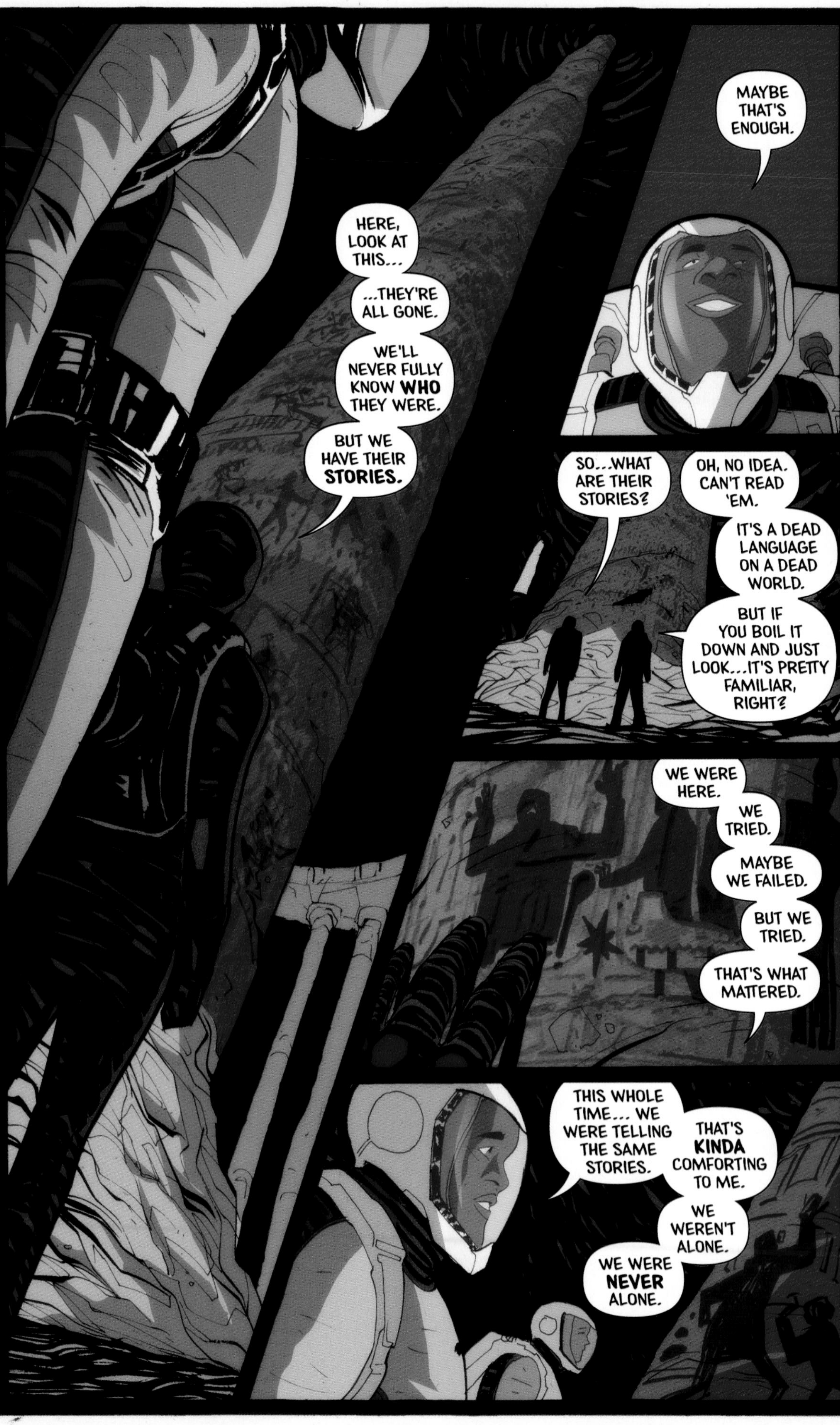
HERE, LOOK AT THIS...
...THEY'RE ALL GONE.
WE'LL NEVER FULLY KNOW **WHO** THEY WERE.
BUT WE HAVE THEIR **STORIES.**
MAYBE THAT'S ENOUGH.
SO...WHAT ARE THEIR STORIES?
OH, NO IDEA. CAN'T READ 'EM.
IT'S A DEAD LANGUAGE ON A DEAD WORLD.
BUT IF YOU BOIL IT DOWN AND JUST LOOK...IT'S PRETTY FAMILIAR, RIGHT?
WE WERE HERE.
WE TRIED.
MAYBE WE FAILED.
BUT WE TRIED.
THAT'S WHAT MATTERED.
THIS WHOLE TIME... WE WERE TELLING THE SAME STORIES.
THAT'S **KINDA** COMFORTING TO ME.
WE WEREN'T ALONE.
WE WERE **NEVER** ALONE.

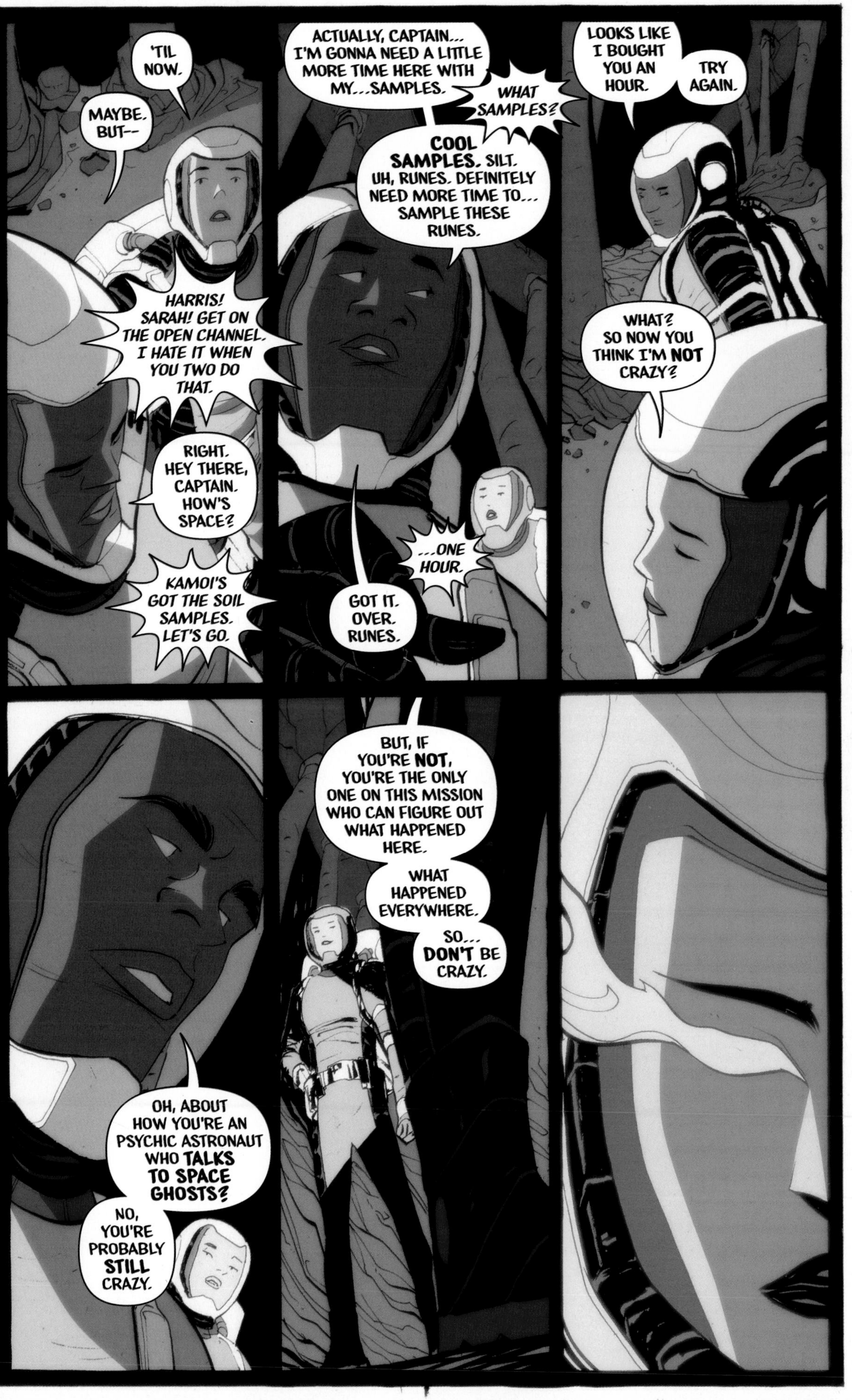
'TIL NOW.
MAYBE. BUT--
HARRIS! SARAH! GET ON THE OPEN CHANNEL. I HATE IT WHEN YOU TWO DO THAT.
RIGHT. HEY THERE, CAPTAIN. HOW'S SPACE?
KAMOI'S GOT THE SOIL SAMPLES. LET'S GO.
ACTUALLY, CAPTAIN... I'M GONNA NEED A LITTLE MORE TIME HERE WITH MY...SAMPLES.
WHAT SAMPLES?
COOL SAMPLES. SILT. UH, RUNES. DEFINITELY NEED MORE TIME TO... SAMPLE THESE RUNES.
...ONE HOUR.
GOT IT. OVER. RUNES.
LOOKS LIKE I BOUGHT YOU AN HOUR.
TRY AGAIN.
WHAT? SO NOW YOU THINK I'M NOT CRAZY?
OH, ABOUT HOW YOU'RE AN PSYCHIC ASTRONAUT WHO TALKS TO SPACE GHOSTS?
NO, YOU'RE PROBABLY STILL CRAZY.
BUT, IF YOU'RE NOT, YOU'RE THE ONLY ONE ON THIS MISSION WHO CAN FIGURE OUT WHAT HAPPENED HERE.
WHAT HAPPENED EVERYWHERE.
SO... DON'T BE CRAZY.

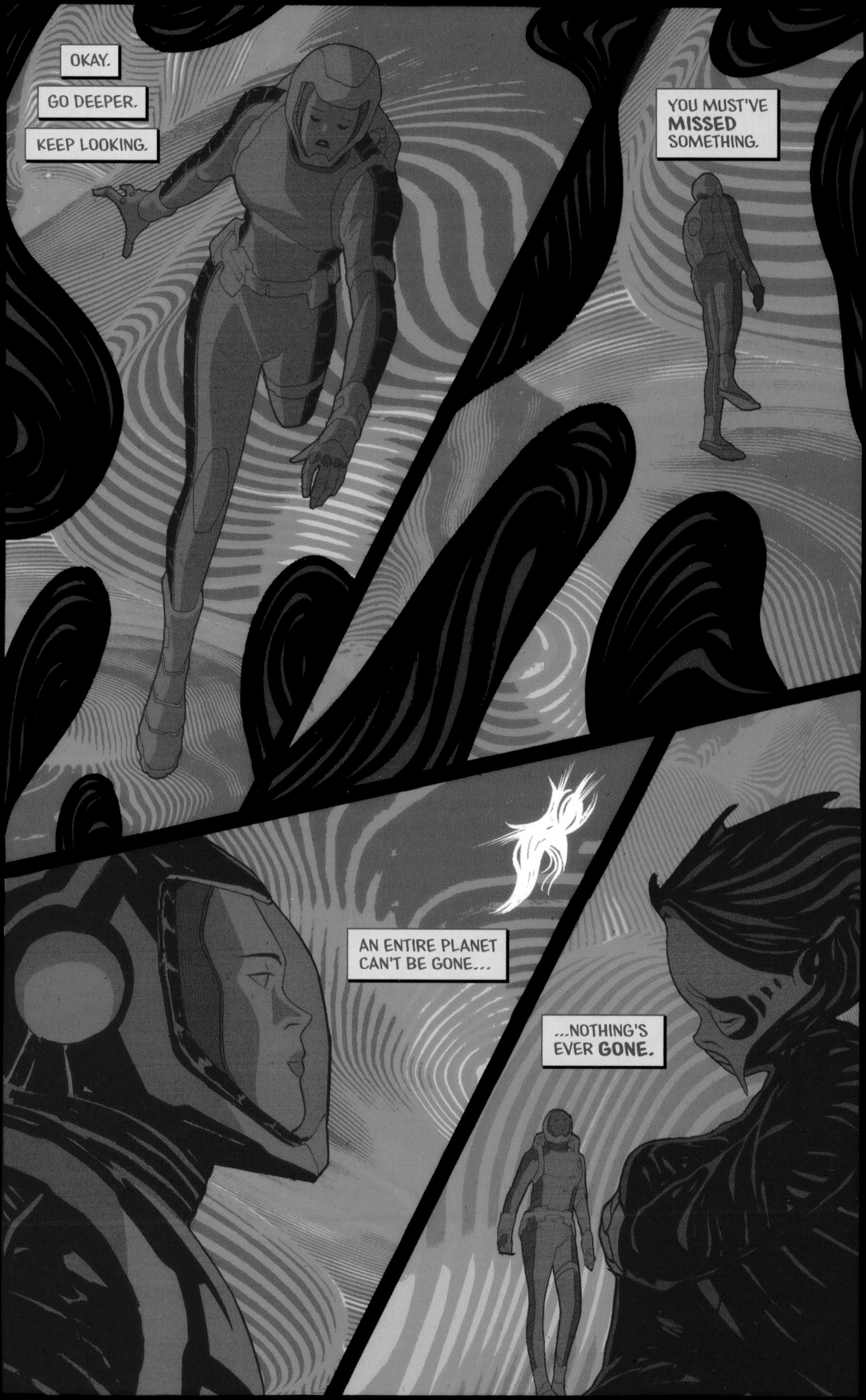
OKAY.
GO DEEPER.
KEEP LOOKING.
YOU MUST'VE MISSED SOMETHING.
AN ENTIRE PLANET CAN'T BE GONE...
...NOTHING'S EVER GONE.

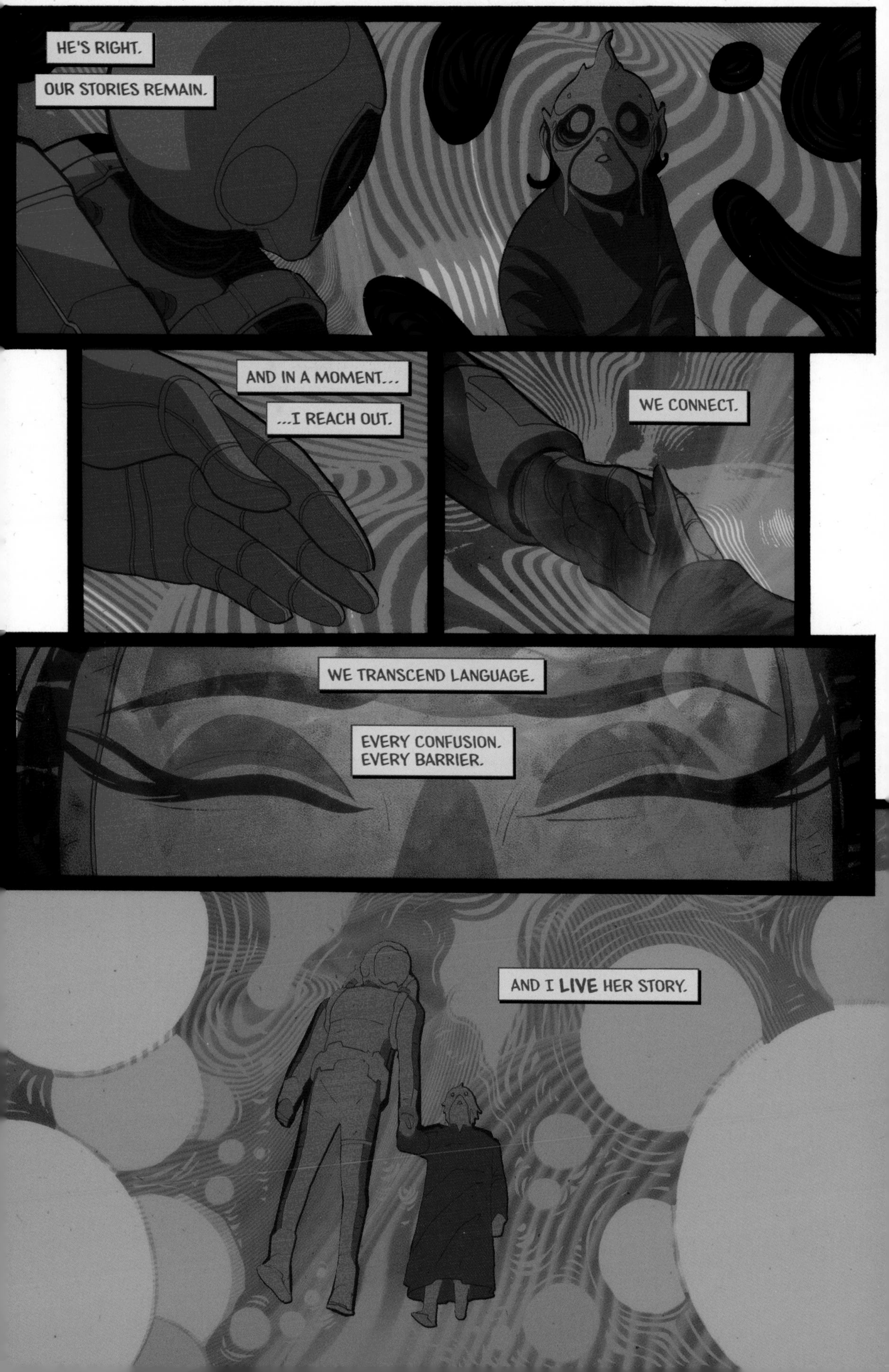
HE'S RIGHT.
OUR STORIES REMAIN.
AND IN A MOMENT...
...I REACH OUT.
WE CONNECT.
WE TRANSCEND LANGUAGE.
EVERY CONFUSION. EVERY BARRIER.
AND I LIVE HER STORY.

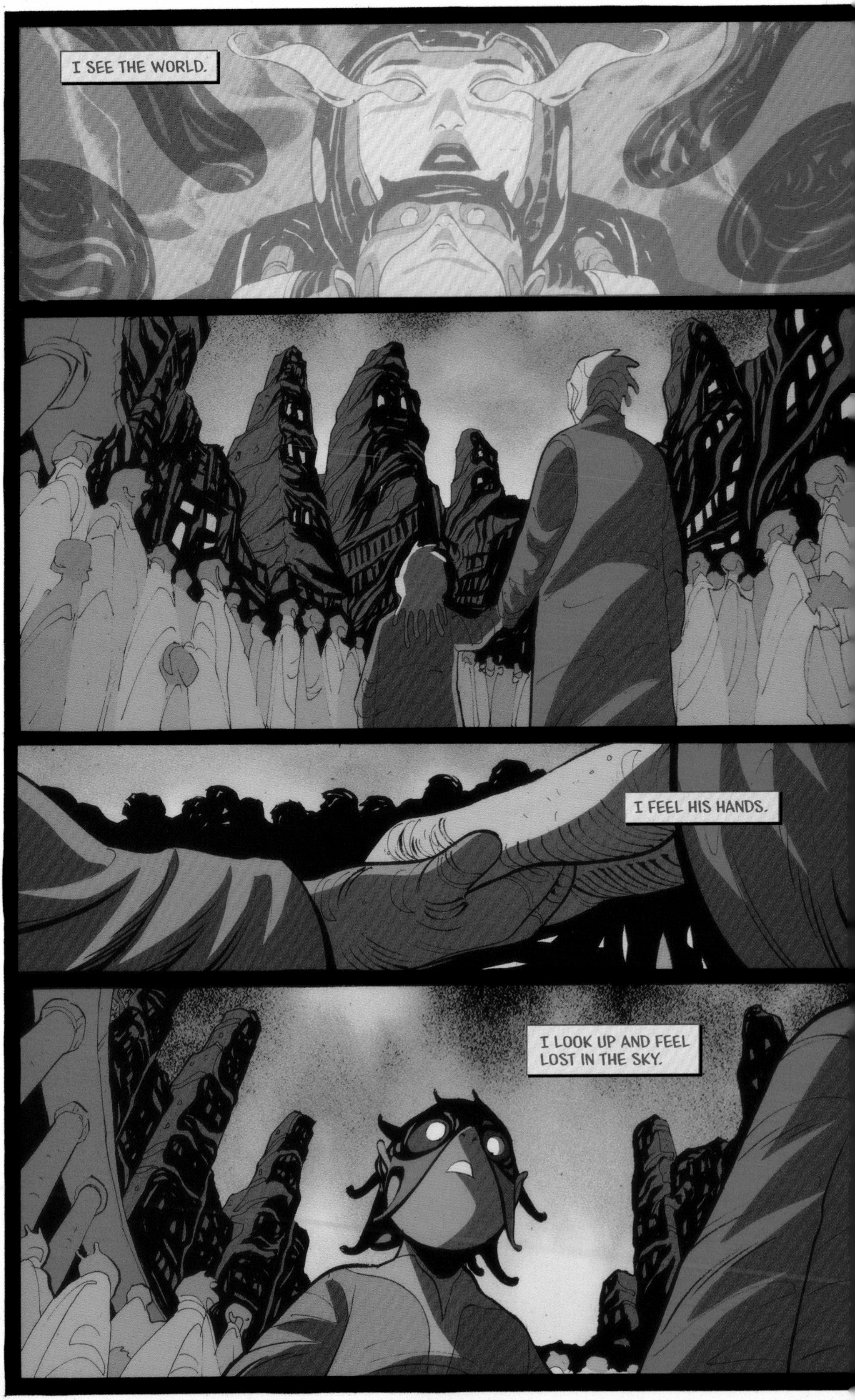
I SEE THE WORLD.
I FEEL HIS HANDS.
I LOOK UP AND FEEL LOST IN THE SKY.

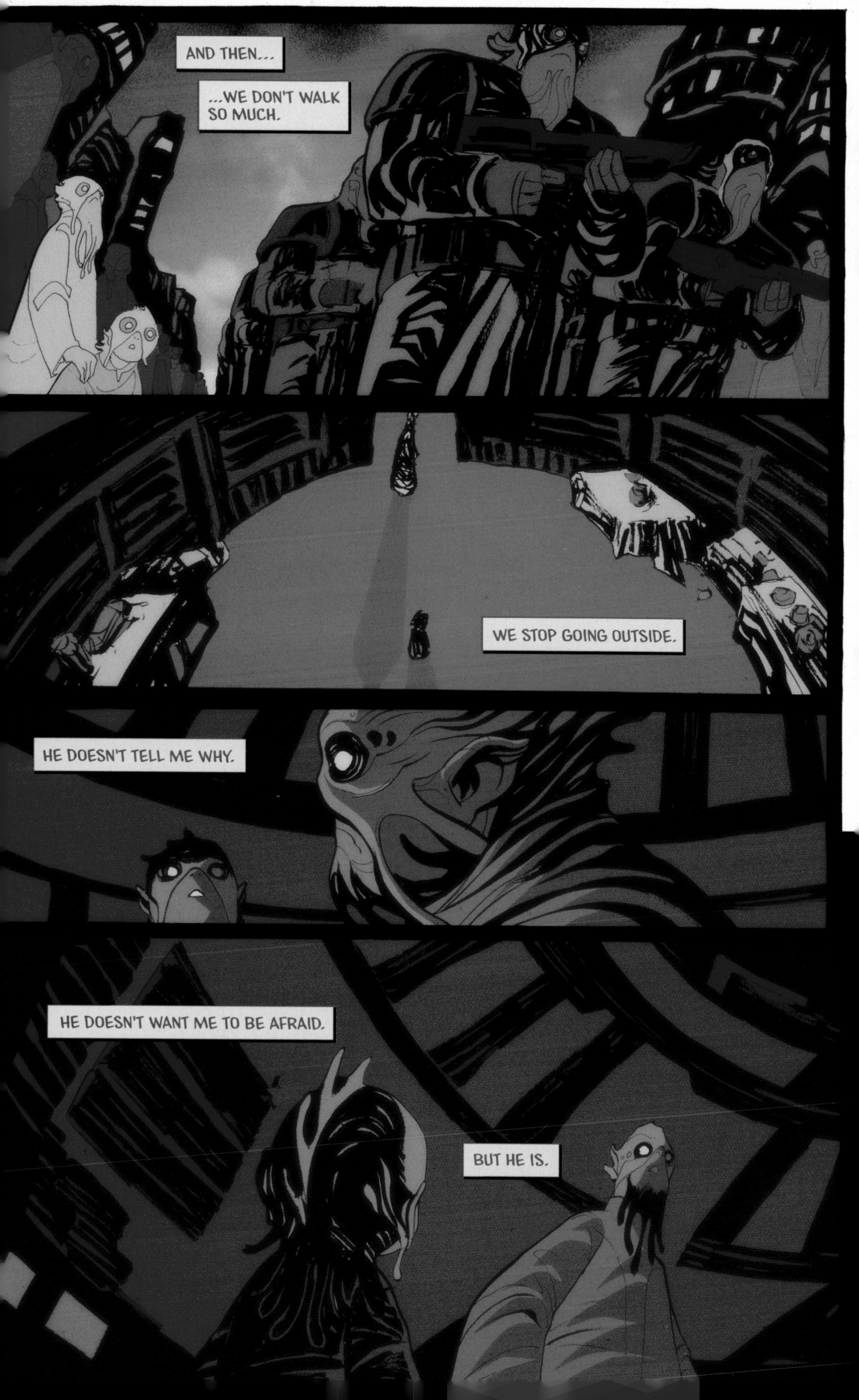
AND THEN...
...WE DON'T WALK SO MUCH.
WE STOP GOING OUTSIDE.
HE DOESN'T TELL ME WHY.
HE DOESN'T WANT ME TO BE AFRAID.
BUT HE IS.

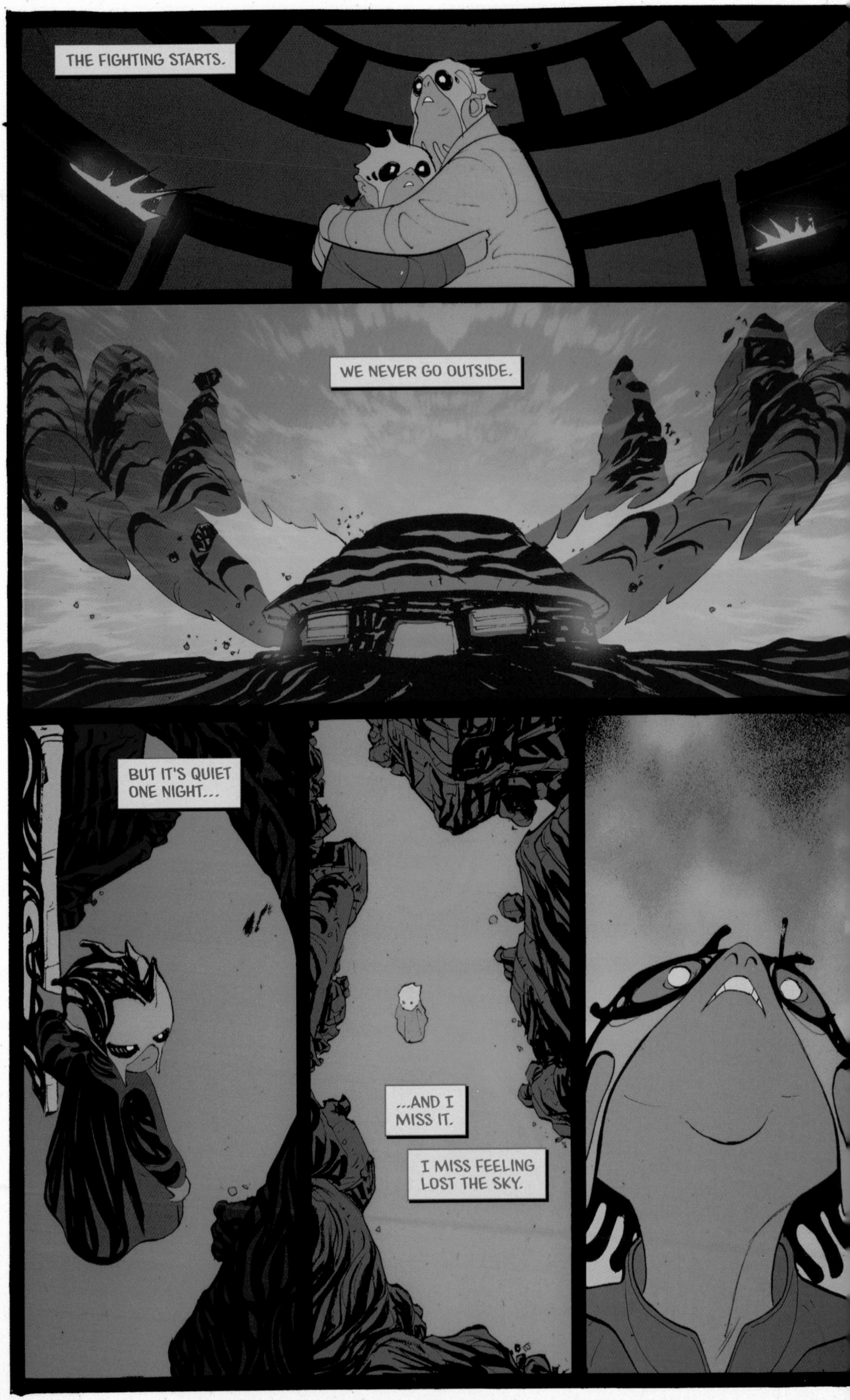
THE FIGHTING STARTS.
WE NEVER GO OUTSIDE.
BUT IT'S QUIET ONE NIGHT...
...AND I MISS IT.
I MISS FEELING LOST THE SKY.

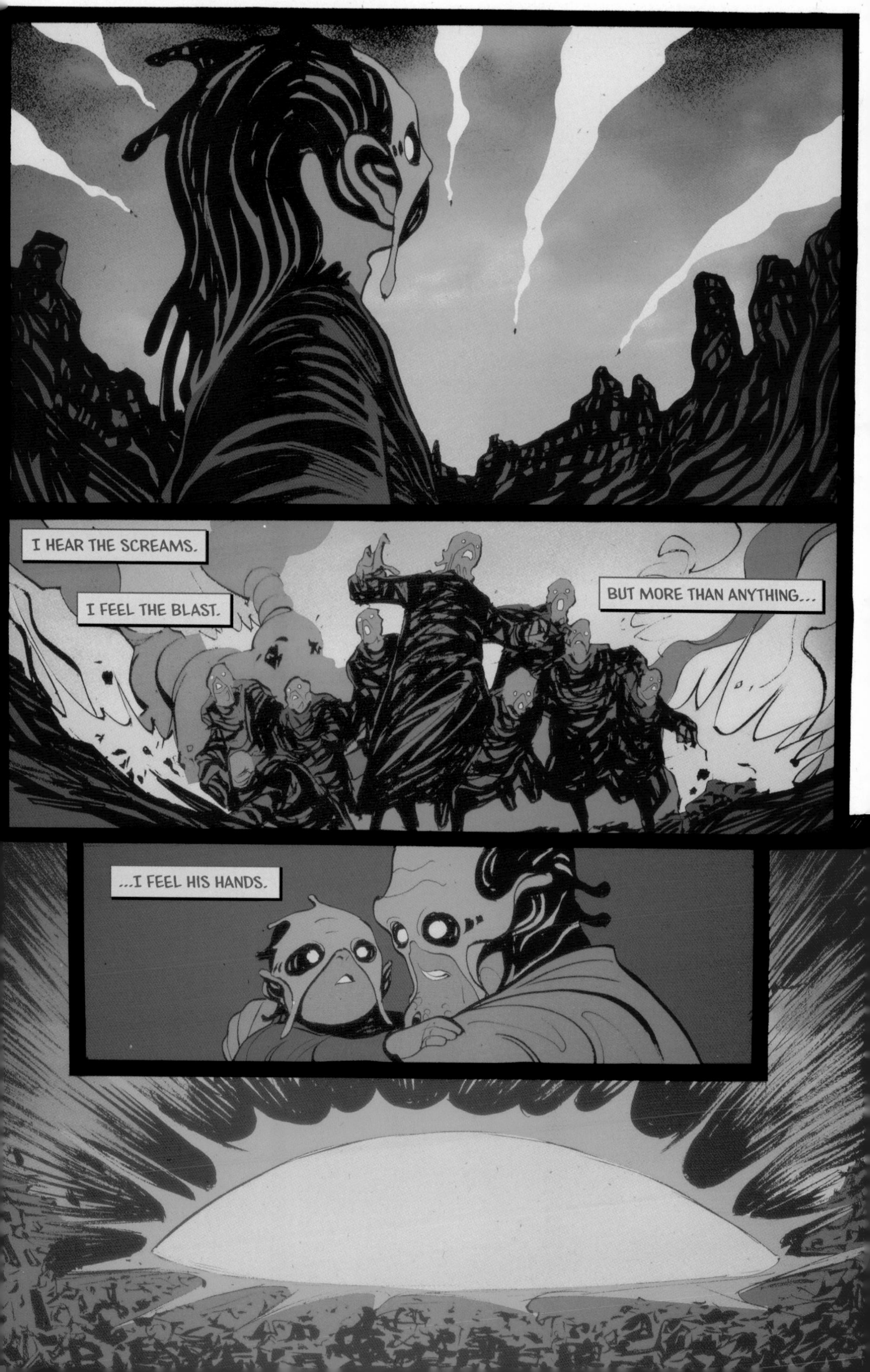
I HEAR THE SCREAMS.
I FEEL THE BLAST.
BUT MORE THAN ANYTHING...
...I FEEL HIS HANDS.

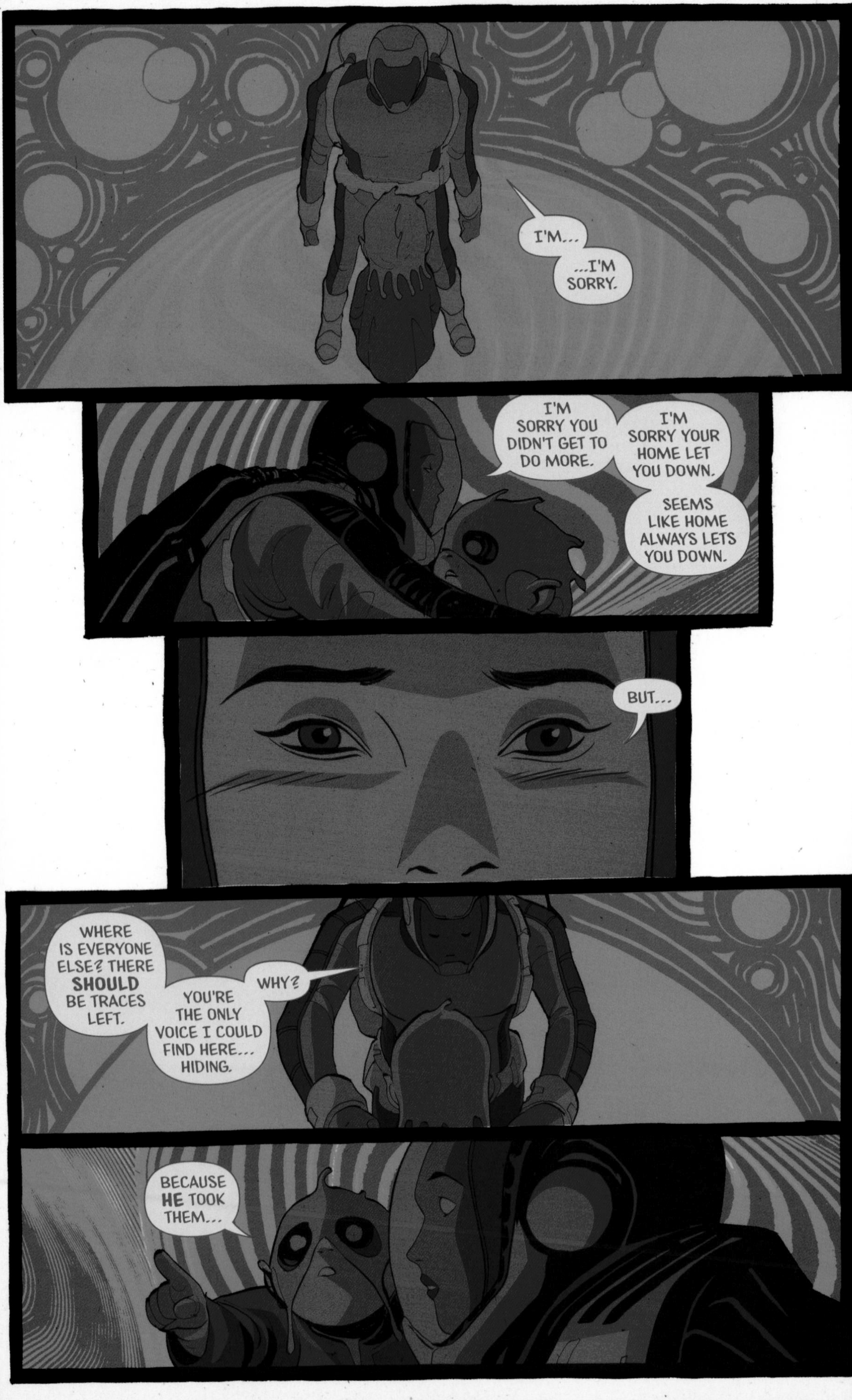
I'M...
...I'M SORRY.
I'M SORRY YOU DIDN'T GET TO DO MORE.
I'M SORRY YOUR HOME LET YOU DOWN.
SEEMS LIKE HOME ALWAYS LETS YOU DOWN.
BUT...
WHERE IS EVERYONE ELSE? THERE **SHOULD** BE TRACES LEFT.
YOU'RE THE ONLY VOICE I COULD FIND HERE... HIDING.
WHY?
BECAUSE **HE** TOOK THEM...

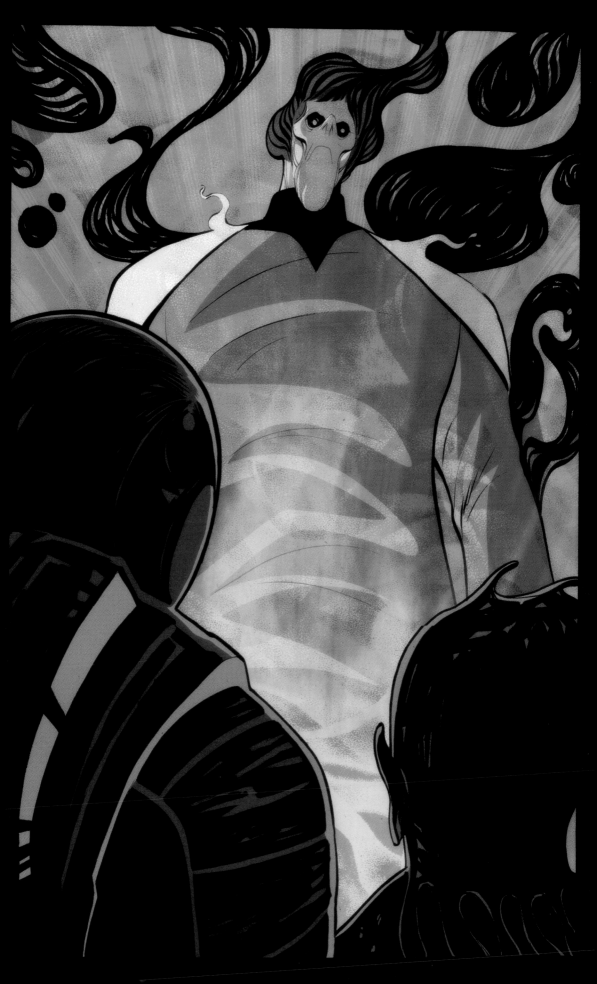

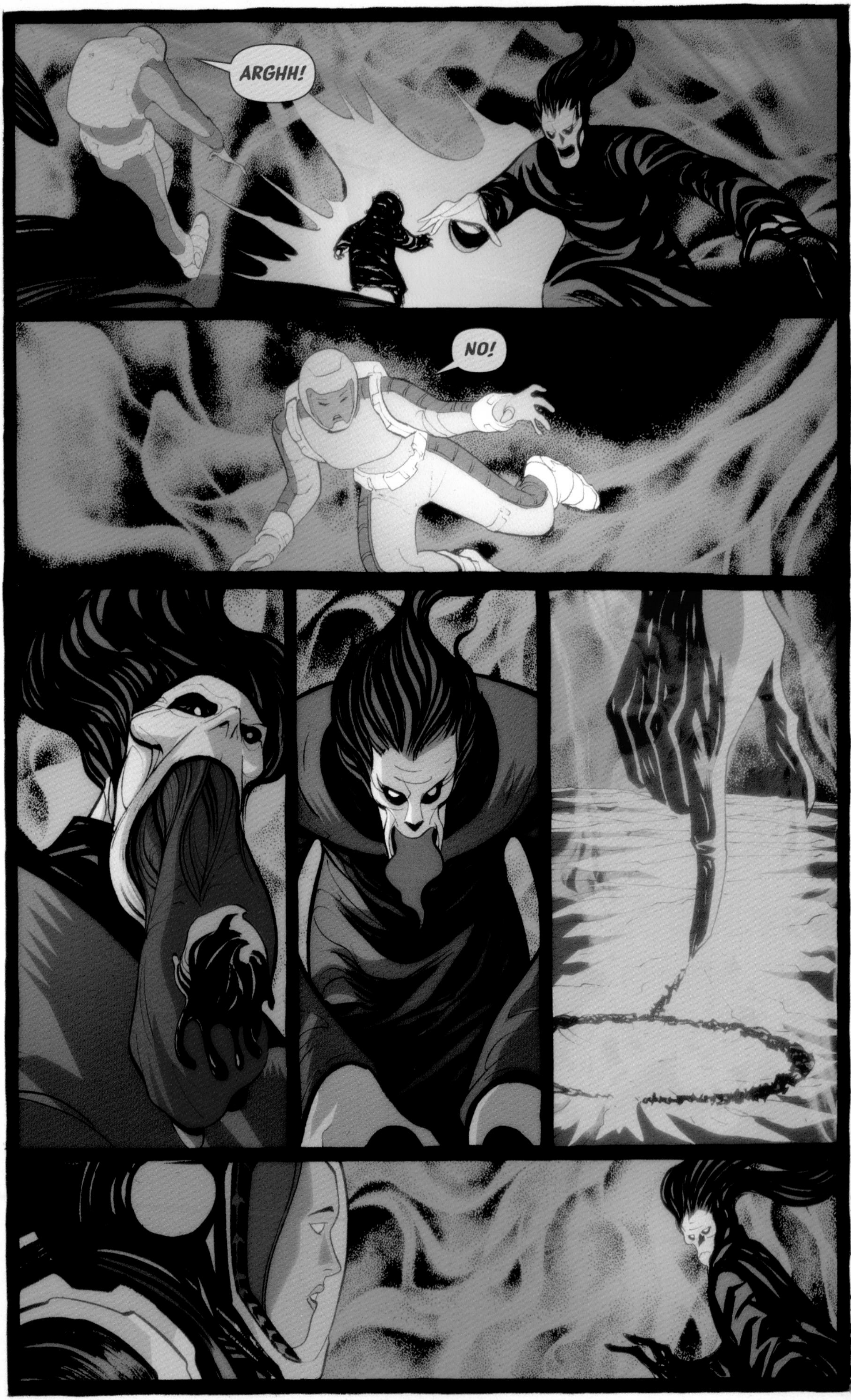
ARGHH!
NO!

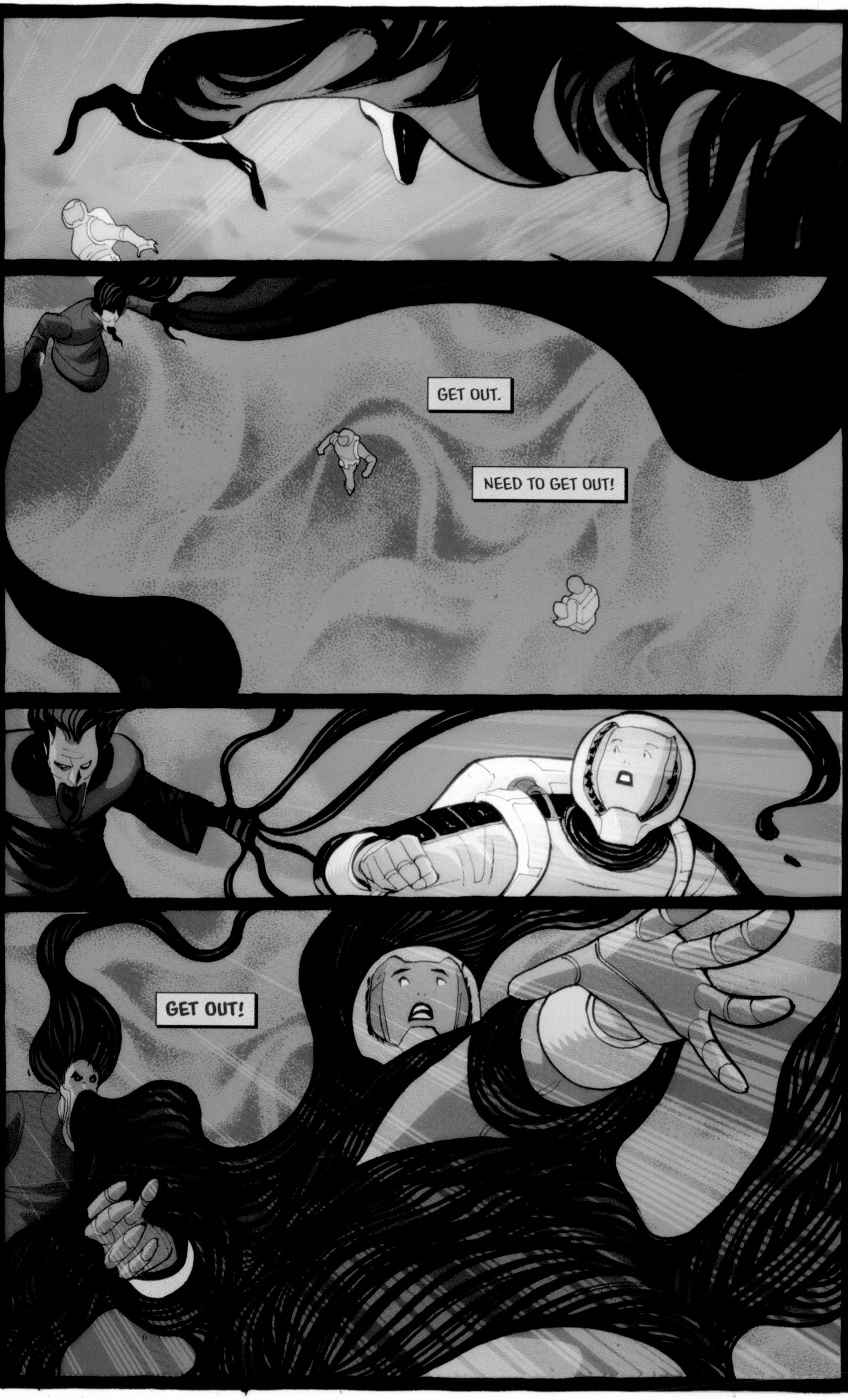
GET OUT.
NEED TO GET OUT!
GET OUT!

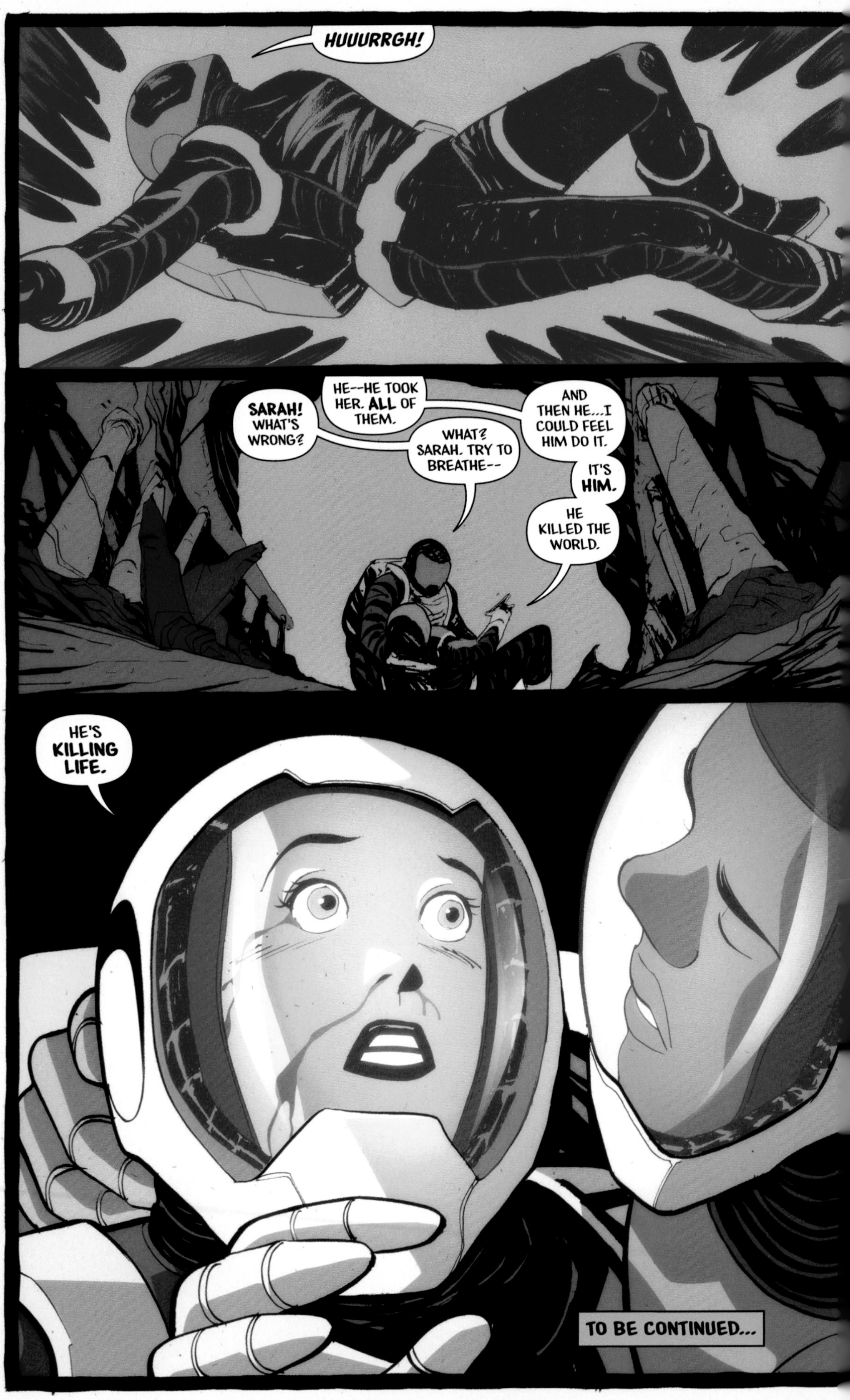
HUUURRGH!
SARAH! WHAT'S WRONG?
HE--HE TOOK HER. ALL OF THEM.
WHAT? SARAH. TRY TO BREATHE--
AND THEN HE...I COULD FEEL HIM DO IT.
IT'S HIM.
HE KILLED THE WORLD.
HE'S KILLING LIFE.
TO BE CONTINUED...

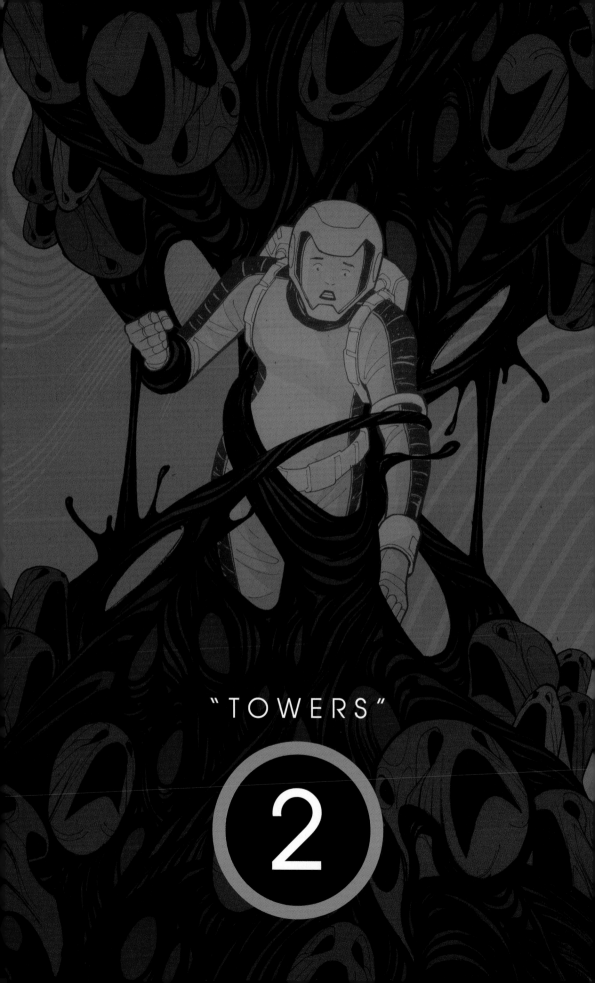

"TOWERS"

2

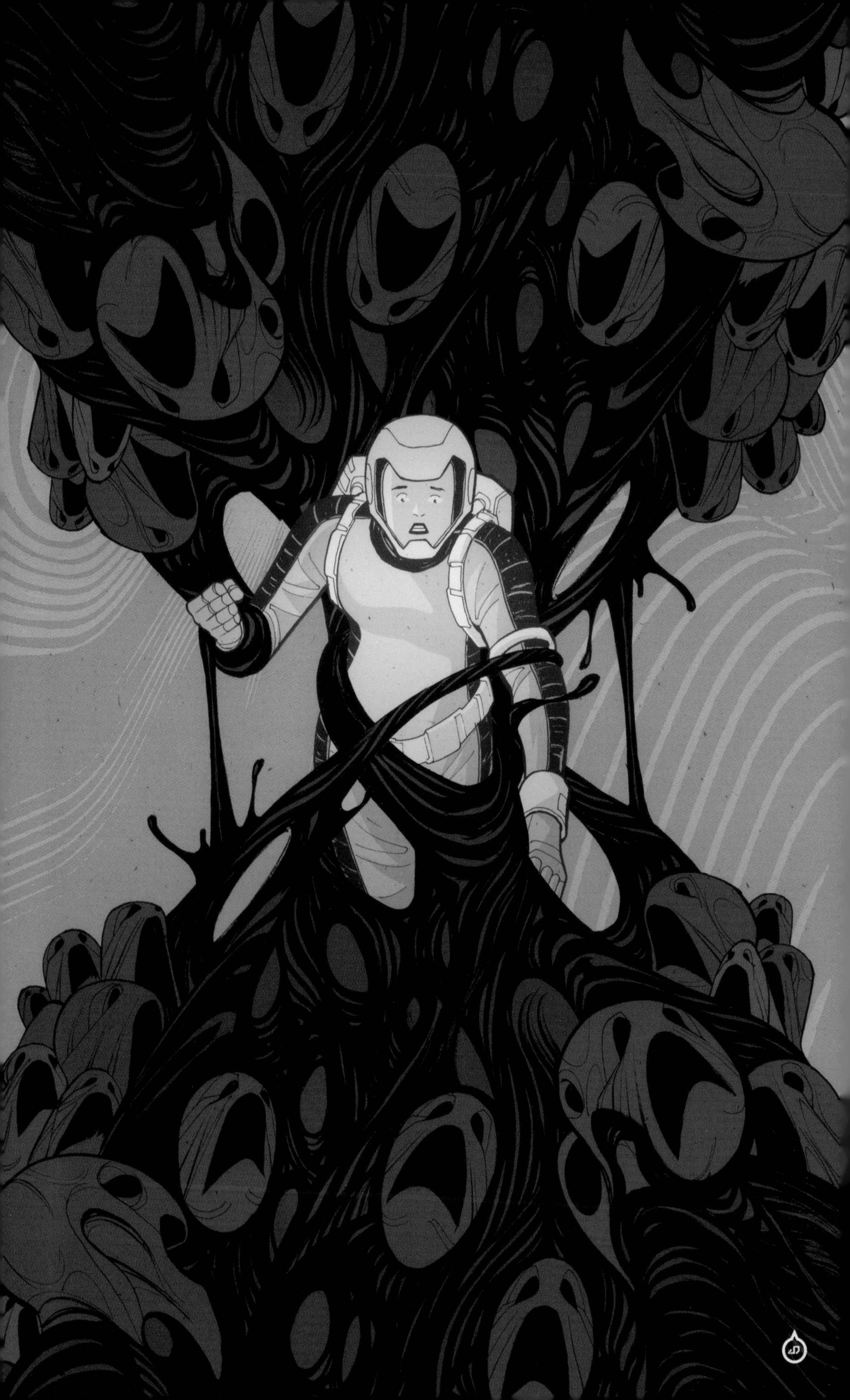

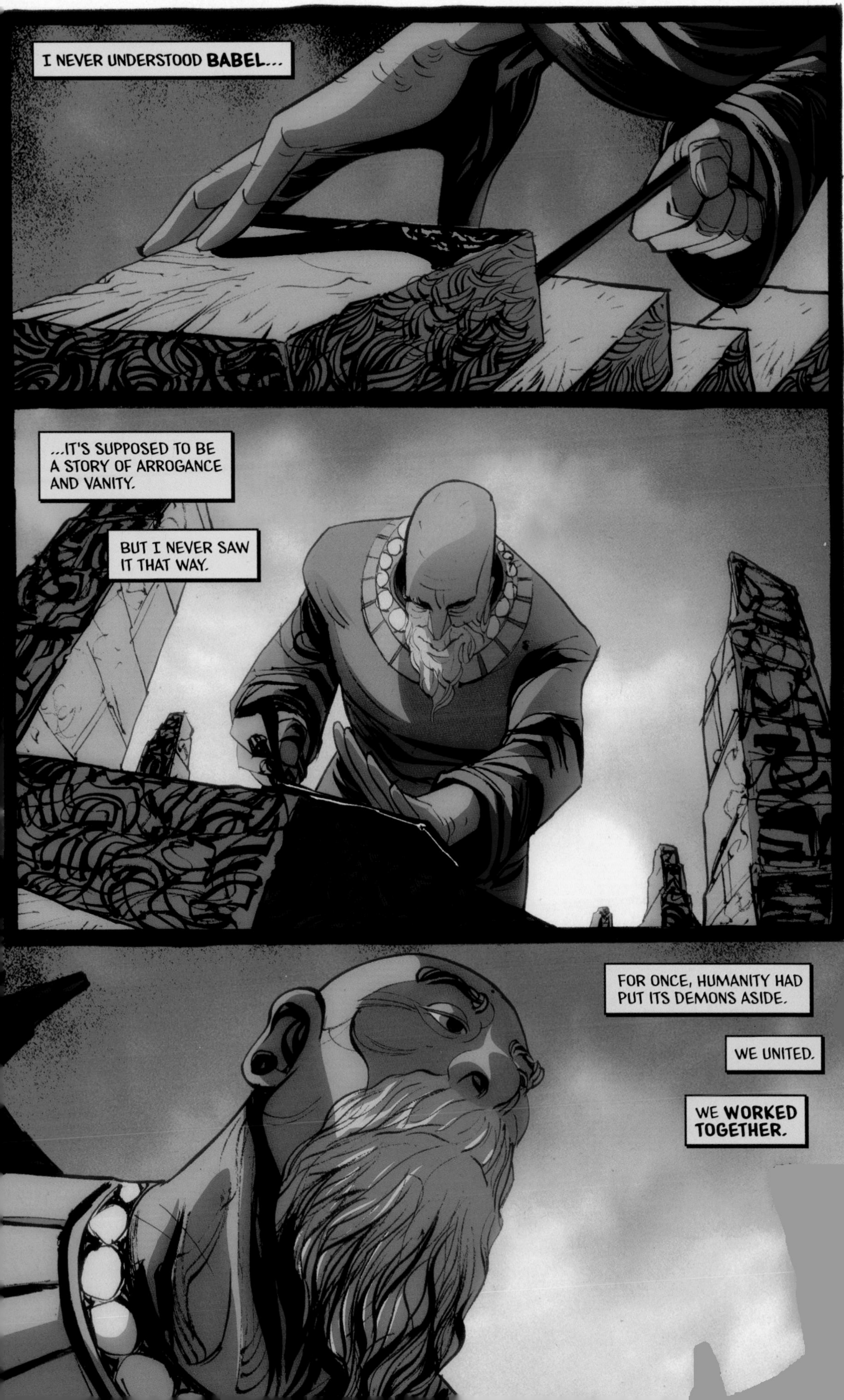
I NEVER UNDERSTOOD BABEL...
...IT'S SUPPOSED TO BE A STORY OF ARROGANCE AND VANITY.
BUT I NEVER SAW IT THAT WAY.
FOR ONCE, HUMANITY HAD PUT ITS DEMONS ASIDE.
WE UNITED.
WE WORKED TOGETHER.

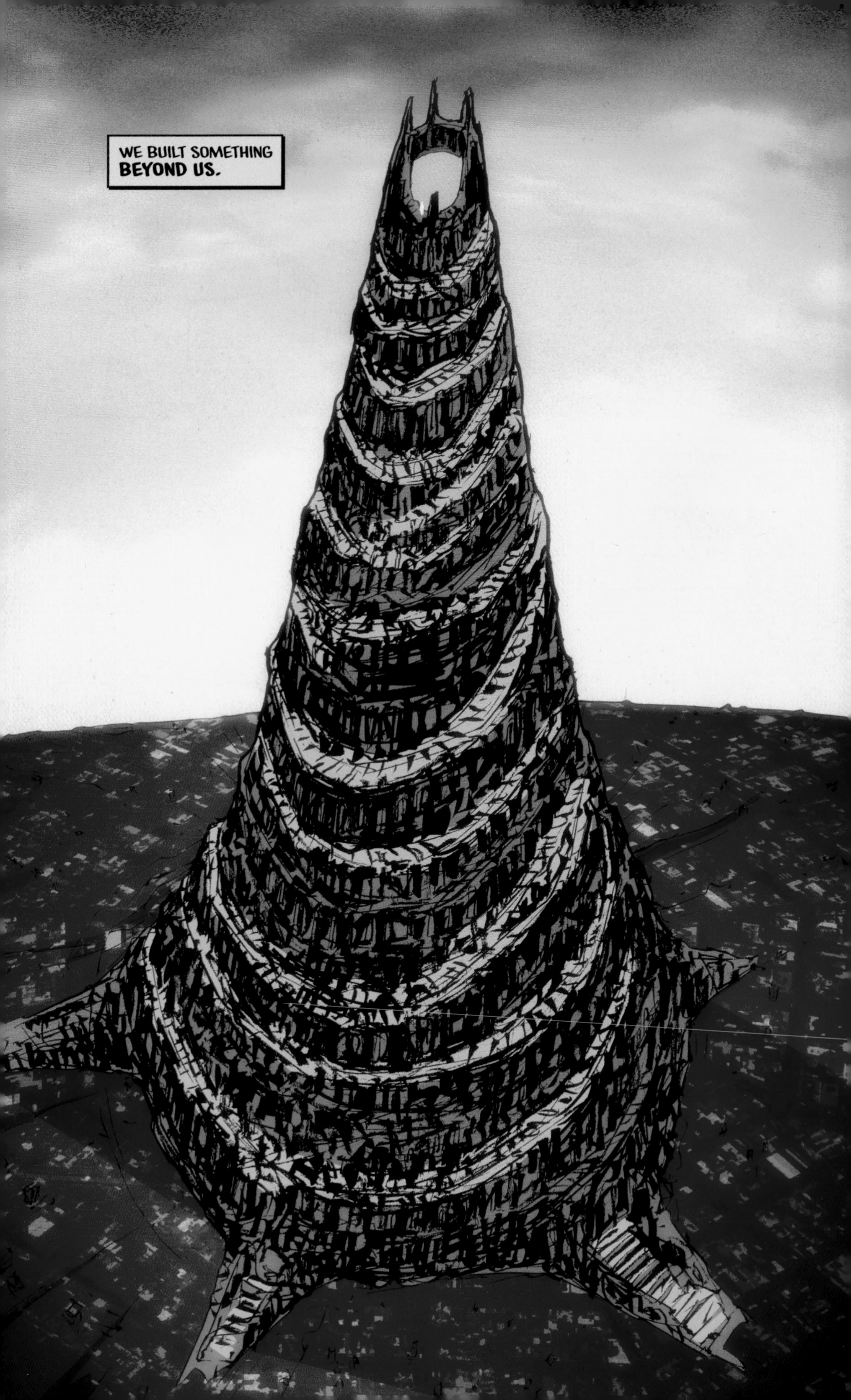
WE BUILT SOMETHING
BEYOND US.

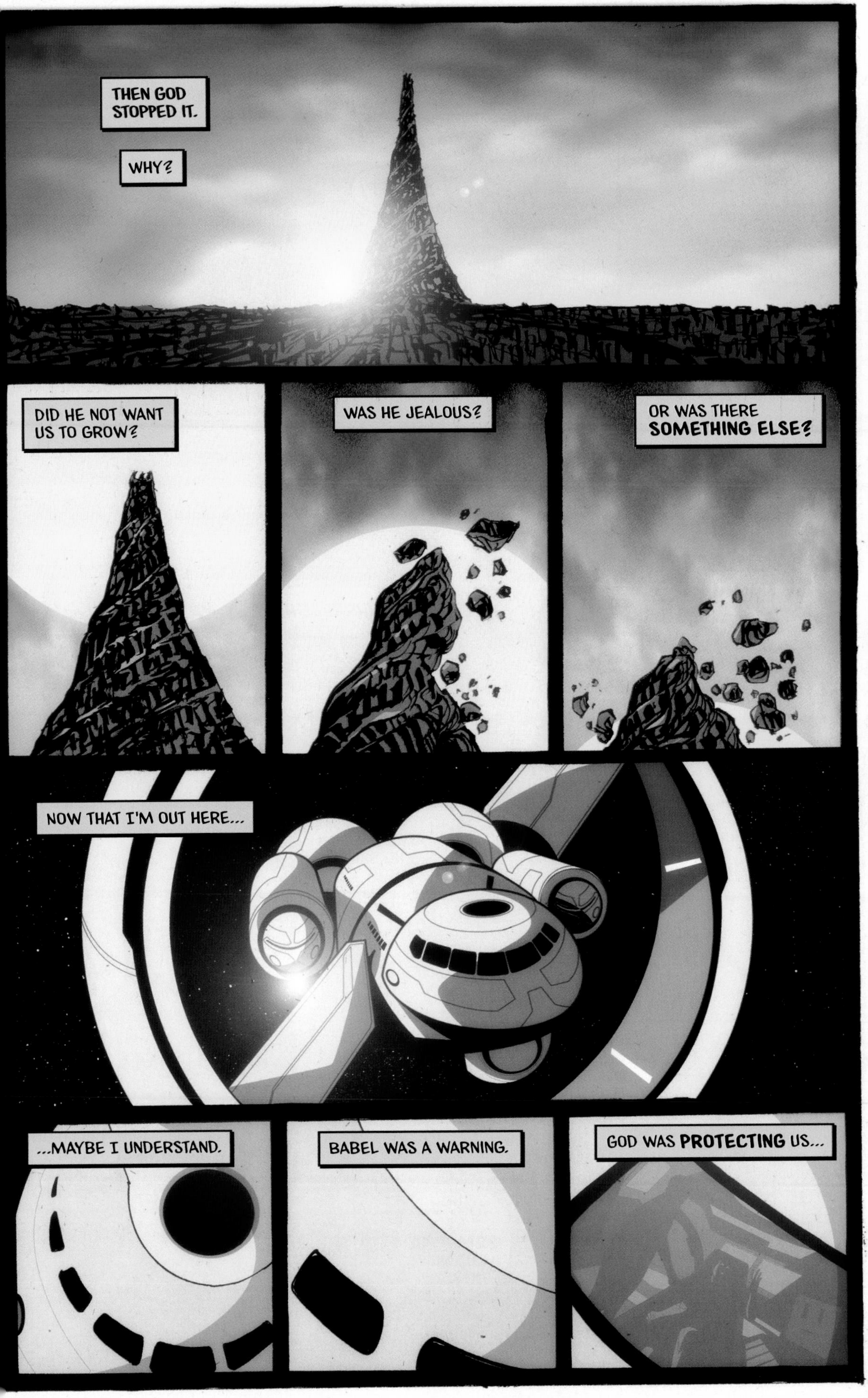
THEN GOD STOPPED IT.
WHY?
DID HE NOT WANT US TO GROW?
WAS HE JEALOUS?
OR WAS THERE **SOMETHING ELSE?**
NOW THAT I'M OUT HERE...
...MAYBE I UNDERSTAND.
BABEL WAS A WARNING.
GOD WAS **PROTECTING** US...

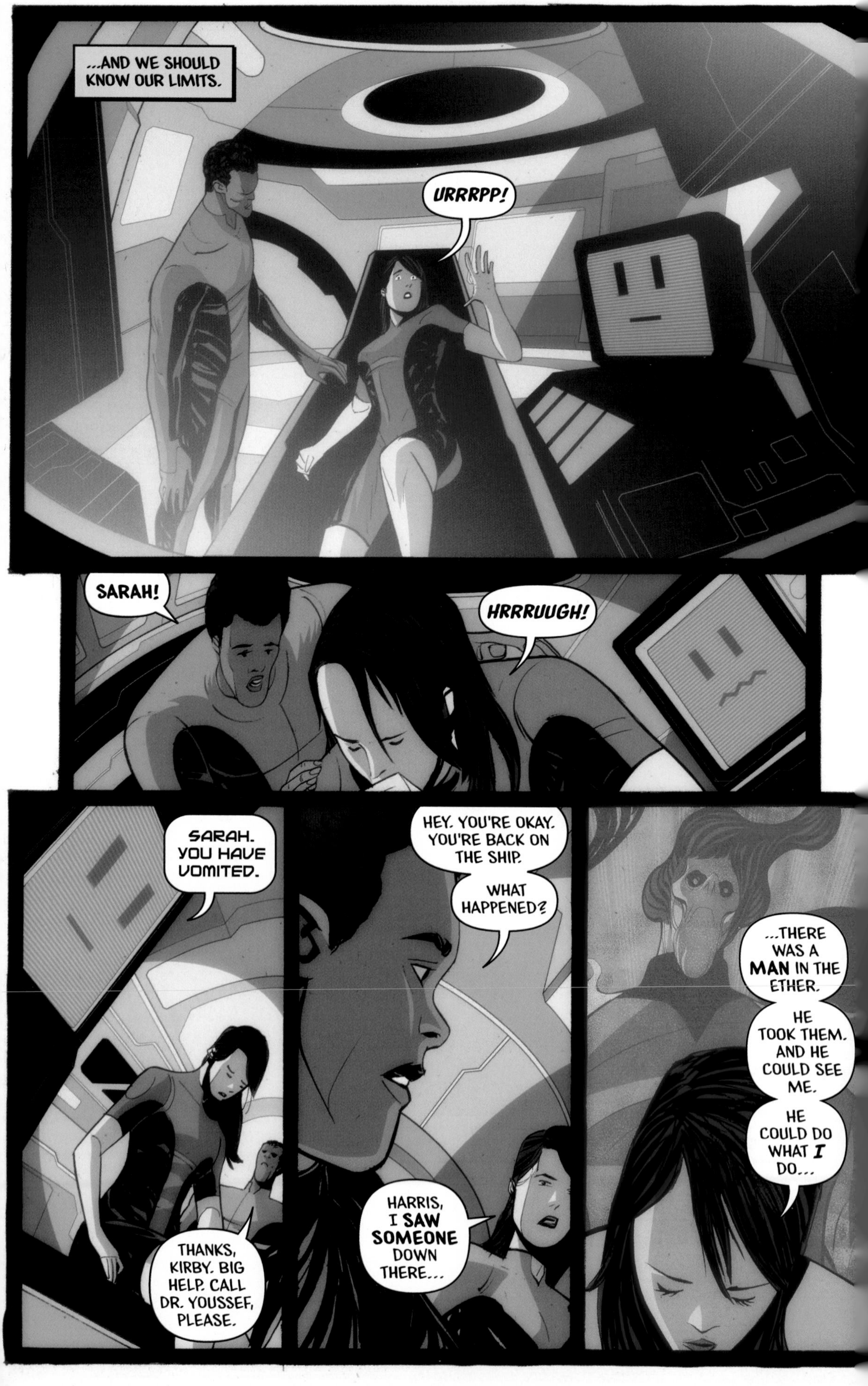
...AND WE SHOULD KNOW OUR LIMITS.
URRRPP!
SARAH!
HRRRUUGH!
SARAH. YOU HAVE VOMITED.
THANKS, KIRBY. BIG HELP. CALL DR. YOUSSEF, PLEASE.
HEY. YOU'RE OKAY. YOU'RE BACK ON THE SHIP.
WHAT HAPPENED?
HARRIS, I SAW SOMEONE DOWN THERE...
...THERE WAS A MAN IN THE ETHER.
HE TOOK THEM. AND HE COULD SEE ME.
HE COULD DO WHAT I DO...

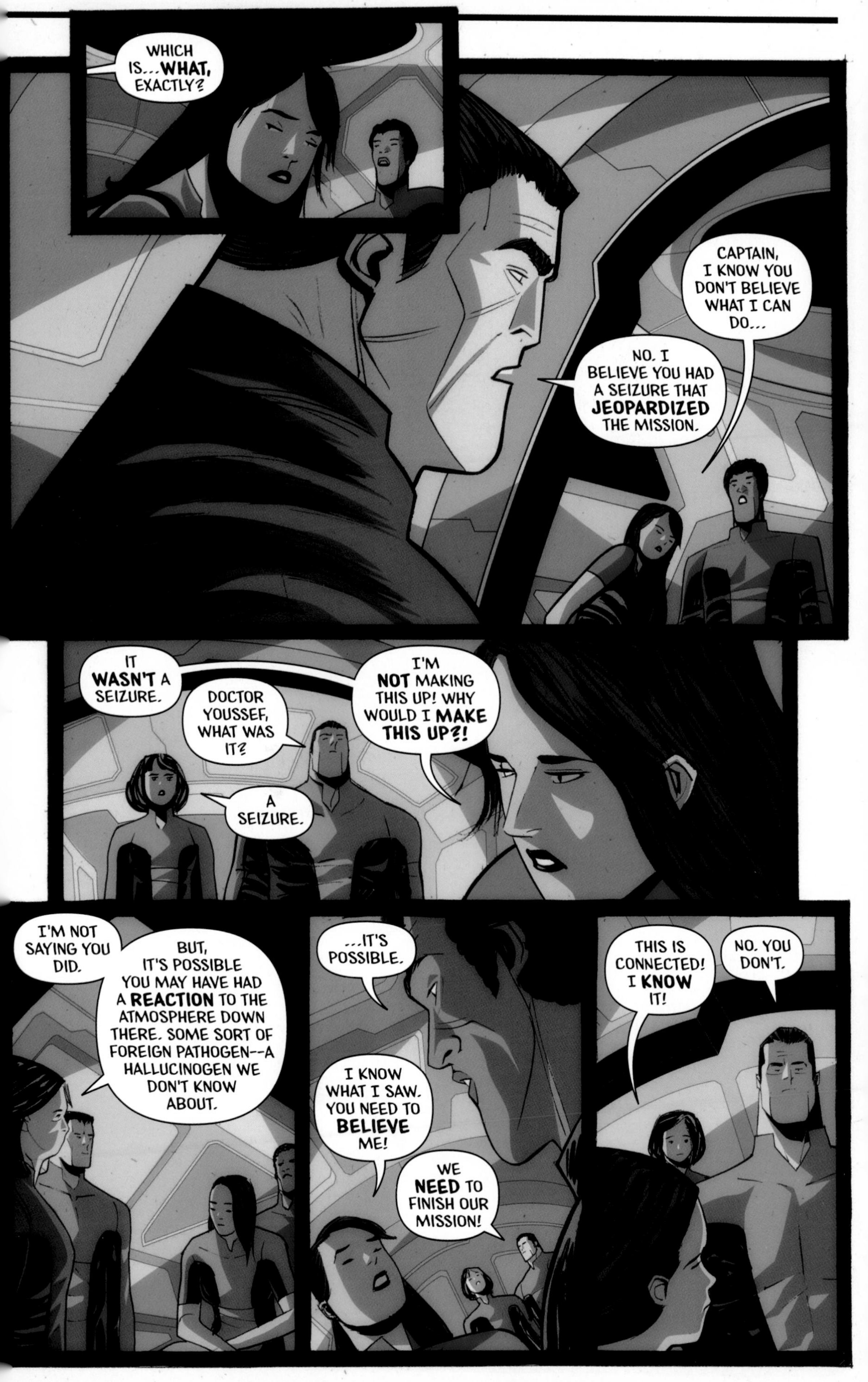
WHICH IS...WHAT, EXACTLY?
CAPTAIN, I KNOW YOU DON'T BELIEVE WHAT I CAN DO...
NO. I BELIEVE YOU HAD A SEIZURE THAT JEOPARDIZED THE MISSION.
IT WASN'T A SEIZURE.
I'M NOT MAKING THIS UP! WHY WOULD I MAKE THIS UP?!
DOCTOR YOUSSEF, WHAT WAS IT?
A SEIZURE.
I'M NOT SAYING YOU DID.
BUT, IT'S POSSIBLE YOU MAY HAVE HAD A REACTION TO THE ATMOSPHERE DOWN THERE. SOME SORT OF FOREIGN PATHOGEN--A HALLUCINOGEN WE DON'T KNOW ABOUT.
...IT'S POSSIBLE.
I KNOW WHAT I SAW. YOU NEED TO BELIEVE ME!
WE NEED TO FINISH OUR MISSION!
THIS IS CONNECTED! I KNOW IT!
NO. YOU DON'T.

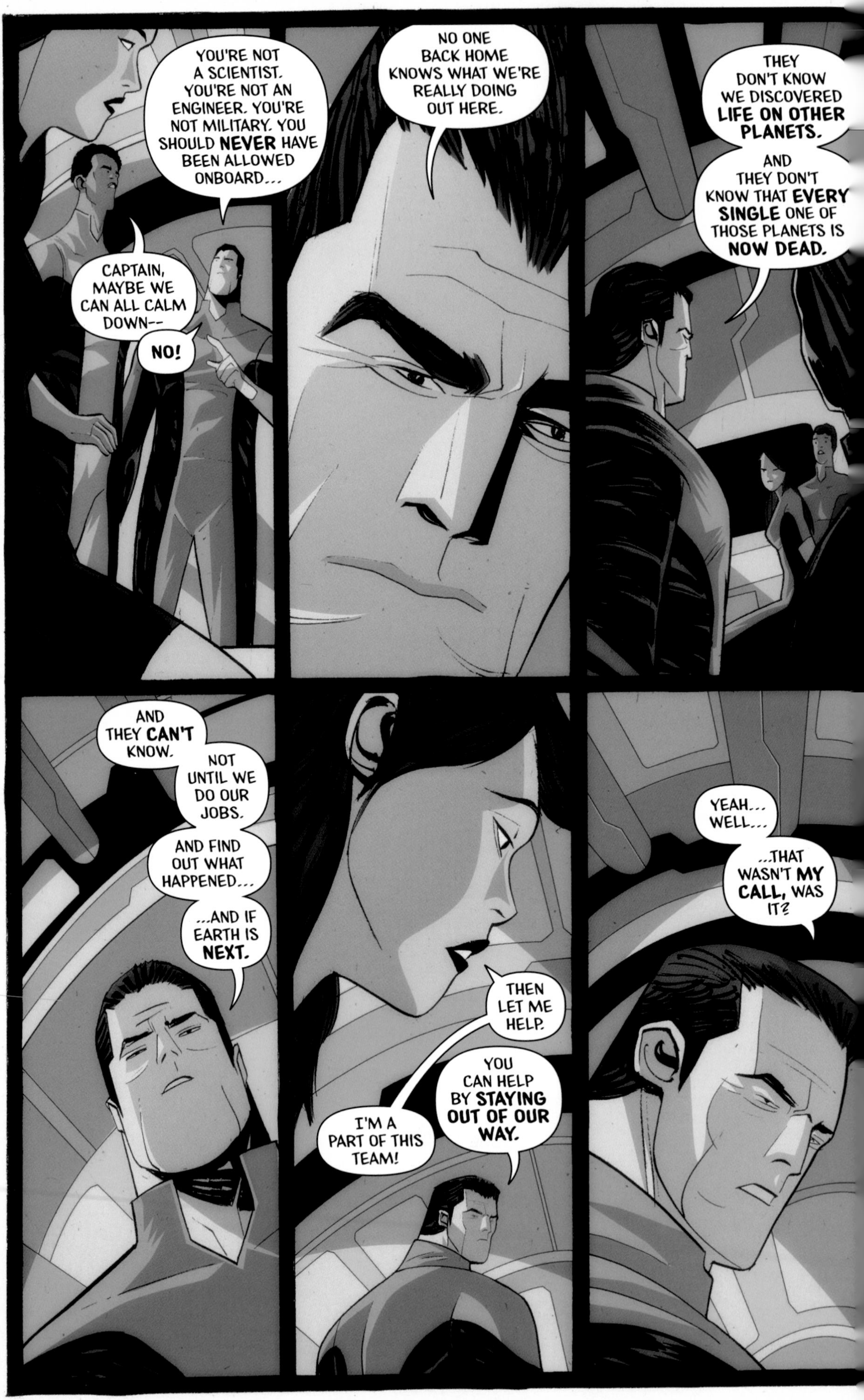
YOU'RE NOT A SCIENTIST. YOU'RE NOT AN ENGINEER. YOU'RE NOT MILITARY. YOU SHOULD NEVER HAVE BEEN ALLOWED ONBOARD...
CAPTAIN, MAYBE WE CAN ALL CALM DOWN--
NO!
NO ONE BACK HOME KNOWS WHAT WE'RE REALLY DOING OUT HERE.
THEY DON'T KNOW WE DISCOVERED LIFE ON OTHER PLANETS.
AND THEY DON'T KNOW THAT EVERY SINGLE ONE OF THOSE PLANETS IS NOW DEAD.
AND THEY CAN'T KNOW.
NOT UNTIL WE DO OUR JOBS.
AND FIND OUT WHAT HAPPENED...
...AND IF EARTH IS NEXT.
THEN LET ME HELP.
YOU CAN HELP BY STAYING OUT OF OUR WAY.
I'M A PART OF THIS TEAM!
YEAH... WELL...
...THAT WASN'T MY CALL, WAS IT?

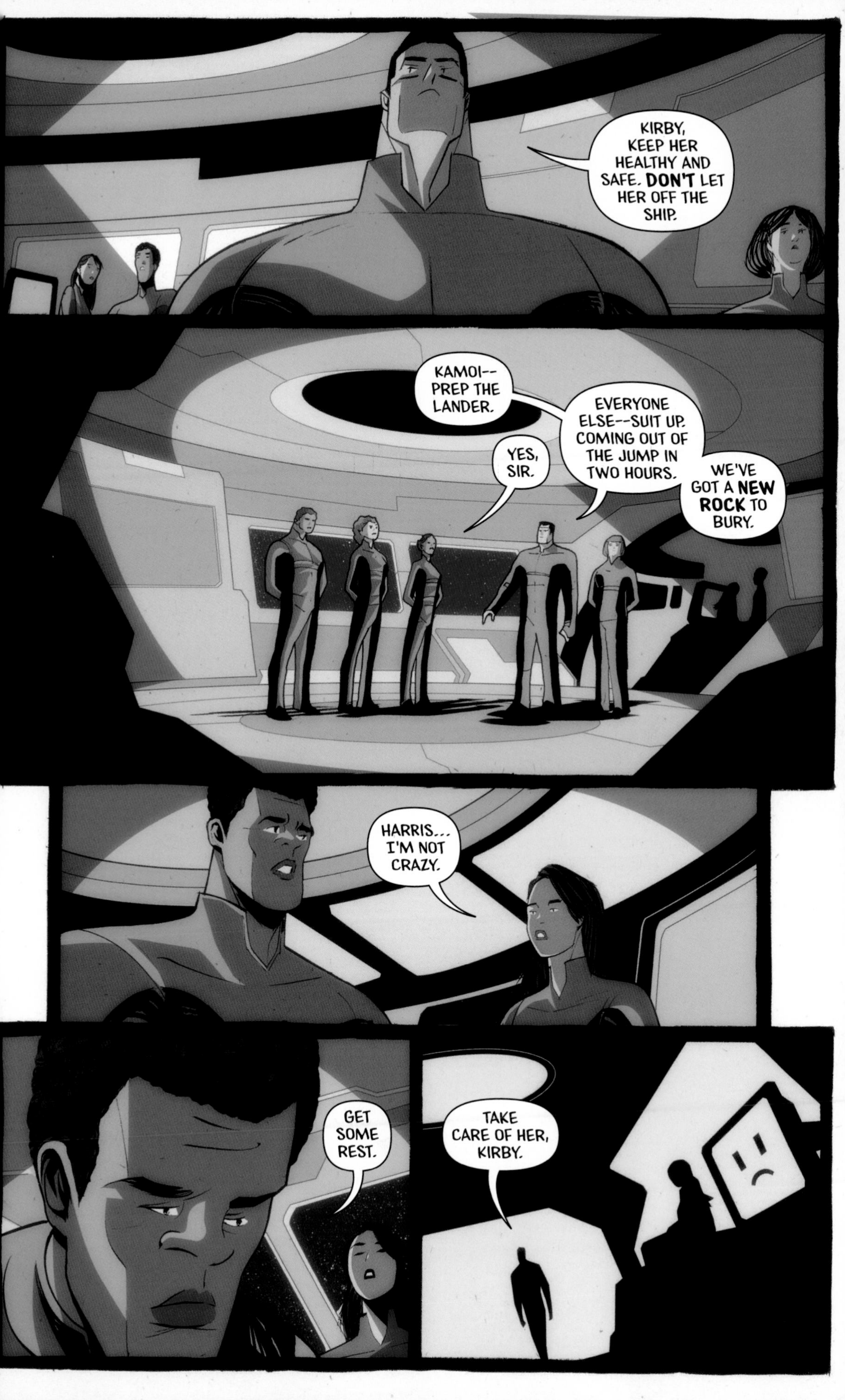
KIRBY, KEEP HER HEALTHY AND SAFE. DON'T LET HER OFF THE SHIP.
KAMOI-- PREP THE LANDER.
EVERYONE ELSE--SUIT UP. COMING OUT OF THE JUMP IN TWO HOURS.
YES, SIR.
WE'VE GOT A NEW ROCK TO BURY.
HARRIS... I'M NOT CRAZY.
GET SOME REST.
TAKE CARE OF HER, KIRBY.

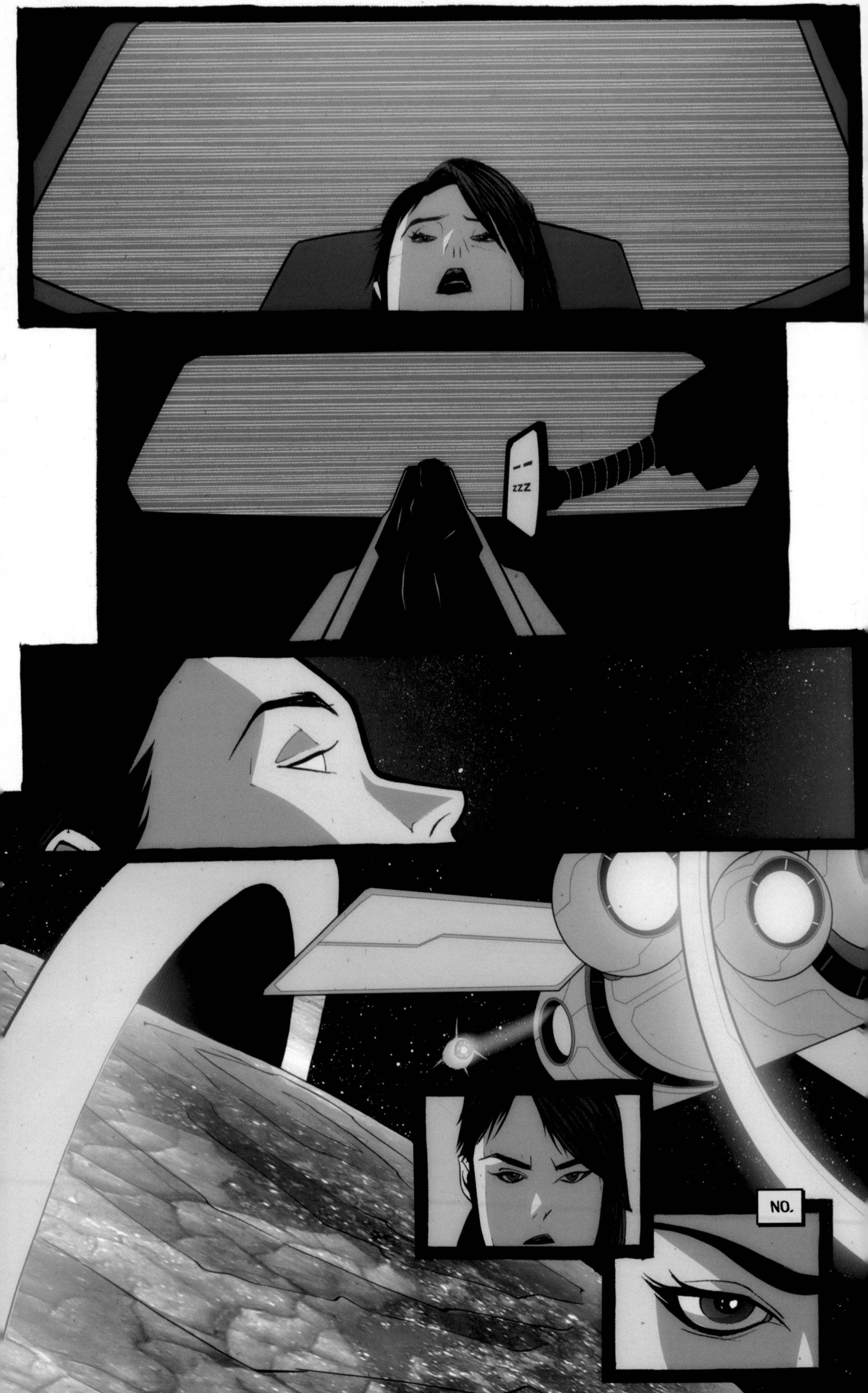
zzZ
NO.

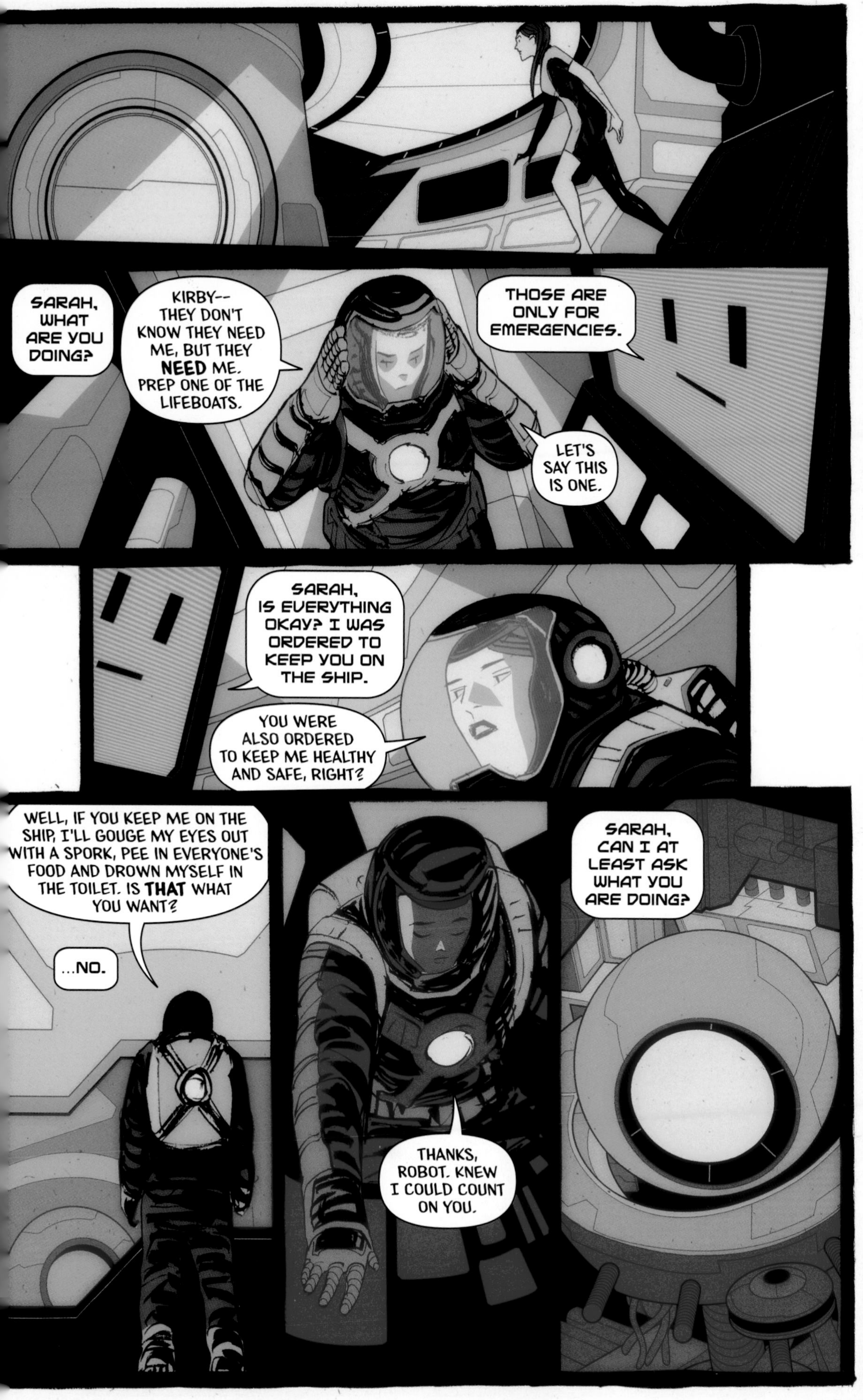
SARAH, WHAT ARE YOU DOING?
KIRBY-- THEY DON'T KNOW THEY NEED ME, BUT THEY **NEED** ME. PREP ONE OF THE LIFEBOATS.
THOSE ARE ONLY FOR EMERGENCIES.
LET'S SAY THIS IS ONE.
SARAH, IS EVERYTHING OKAY? I WAS ORDERED TO KEEP YOU ON THE SHIP.
YOU WERE ALSO ORDERED TO KEEP ME HEALTHY AND SAFE, RIGHT?
WELL, IF YOU KEEP ME ON THE SHIP, I'LL GOUGE MY EYES OUT WITH A SPORK, PEE IN EVERYONE'S FOOD AND DROWN MYSELF IN THE TOILET. IS **THAT** WHAT YOU WANT?
...NO.
THANKS, ROBOT. KNEW I COULD COUNT ON YOU.
SARAH, CAN I AT LEAST ASK WHAT YOU ARE DOING?

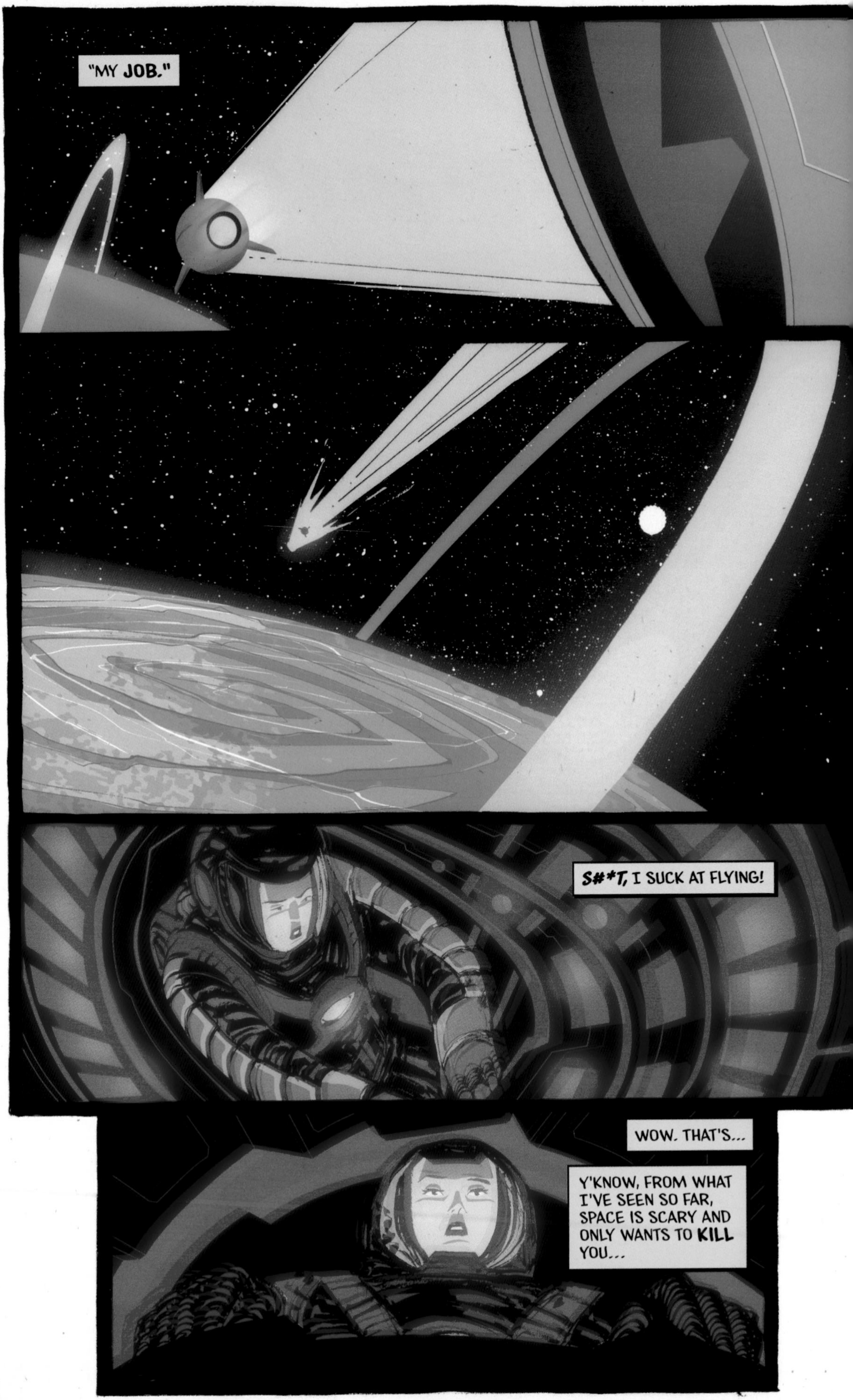
"MY JOB."
S#*T, I SUCK AT FLYING!
WOW. THAT'S...
Y'KNOW, FROM WHAT I'VE SEEN SO FAR, SPACE IS SCARY AND ONLY WANTS TO KILL YOU...

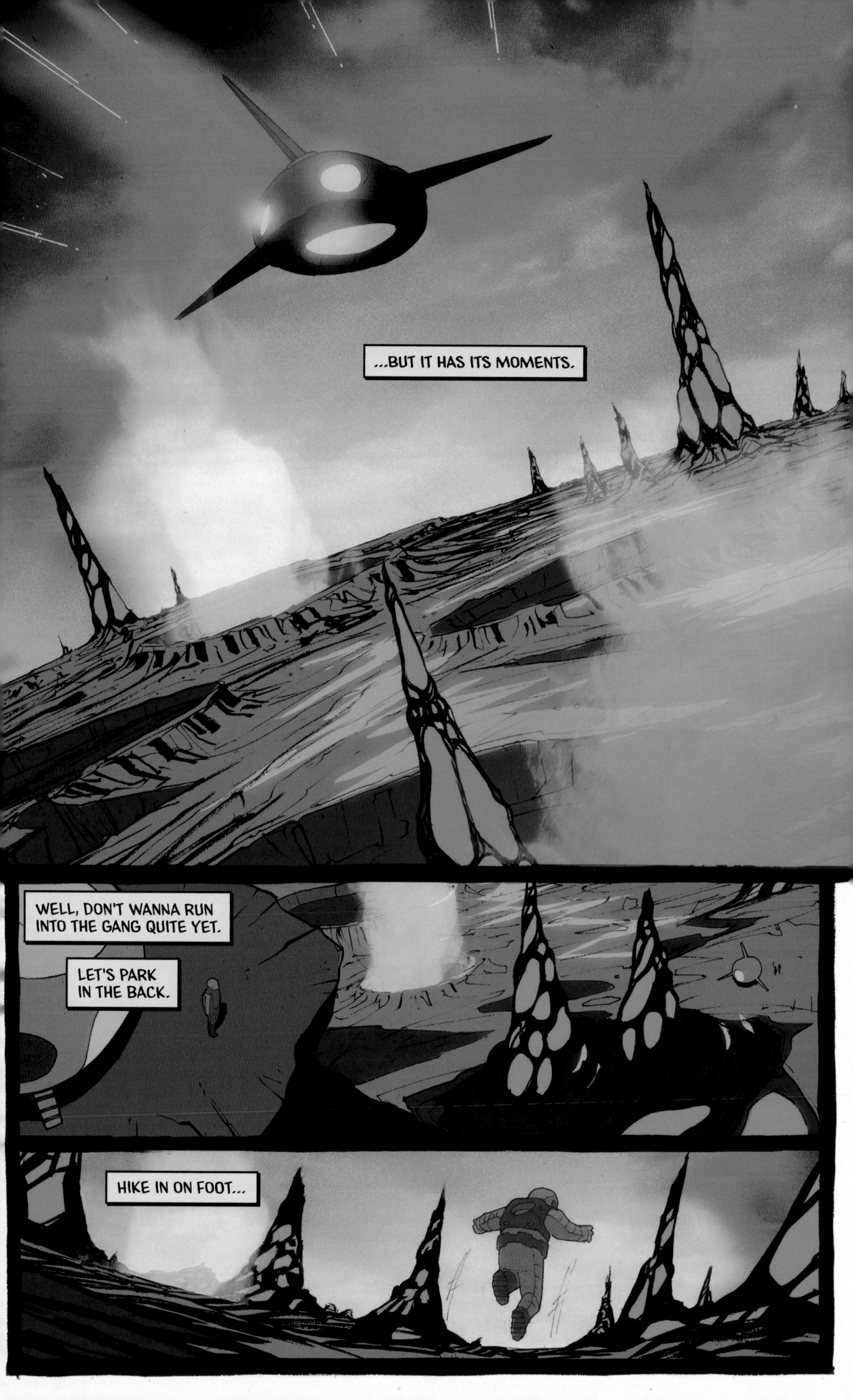
...BUT IT HAS ITS MOMENTS.
WELL, DON'T WANNA RUN INTO THE GANG QUITE YET.
LET'S PARK IN THE BACK.
HIKE IN ON FOOT...

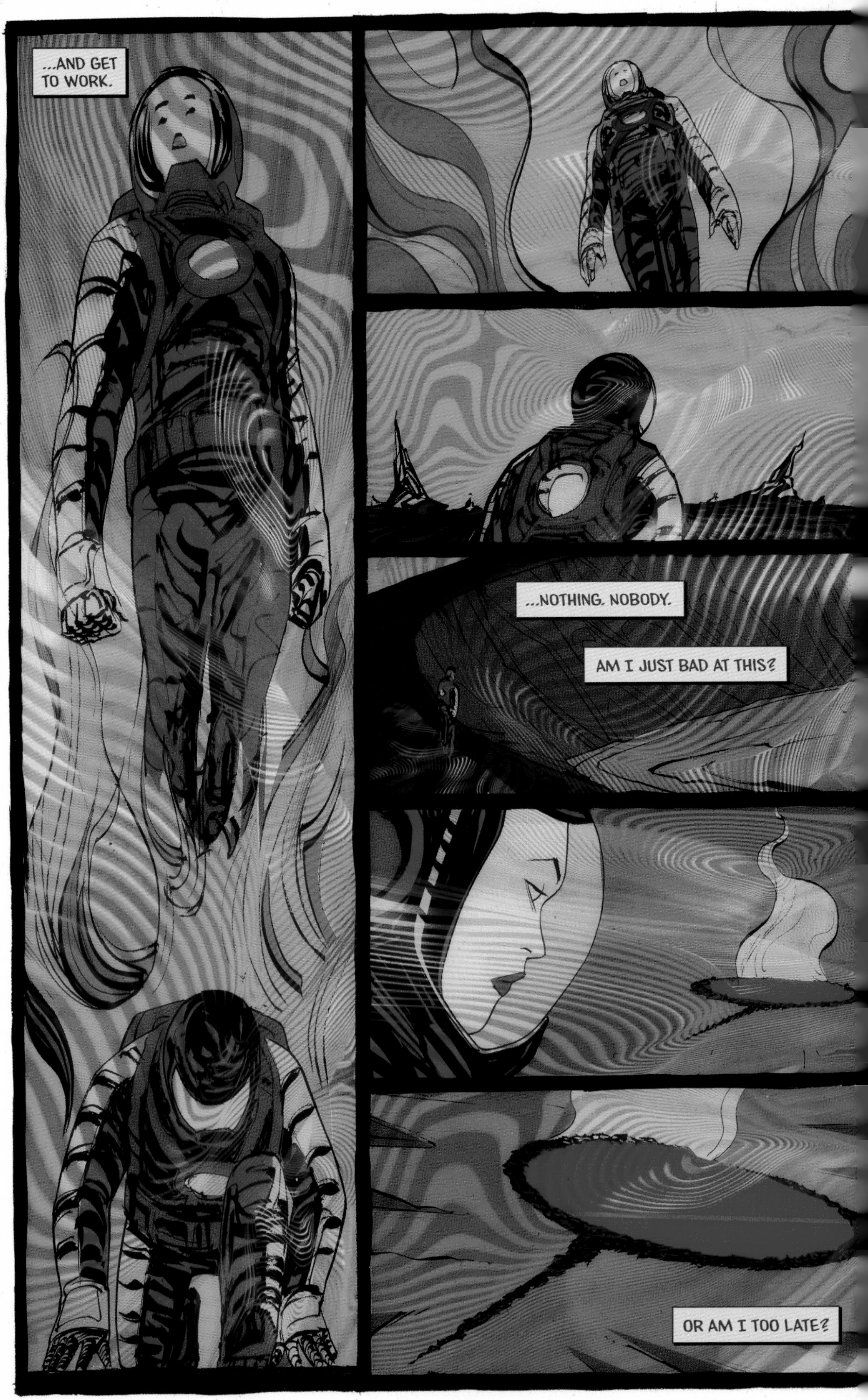
...AND GET TO WORK.
...NOTHING. NOBODY.
AM I JUST BAD AT THIS?
OR AM I TOO LATE?

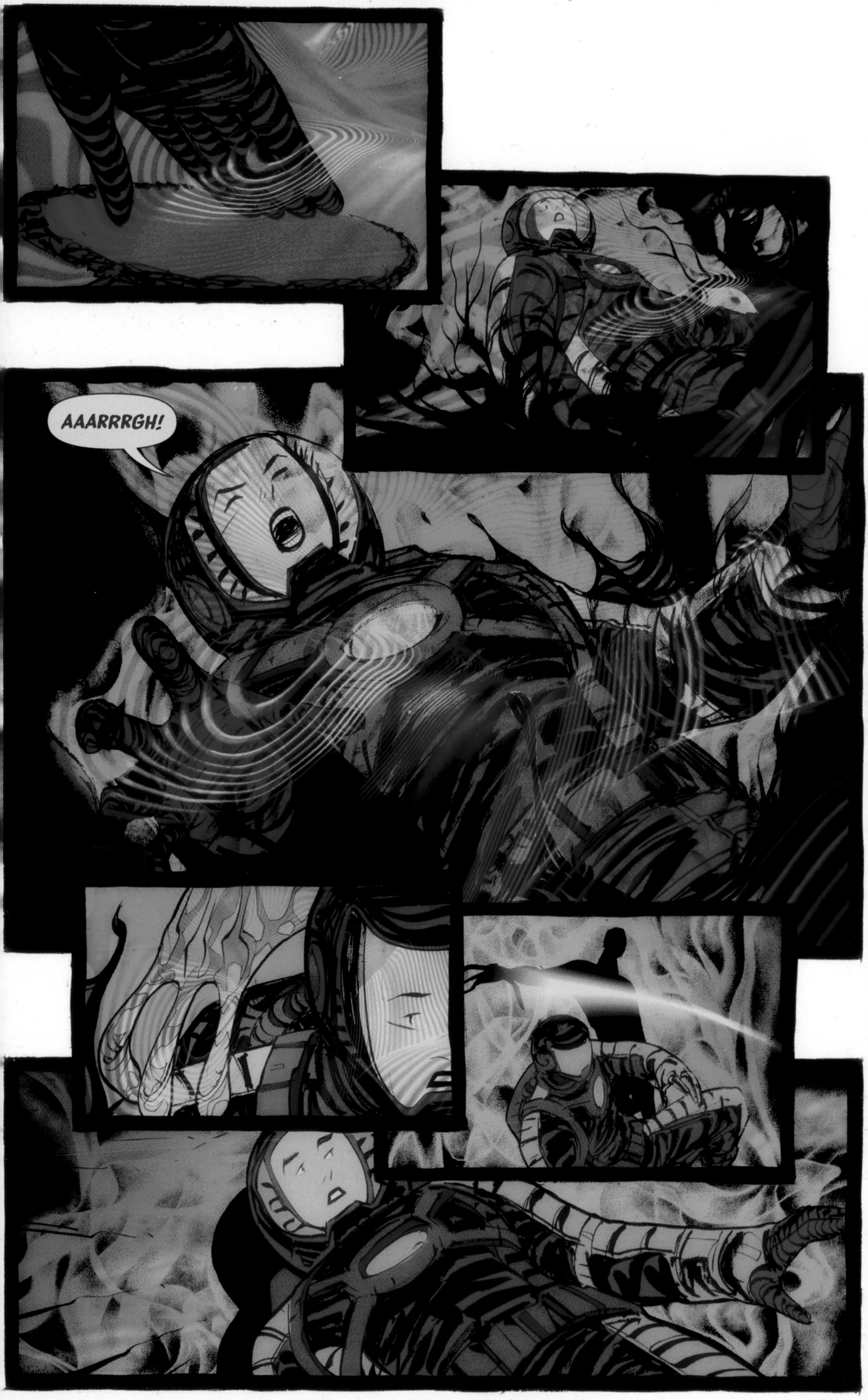
AAARRRGH!

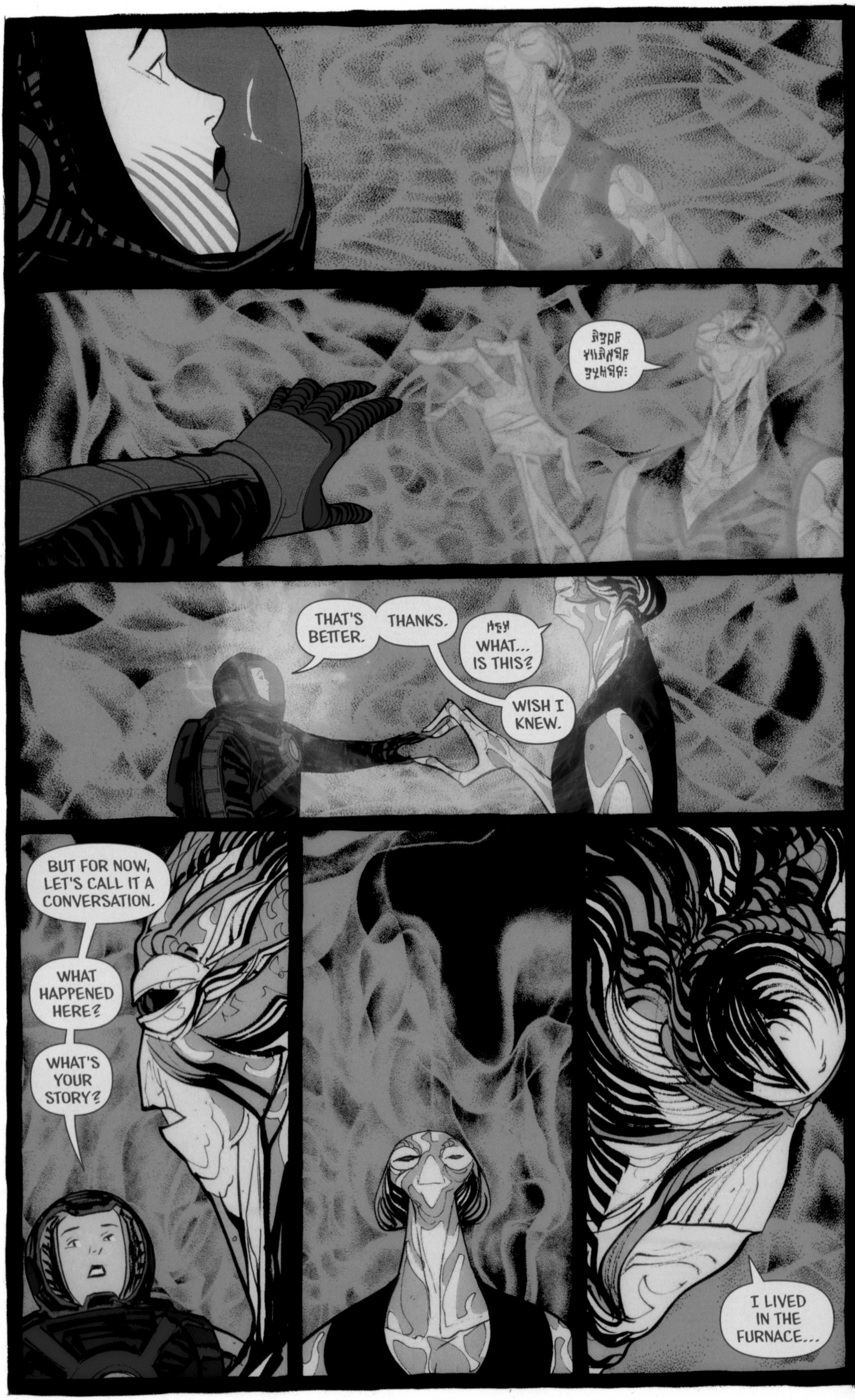
THAT'S BETTER.
THANKS.
WHAT... IS THIS?
WISH I KNEW.
BUT FOR NOW, LET'S CALL IT A CONVERSATION.
WHAT HAPPENED HERE?
WHAT'S YOUR STORY?
I LIVED IN THE FURNACE...

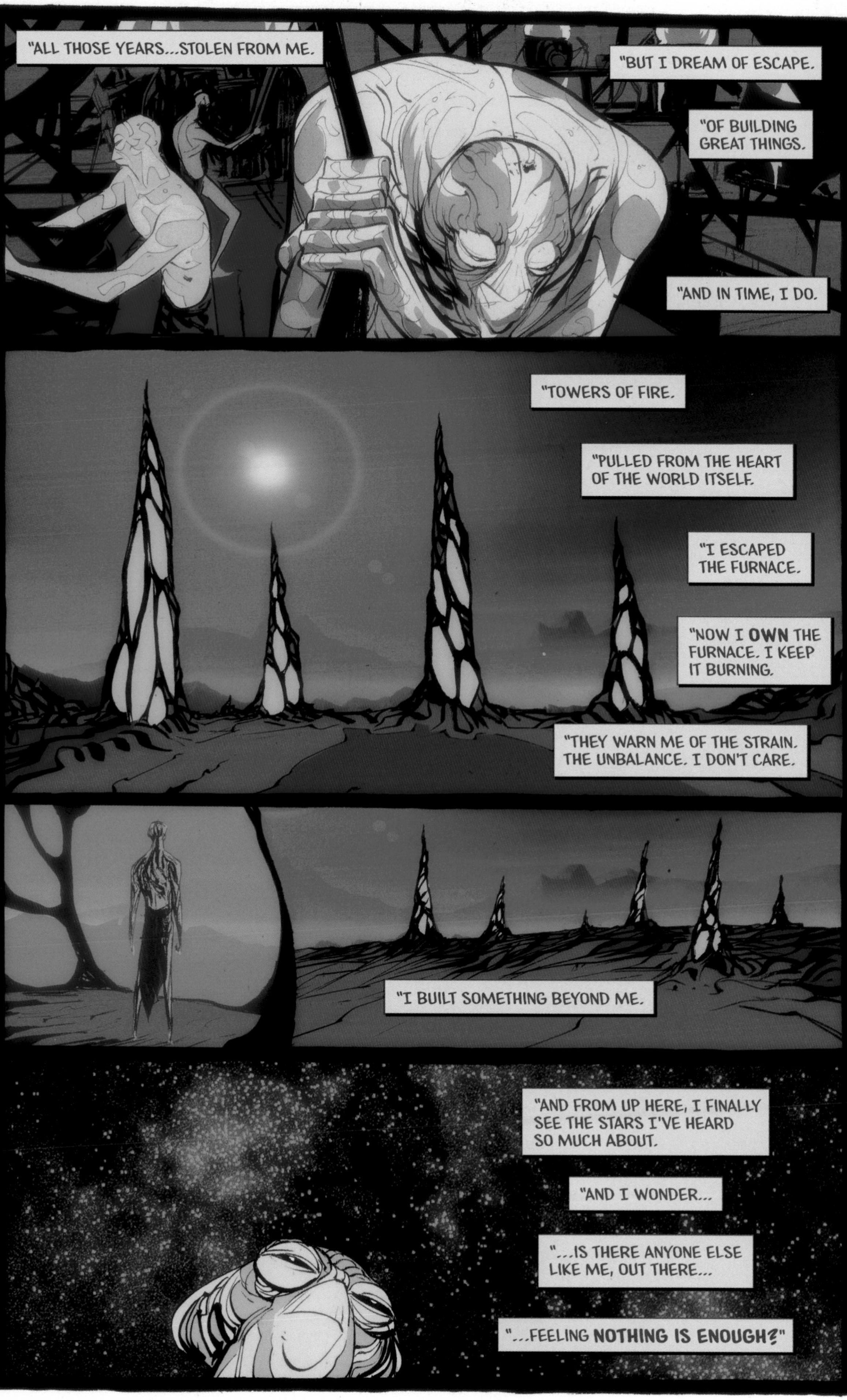
"ALL THOSE YEARS...STOLEN FROM ME.
"BUT I DREAM OF ESCAPE.
"OF BUILDING GREAT THINGS.
"AND IN TIME, I DO.
"TOWERS OF FIRE.
"PULLED FROM THE HEART OF THE WORLD ITSELF.
"I ESCAPED THE FURNACE.
"NOW I **OWN** THE FURNACE. I KEEP IT BURNING.
"THEY WARN ME OF THE STRAIN. THE UNBALANCE. I DON'T CARE.
"I BUILT SOMETHING BEYOND ME.
"AND FROM UP HERE, I FINALLY SEE THE STARS I'VE HEARD SO MUCH ABOUT.
"AND I WONDER...
"...IS THERE ANYONE ELSE LIKE ME, OUT THERE...
"...FEELING **NOTHING IS ENOUGH?**"

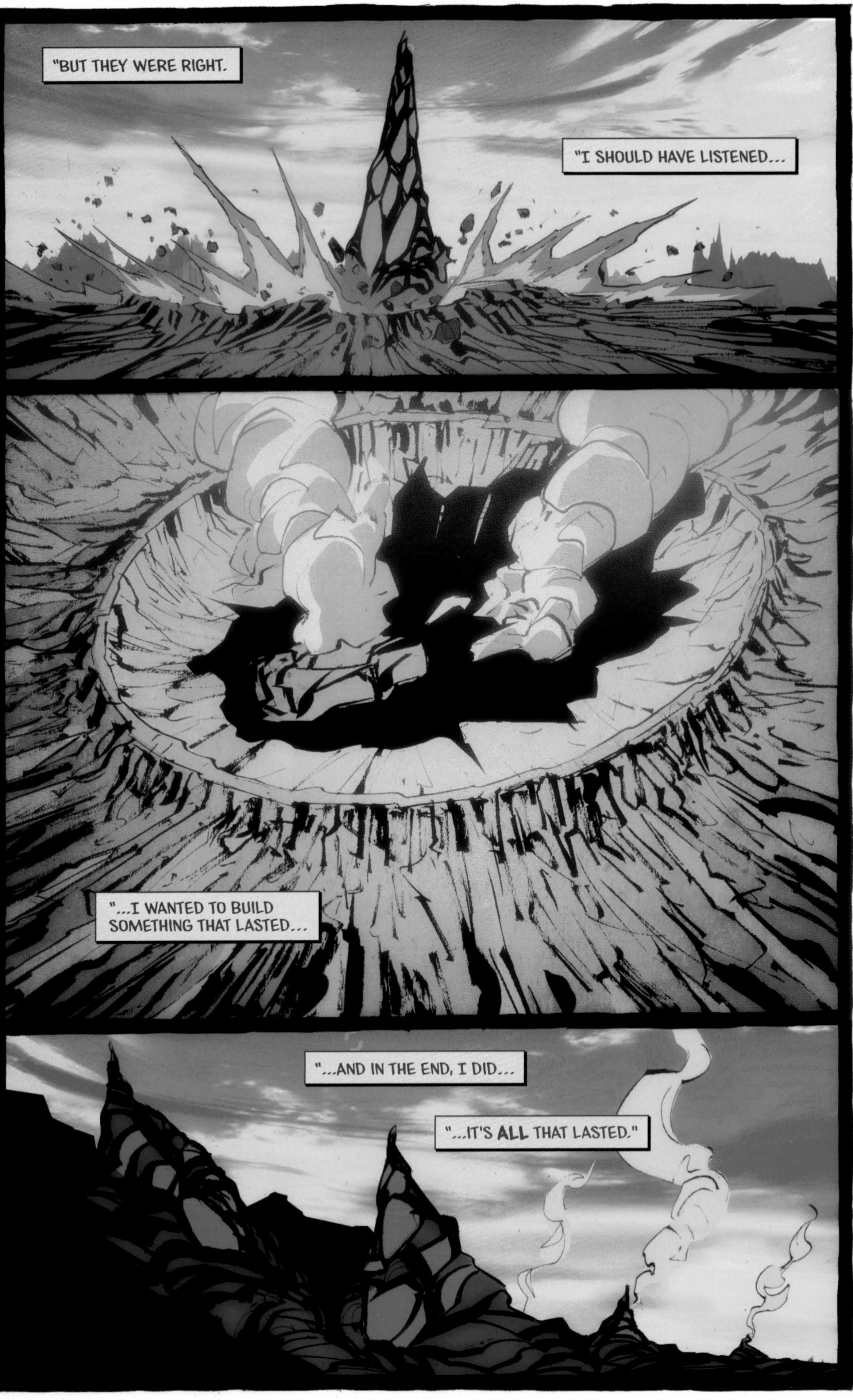
"BUT THEY WERE RIGHT.
"I SHOULD HAVE LISTENED...
"...I WANTED TO BUILD SOMETHING THAT LASTED...
"...AND IN THE END, I DID...
"...IT'S ALL THAT LASTED."

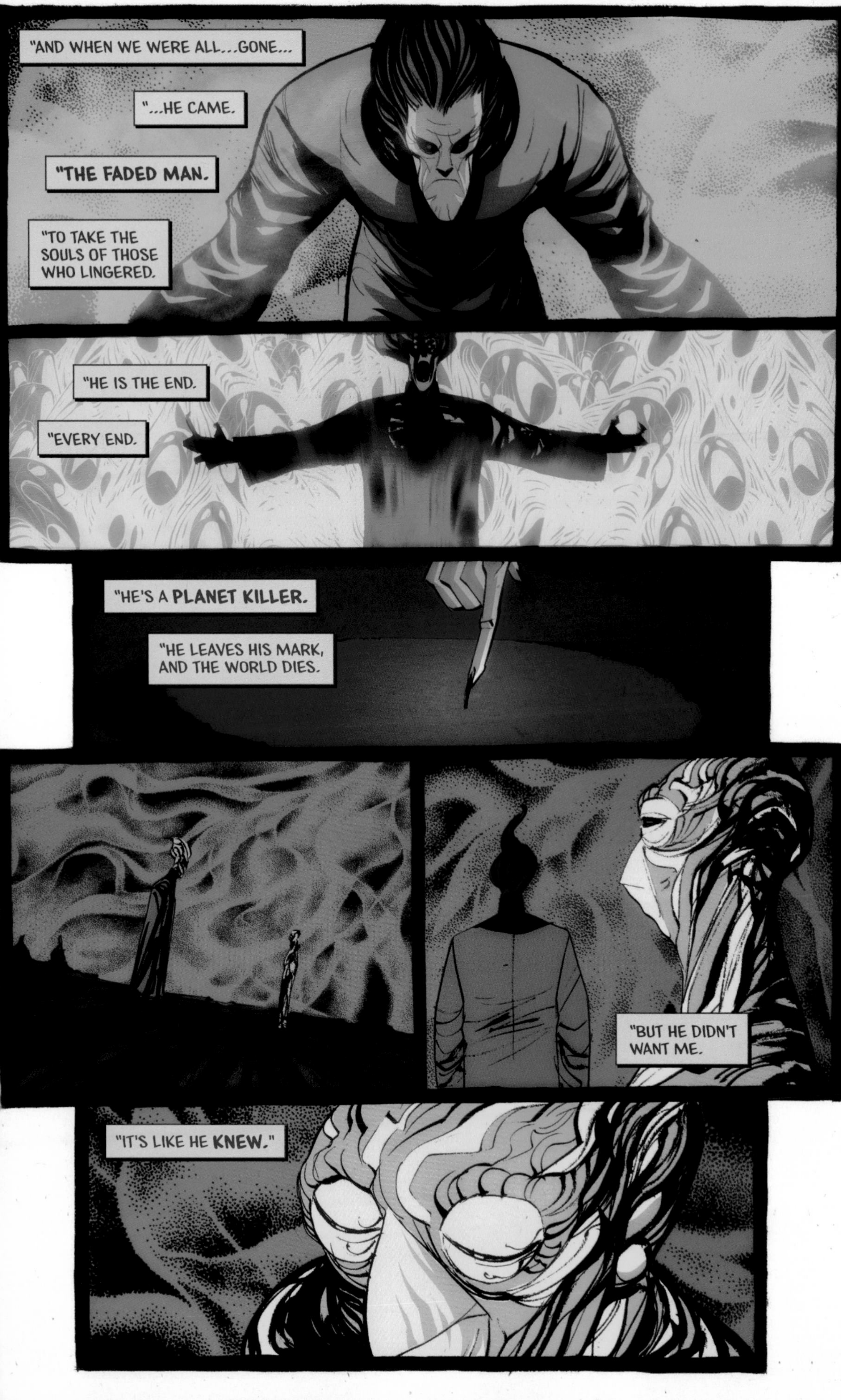
"AND WHEN WE WERE ALL...GONE...
"...HE CAME.
"THE FADED MAN.
"TO TAKE THE SOULS OF THOSE WHO LINGERED.
"HE IS THE END.
"EVERY END.
"HE'S A PLANET KILLER.
"HE LEAVES HIS MARK, AND THE WORLD DIES.
"BUT HE DIDN'T WANT ME.
"IT'S LIKE HE KNEW."

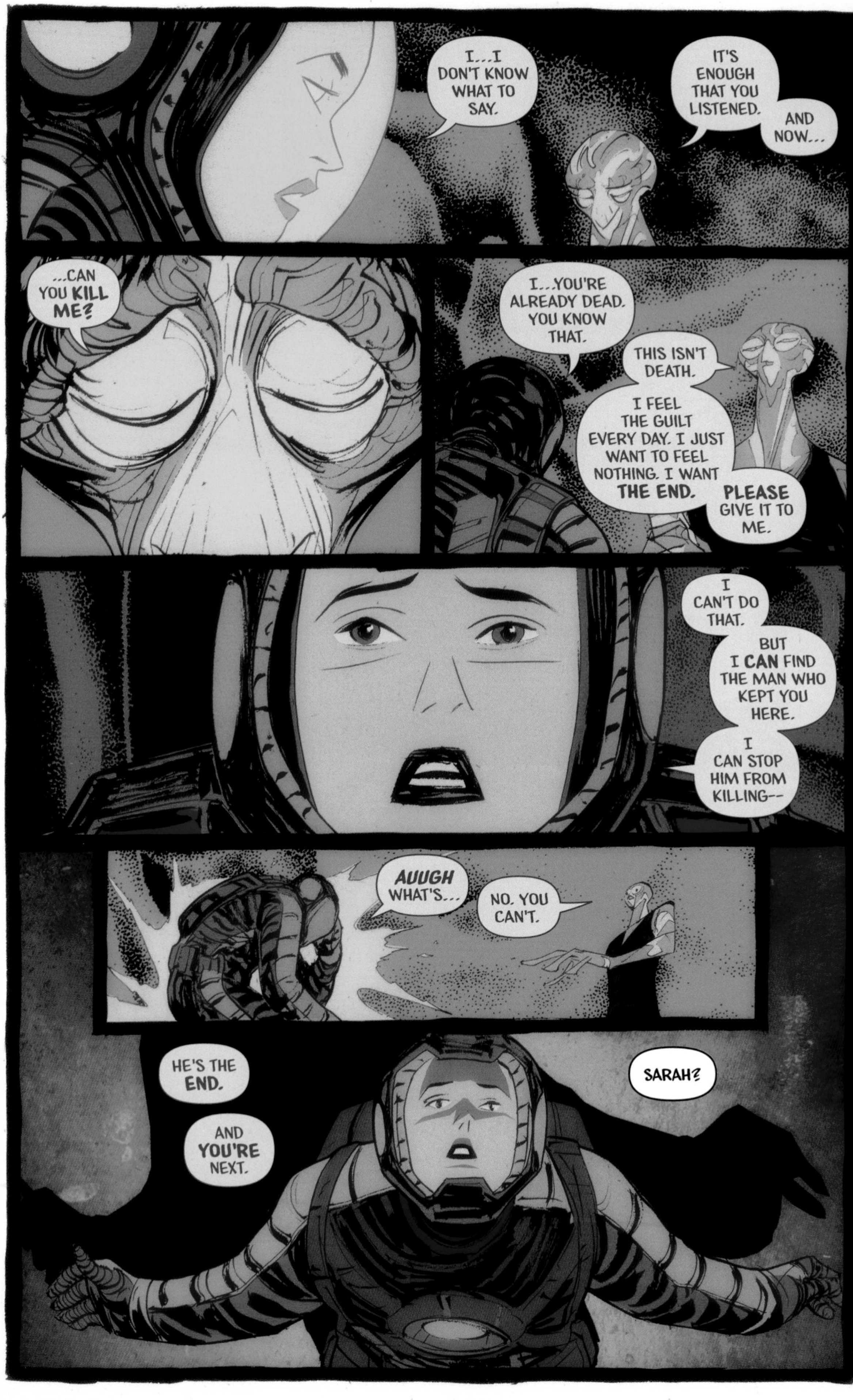
I...I DON'T KNOW WHAT TO SAY.
IT'S ENOUGH THAT YOU LISTENED.
AND NOW...
...CAN YOU KILL ME?
I...YOU'RE ALREADY DEAD. YOU KNOW THAT.
THIS ISN'T DEATH.
I FEEL THE GUILT EVERY DAY. I JUST WANT TO FEEL NOTHING. I WANT THE END.
PLEASE GIVE IT TO ME.
I CAN'T DO THAT.
BUT I CAN FIND THE MAN WHO KEPT YOU HERE.
I CAN STOP HIM FROM KILLING--
AUUGH WHAT'S...
NO. YOU CAN'T.
HE'S THE END.
AND YOU'RE NEXT.
SARAH?

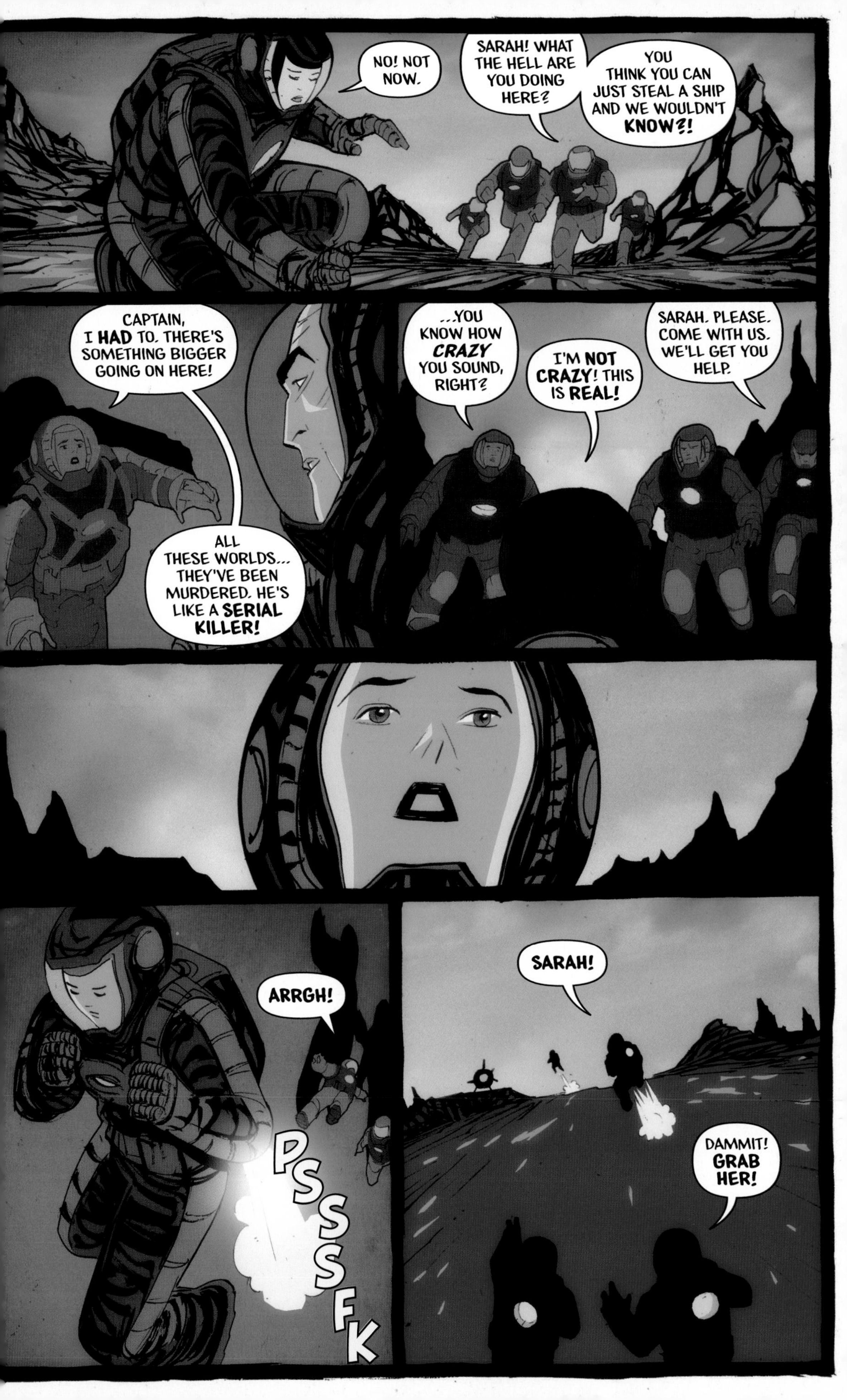
NO! NOT NOW.
SARAH! WHAT THE HELL ARE YOU DOING HERE?
YOU THINK YOU CAN JUST STEAL A SHIP AND WE WOULDN'T KNOW?!
CAPTAIN, I HAD TO. THERE'S SOMETHING BIGGER GOING ON HERE!
ALL THESE WORLDS... THEY'VE BEEN MURDERED. HE'S LIKE A SERIAL KILLER!
...YOU KNOW HOW CRAZY YOU SOUND, RIGHT?
I'M NOT CRAZY! THIS IS REAL!
SARAH. PLEASE. COME WITH US. WE'LL GET YOU HELP.
ARRGH!
PSSSFK
SARAH!
DAMMIT! GRAB HER!

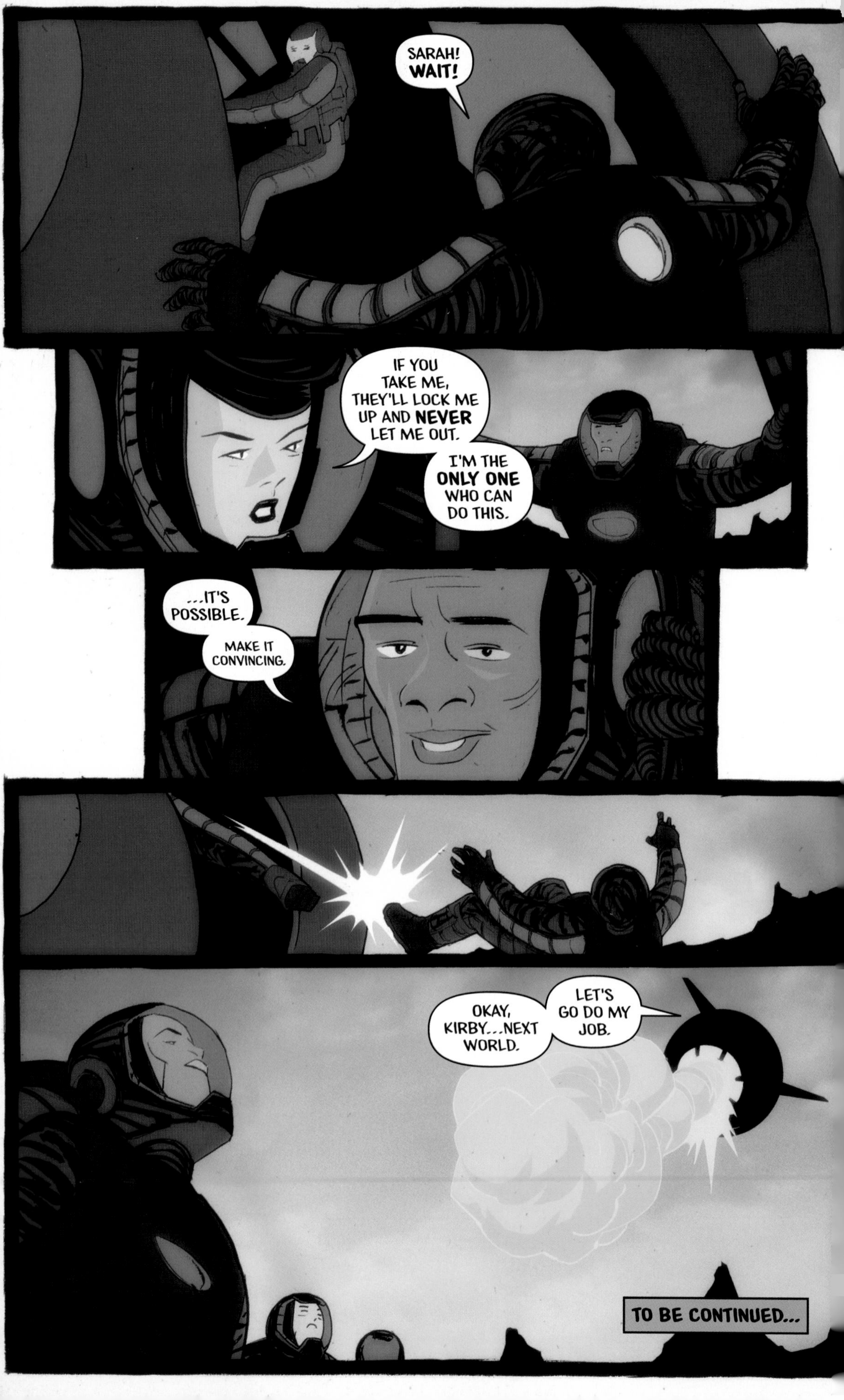
SARAH! WAIT!
IF YOU TAKE ME, THEY'LL LOCK ME UP AND NEVER LET ME OUT.
I'M THE ONLY ONE WHO CAN DO THIS.
...IT'S POSSIBLE.
MAKE IT CONVINCING.
OKAY, KIRBY...NEXT WORLD.
LET'S GO DO MY JOB.
TO BE CONTINUED...

3

"PAUL"

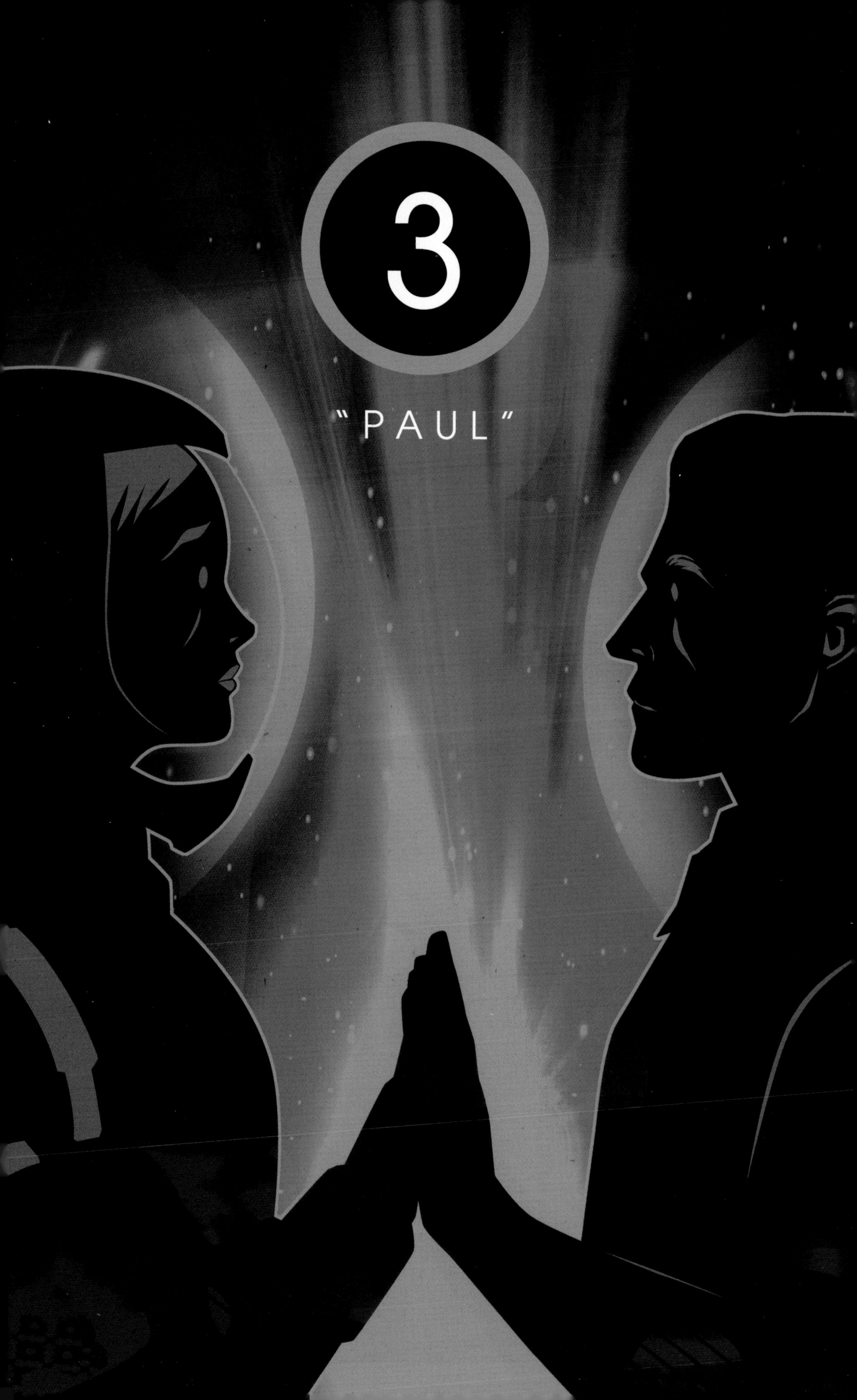

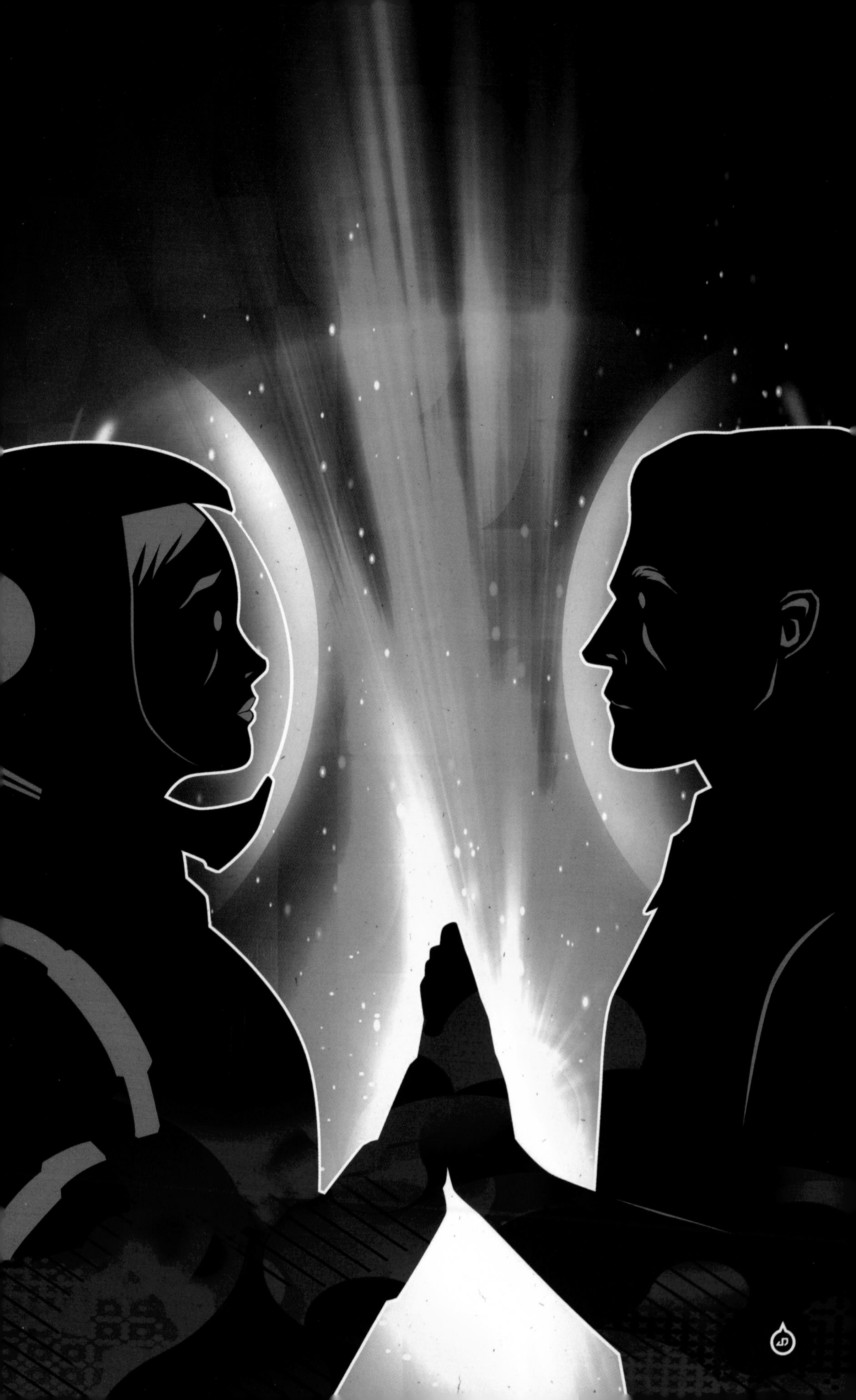

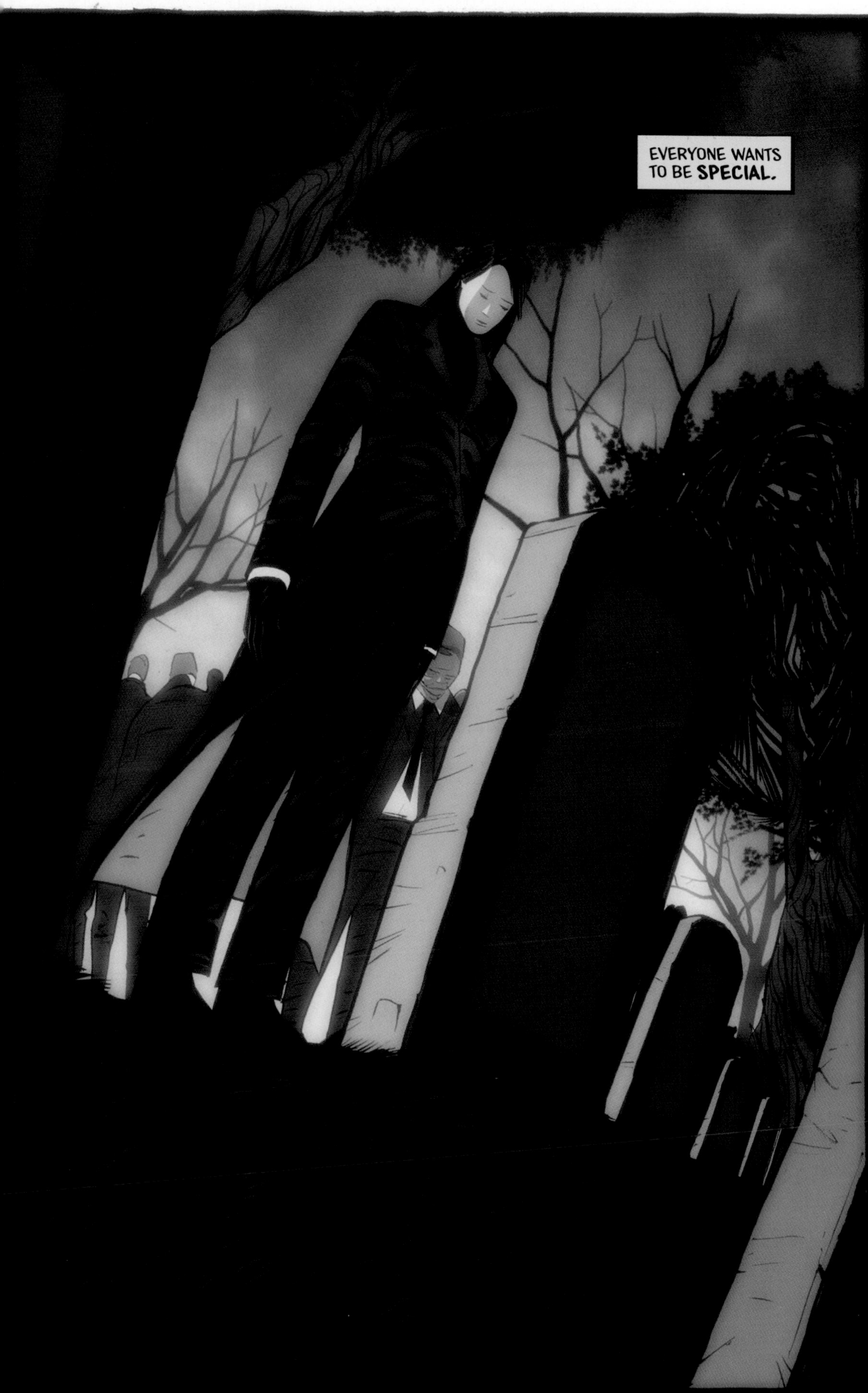
EVERYONE WANTS
TO BE SPECIAL.

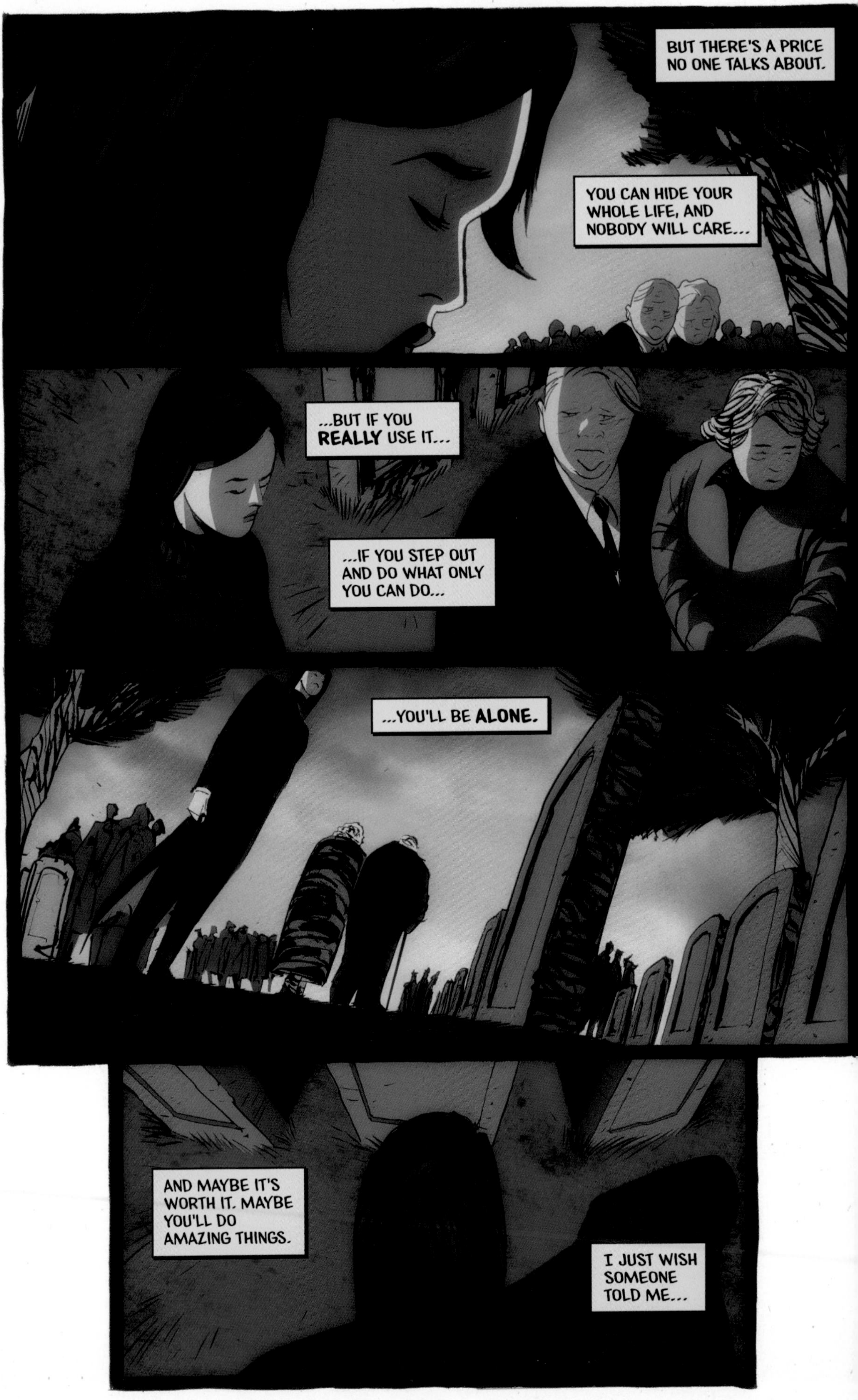
BUT THERE'S A PRICE NO ONE TALKS ABOUT.
YOU CAN HIDE YOUR WHOLE LIFE, AND NOBODY WILL CARE...
...BUT IF YOU **REALLY** USE IT...
...IF YOU STEP OUT AND DO WHAT ONLY YOU CAN DO...
...YOU'LL BE **ALONE.**
AND MAYBE IT'S WORTH IT. MAYBE YOU'LL DO AMAZING THINGS.
I JUST WISH SOMEONE TOLD ME...

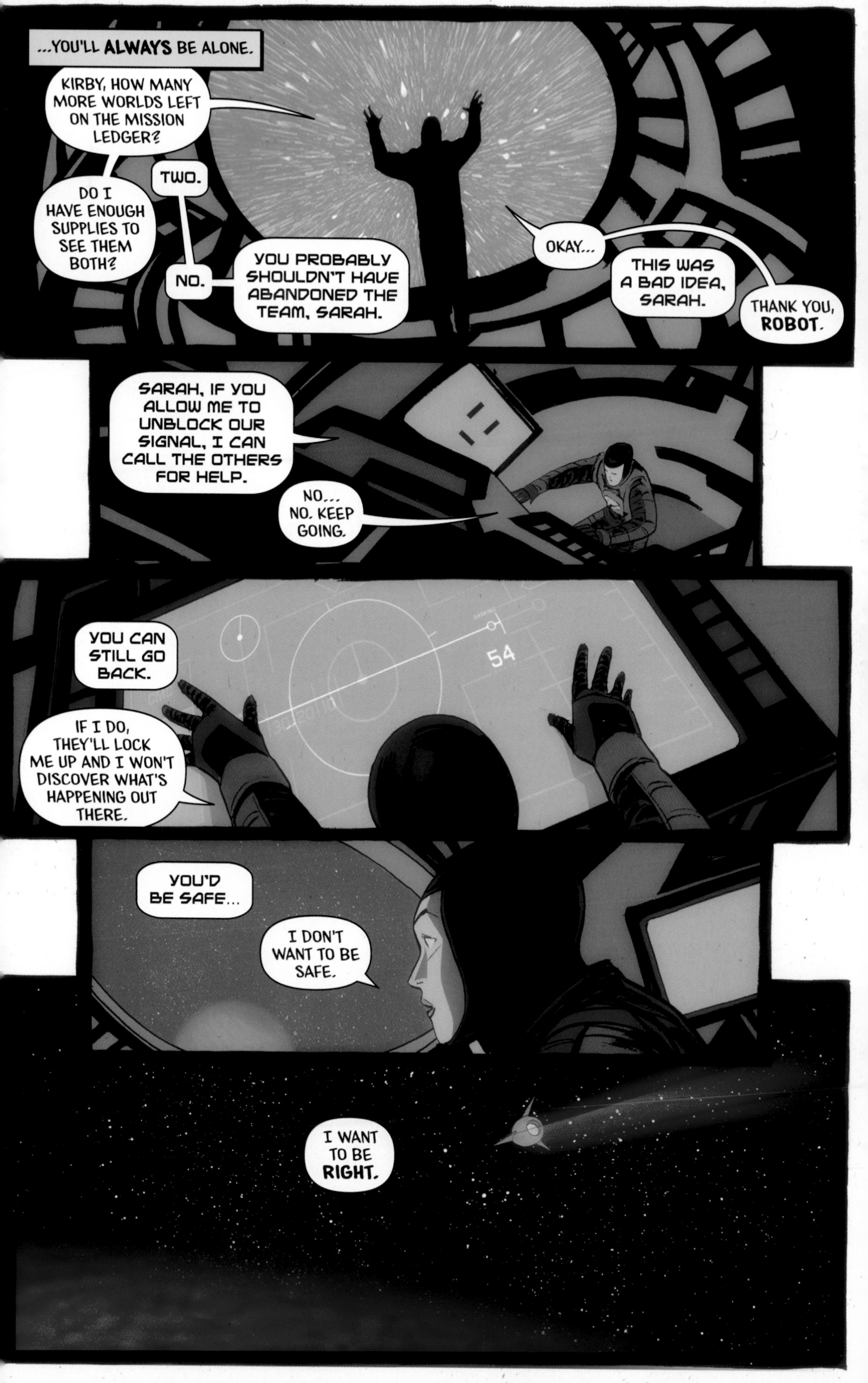
...YOU'LL ALWAYS BE ALONE.
KIRBY, HOW MANY MORE WORLDS LEFT ON THE MISSION LEDGER?
TWO.
DO I HAVE ENOUGH SUPPLIES TO SEE THEM BOTH?
NO.
YOU PROBABLY SHOULDN'T HAVE ABANDONED THE TEAM, SARAH.
OKAY...
THIS WAS A BAD IDEA, SARAH.
THANK YOU, ROBOT.
SARAH, IF YOU ALLOW ME TO UNBLOCK OUR SIGNAL, I CAN CALL THE OTHERS FOR HELP.
NO... NO. KEEP GOING.
YOU CAN STILL GO BACK.
54
IF I DO, THEY'LL LOCK ME UP AND I WON'T DISCOVER WHAT'S HAPPENING OUT THERE.
YOU'D BE SAFE...
I DON'T WANT TO BE SAFE.
I WANT TO BE RIGHT.

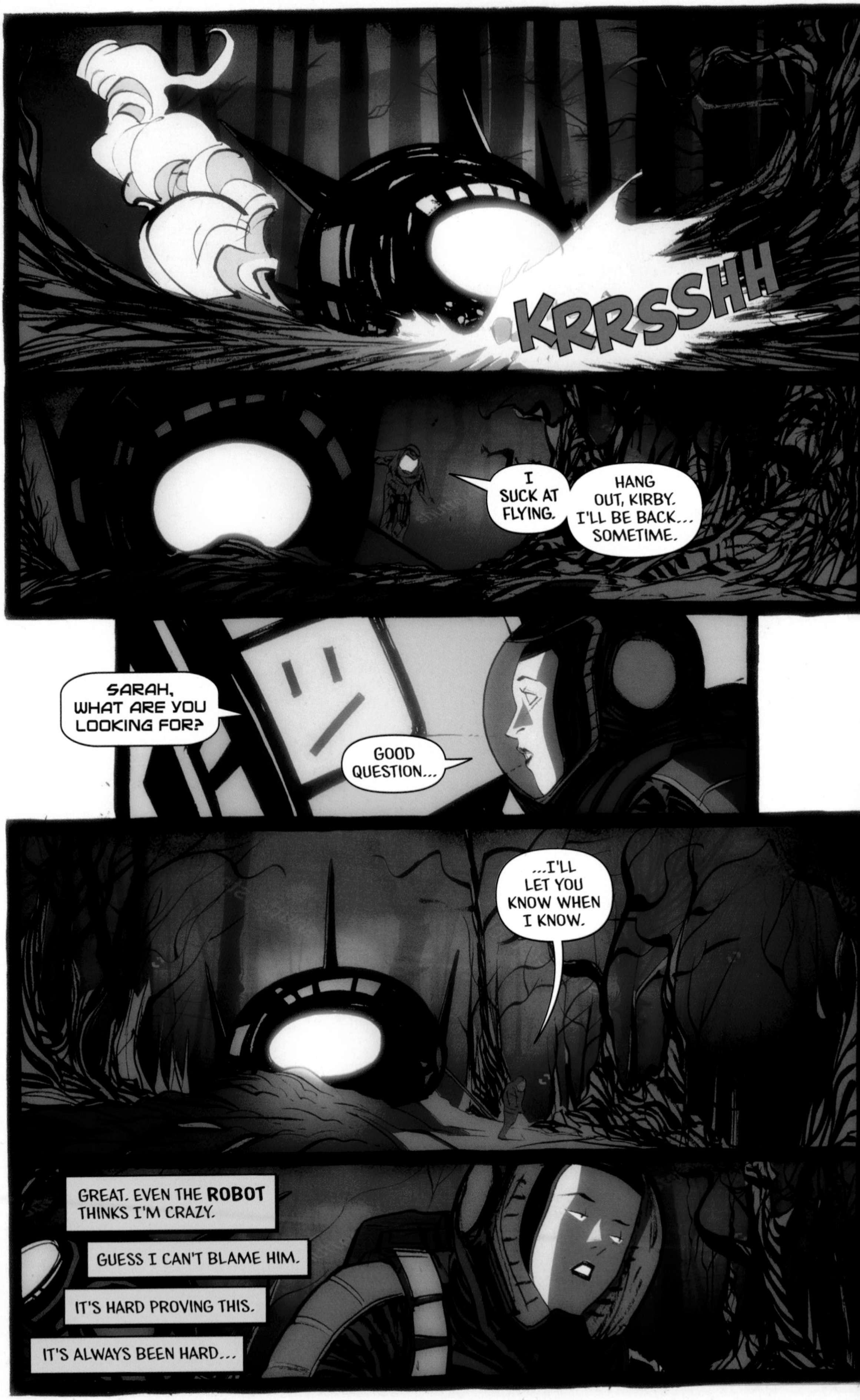
KRRSSHH
I SUCK AT FLYING.
HANG OUT, KIRBY. I'LL BE BACK... SOMETIME.
SARAH, WHAT ARE YOU LOOKING FOR?
GOOD QUESTION...
...I'LL LET YOU KNOW WHEN I KNOW.
GREAT. EVEN THE **ROBOT** THINKS I'M CRAZY.
GUESS I CAN'T BLAME HIM.
IT'S HARD PROVING THIS.
IT'S ALWAYS BEEN HARD...

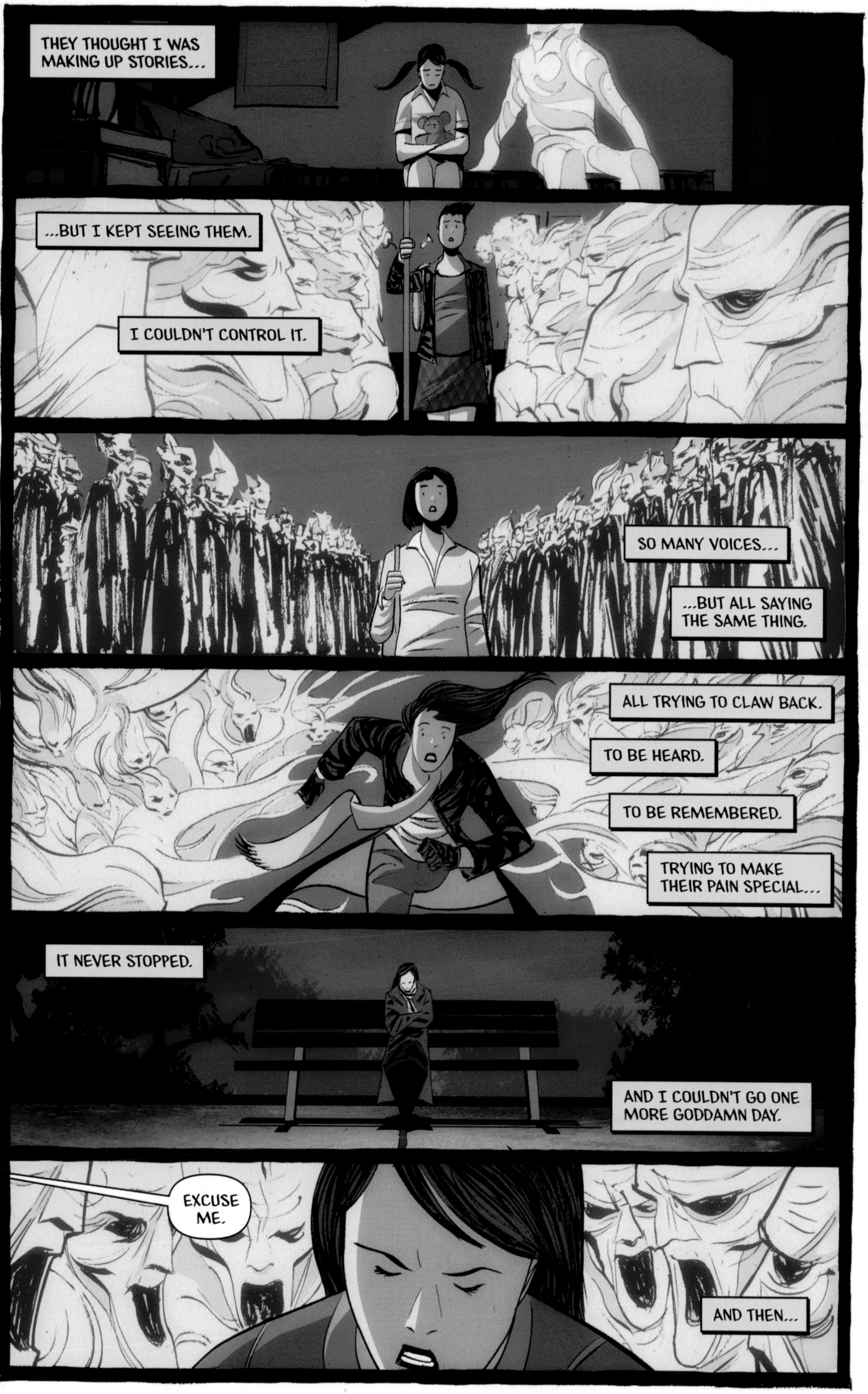
THEY THOUGHT I WAS MAKING UP STORIES...
...BUT I KEPT SEEING THEM.
I COULDN'T CONTROL IT.
SO MANY VOICES...
...BUT ALL SAYING THE SAME THING.
ALL TRYING TO CLAW BACK.
TO BE HEARD.
TO BE REMEMBERED.
TRYING TO MAKE THEIR PAIN SPECIAL...
IT NEVER STOPPED.
AND I COULDN'T GO ONE MORE GODDAMN DAY.
EXCUSE ME.
AND THEN...

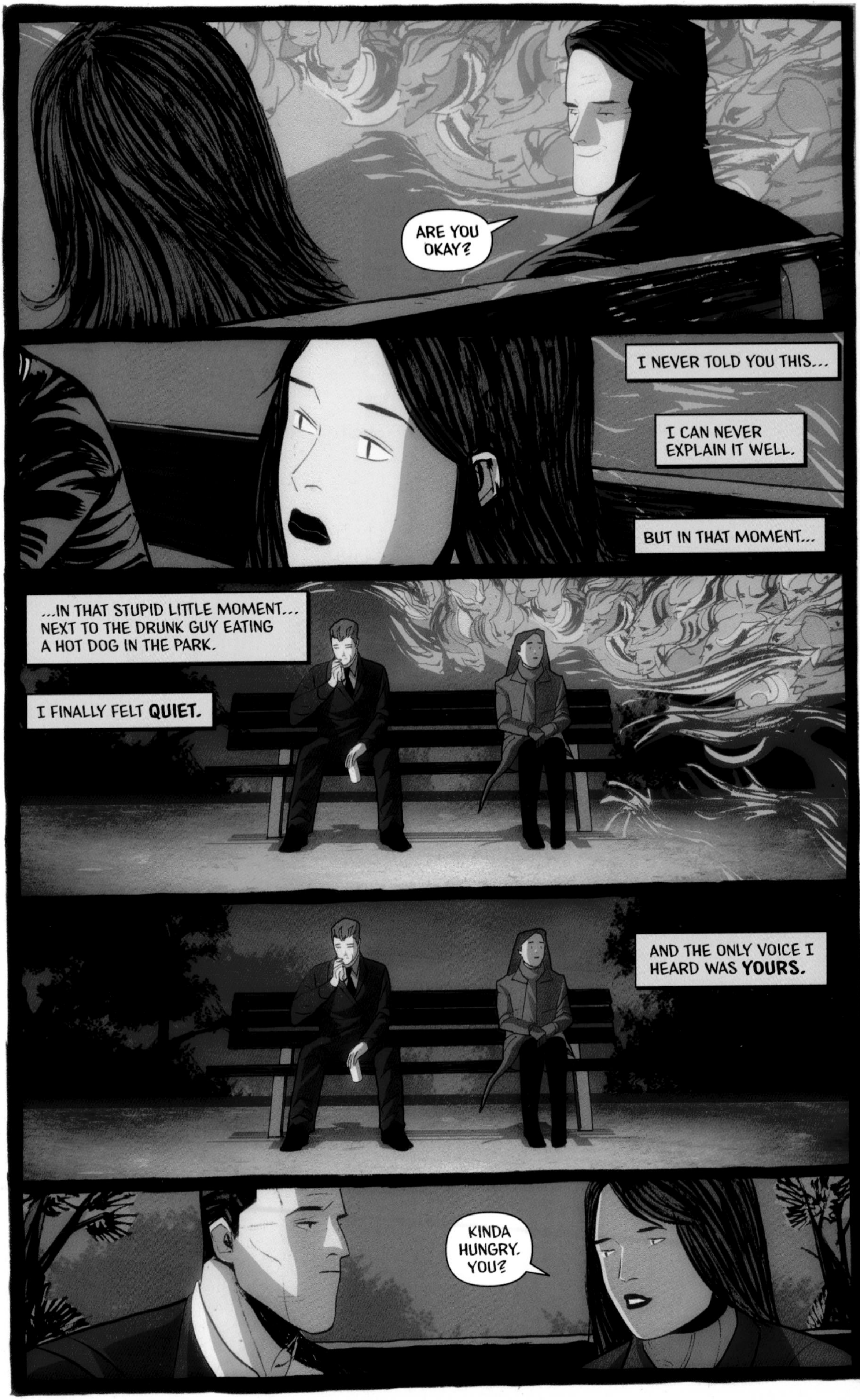
ARE YOU OKAY?
I NEVER TOLD YOU THIS...
I CAN NEVER EXPLAIN IT WELL.
BUT IN THAT MOMENT...
...IN THAT STUPID LITTLE MOMENT... NEXT TO THE DRUNK GUY EATING A HOT DOG IN THE PARK.
I FINALLY FELT **QUIET.**
AND THE ONLY VOICE I HEARD WAS **YOURS.**
KINDA HUNGRY. YOU?

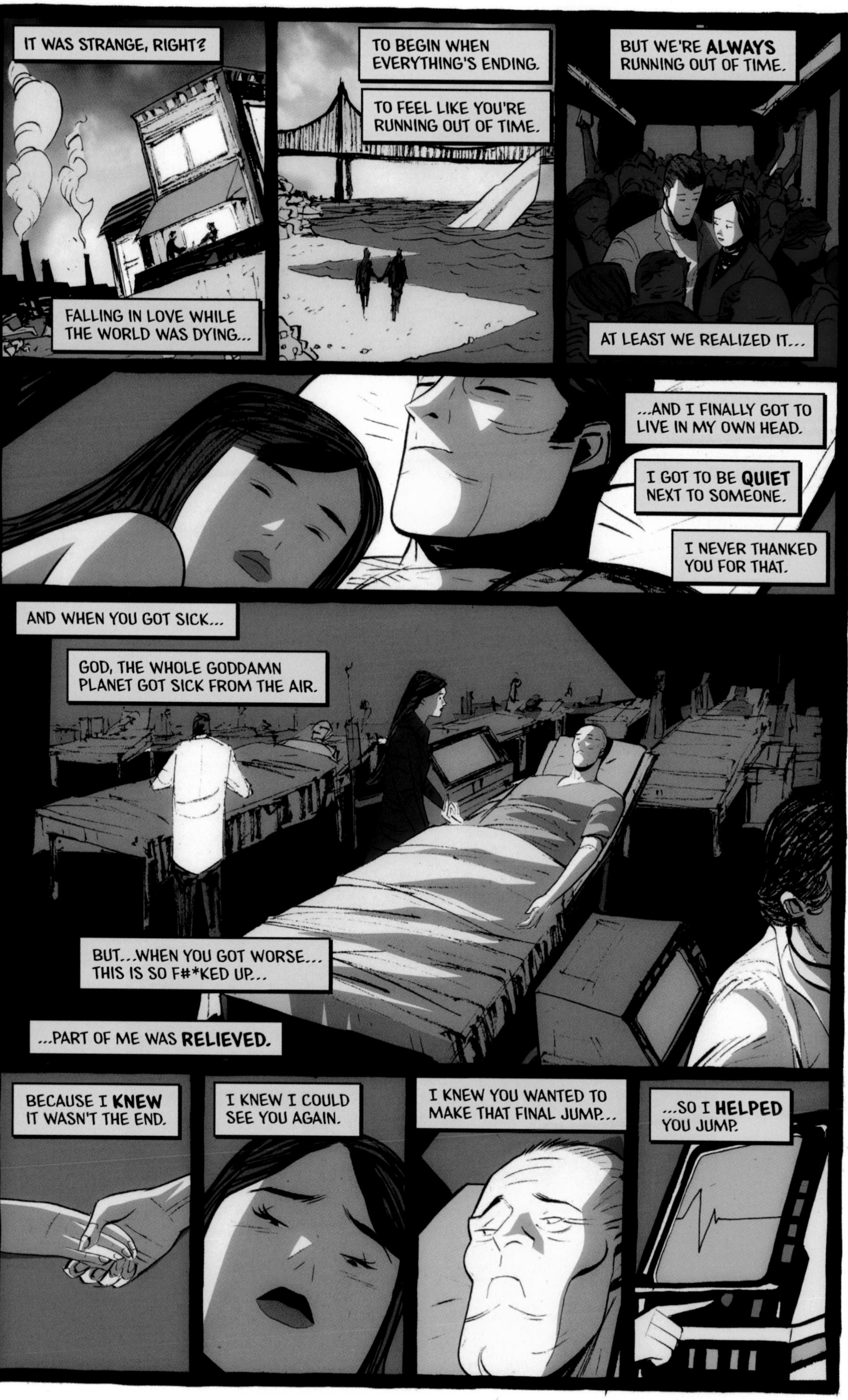
IT WAS STRANGE, RIGHT?
FALLING IN LOVE WHILE THE WORLD WAS DYING...
TO BEGIN WHEN EVERYTHING'S ENDING.
TO FEEL LIKE YOU'RE RUNNING OUT OF TIME.
BUT WE'RE ALWAYS RUNNING OUT OF TIME.
AT LEAST WE REALIZED IT...
...AND I FINALLY GOT TO LIVE IN MY OWN HEAD.
I GOT TO BE QUIET NEXT TO SOMEONE.
I NEVER THANKED YOU FOR THAT.
AND WHEN YOU GOT SICK...
GOD, THE WHOLE GODDAMN PLANET GOT SICK FROM THE AIR.
BUT...WHEN YOU GOT WORSE... THIS IS SO F#*KED UP...
...PART OF ME WAS RELIEVED.
BECAUSE I KNEW IT WASN'T THE END.
I KNEW I COULD SEE YOU AGAIN.
I KNEW YOU WANTED TO MAKE THAT FINAL JUMP...
...SO I HELPED YOU JUMP.

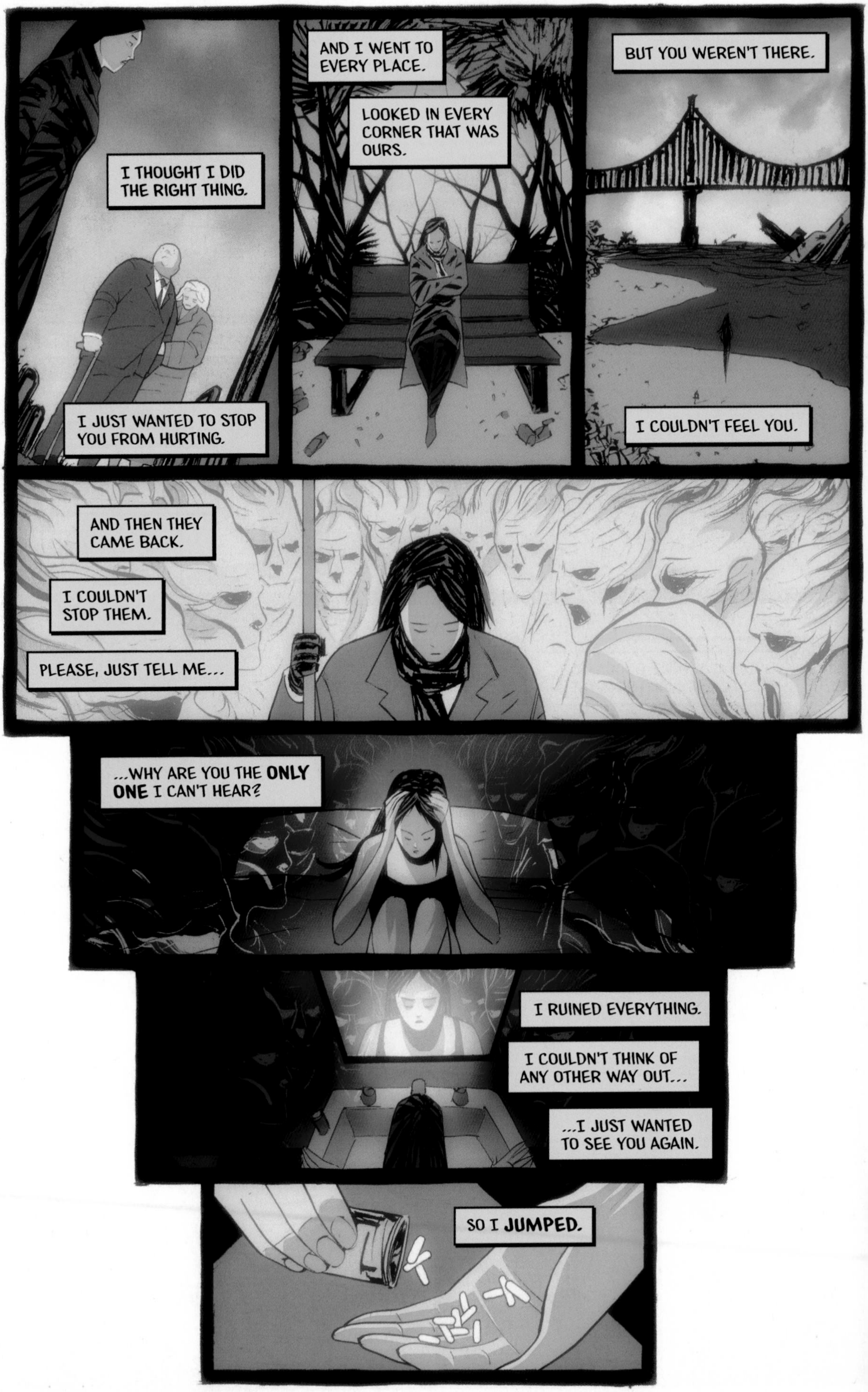
I THOUGHT I DID THE RIGHT THING.
I JUST WANTED TO STOP YOU FROM HURTING.
AND I WENT TO EVERY PLACE.
LOOKED IN EVERY CORNER THAT WAS OURS.
BUT YOU WEREN'T THERE.
I COULDN'T FEEL YOU.
AND THEN THEY CAME BACK.
I COULDN'T STOP THEM.
PLEASE, JUST TELL ME...
...WHY ARE YOU THE ONLY ONE I CAN'T HEAR?
I RUINED EVERYTHING.
I COULDN'T THINK OF ANY OTHER WAY OUT...
...I JUST WANTED TO SEE YOU AGAIN.
SO I JUMPED.

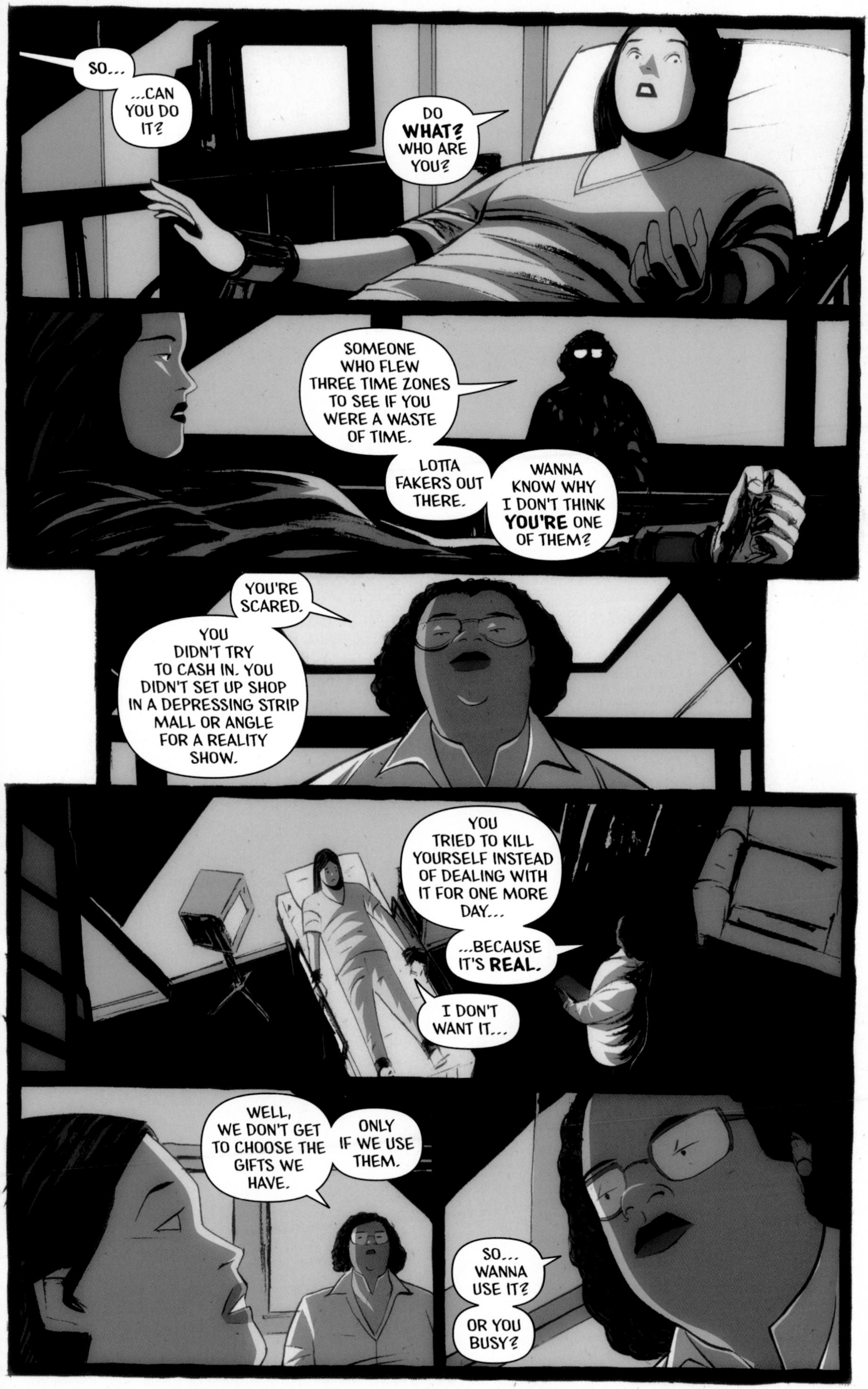

SO...
...CAN YOU DO IT?
DO **WHAT?** WHO ARE YOU?
SOMEONE WHO FLEW THREE TIME ZONES TO SEE IF YOU WERE A WASTE OF TIME.
LOTTA FAKERS OUT THERE.
WANNA KNOW WHY I DON'T THINK **YOU'RE** ONE OF THEM?
YOU'RE SCARED.
YOU DIDN'T TRY TO CASH IN. YOU DIDN'T SET UP SHOP IN A DEPRESSING STRIP MALL OR ANGLE FOR A REALITY SHOW.
YOU TRIED TO KILL YOURSELF INSTEAD OF DEALING WITH IT FOR ONE MORE DAY...
...BECAUSE IT'S **REAL.**
I DON'T WANT IT...
WELL, WE DON'T GET TO CHOOSE THE GIFTS WE HAVE.
ONLY IF WE USE THEM.
SO... WANNA USE IT?
OR YOU BUSY?

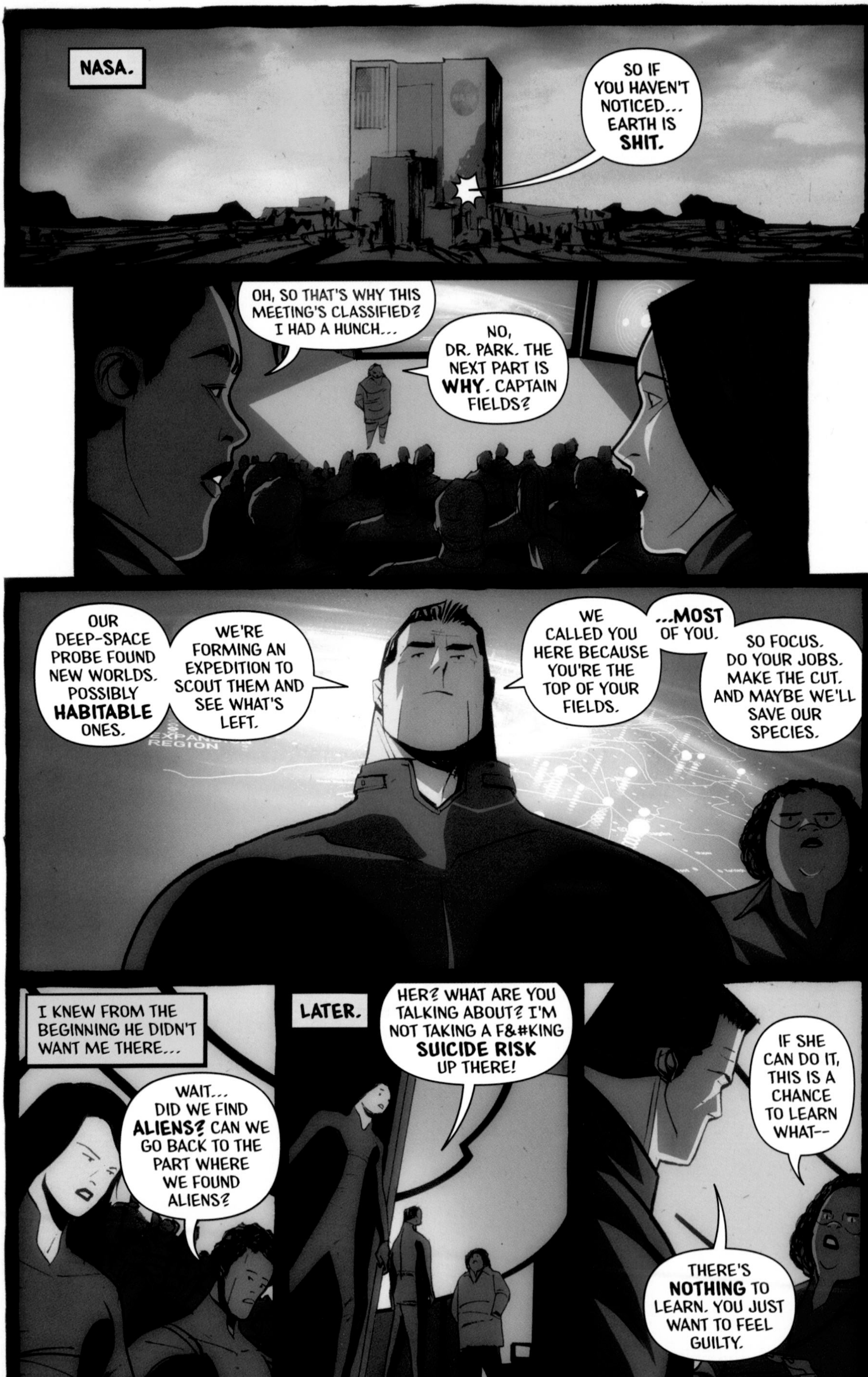
NASA.
SO IF YOU HAVEN'T NOTICED... EARTH IS SHIT.
OH, SO THAT'S WHY THIS MEETING'S CLASSIFIED? I HAD A HUNCH...
NO, DR. PARK. THE NEXT PART IS WHY. CAPTAIN FIELDS?
OUR DEEP-SPACE PROBE FOUND NEW WORLDS. POSSIBLY HABITABLE ONES.
WE'RE FORMING AN EXPEDITION TO SCOUT THEM AND SEE WHAT'S LEFT.
WE CALLED YOU HERE BECAUSE YOU'RE THE TOP OF YOUR FIELDS.
...MOST OF YOU.
SO FOCUS. DO YOUR JOBS. MAKE THE CUT. AND MAYBE WE'LL SAVE OUR SPECIES.
I KNEW FROM THE BEGINNING HE DIDN'T WANT ME THERE...
WAIT... DID WE FIND ALIENS? CAN WE GO BACK TO THE PART WHERE WE FOUND ALIENS?
LATER.
HER? WHAT ARE YOU TALKING ABOUT? I'M NOT TAKING A F&#KING SUICIDE RISK UP THERE!
IF SHE CAN DO IT, THIS IS A CHANCE TO LEARN WHAT--
THERE'S NOTHING TO LEARN. YOU JUST WANT TO FEEL GUILTY.

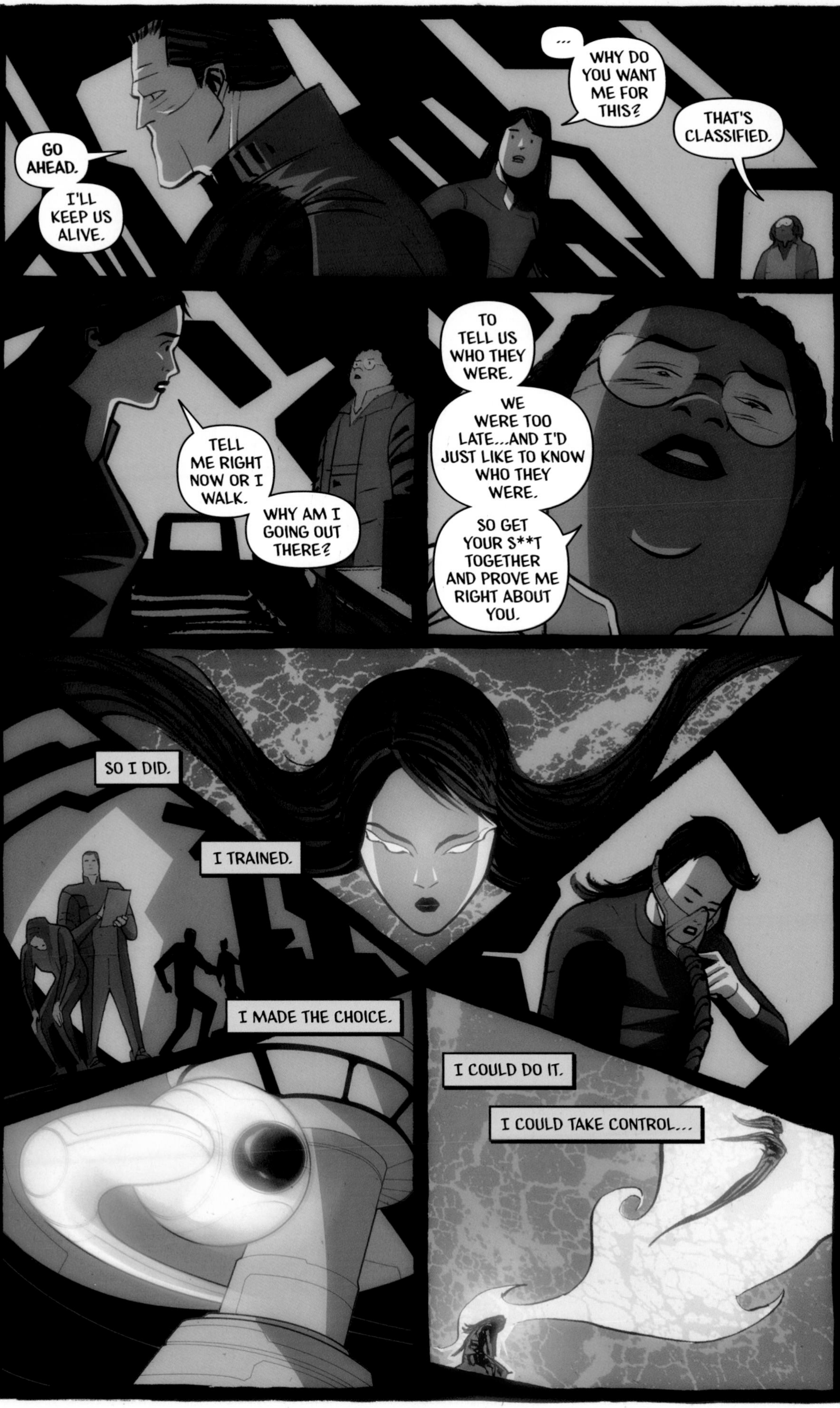
GO AHEAD.
I'LL KEEP US ALIVE.
...
WHY DO YOU WANT ME FOR THIS?
THAT'S CLASSIFIED.
TELL ME RIGHT NOW OR I WALK.
WHY AM I GOING OUT THERE?
TO TELL US WHO THEY WERE.
WE WERE TOO LATE...AND I'D JUST LIKE TO KNOW WHO THEY WERE.
SO GET YOUR S**T TOGETHER AND PROVE ME RIGHT ABOUT YOU.
SO I DID.
I TRAINED.
I MADE THE CHOICE.
I COULD DO IT.
I COULD TAKE CONTROL...

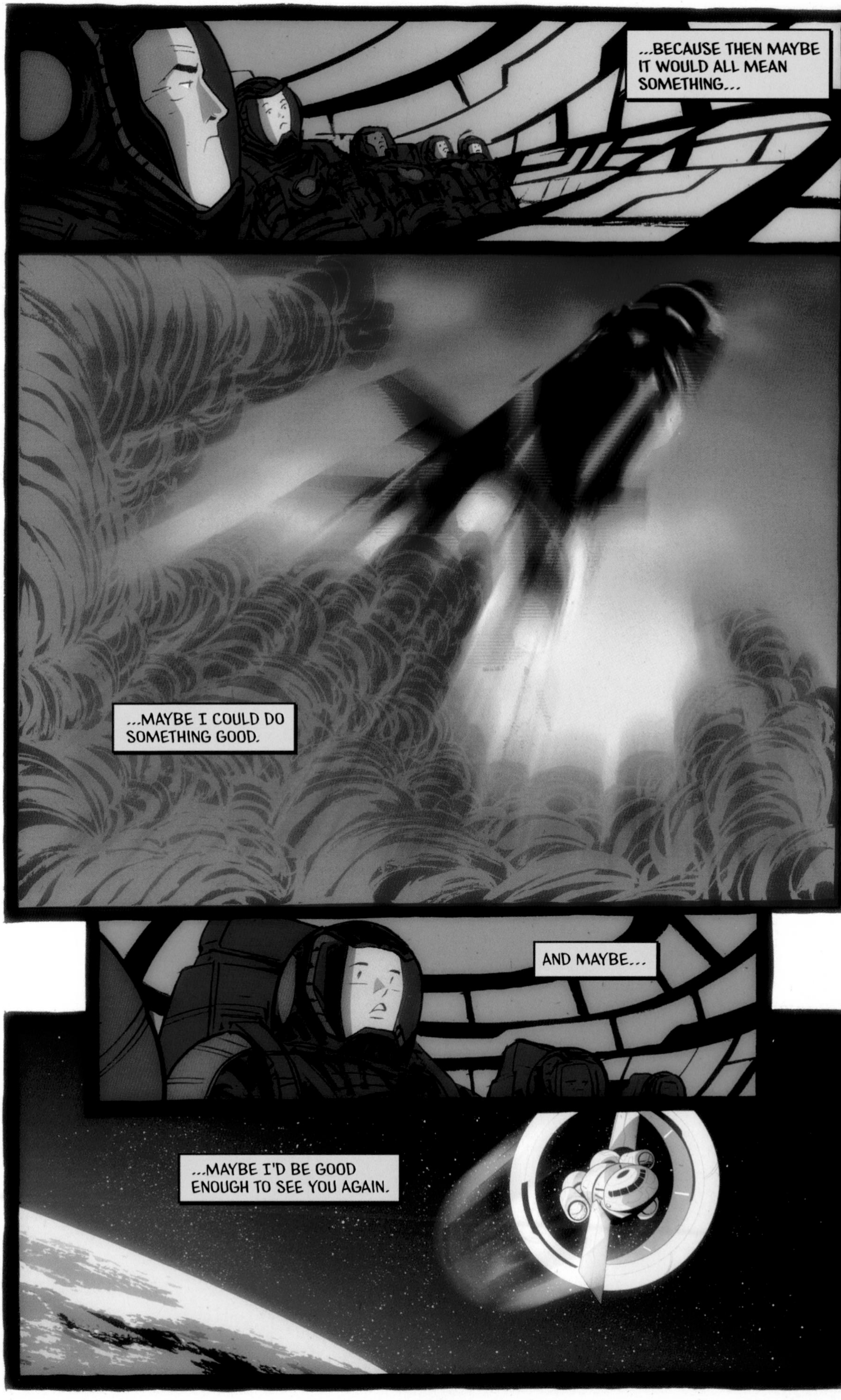
...BECAUSE THEN MAYBE IT WOULD ALL MEAN SOMETHING...
...MAYBE I COULD DO SOMETHING GOOD.
AND MAYBE...
...MAYBE I'D BE GOOD ENOUGH TO SEE YOU AGAIN.

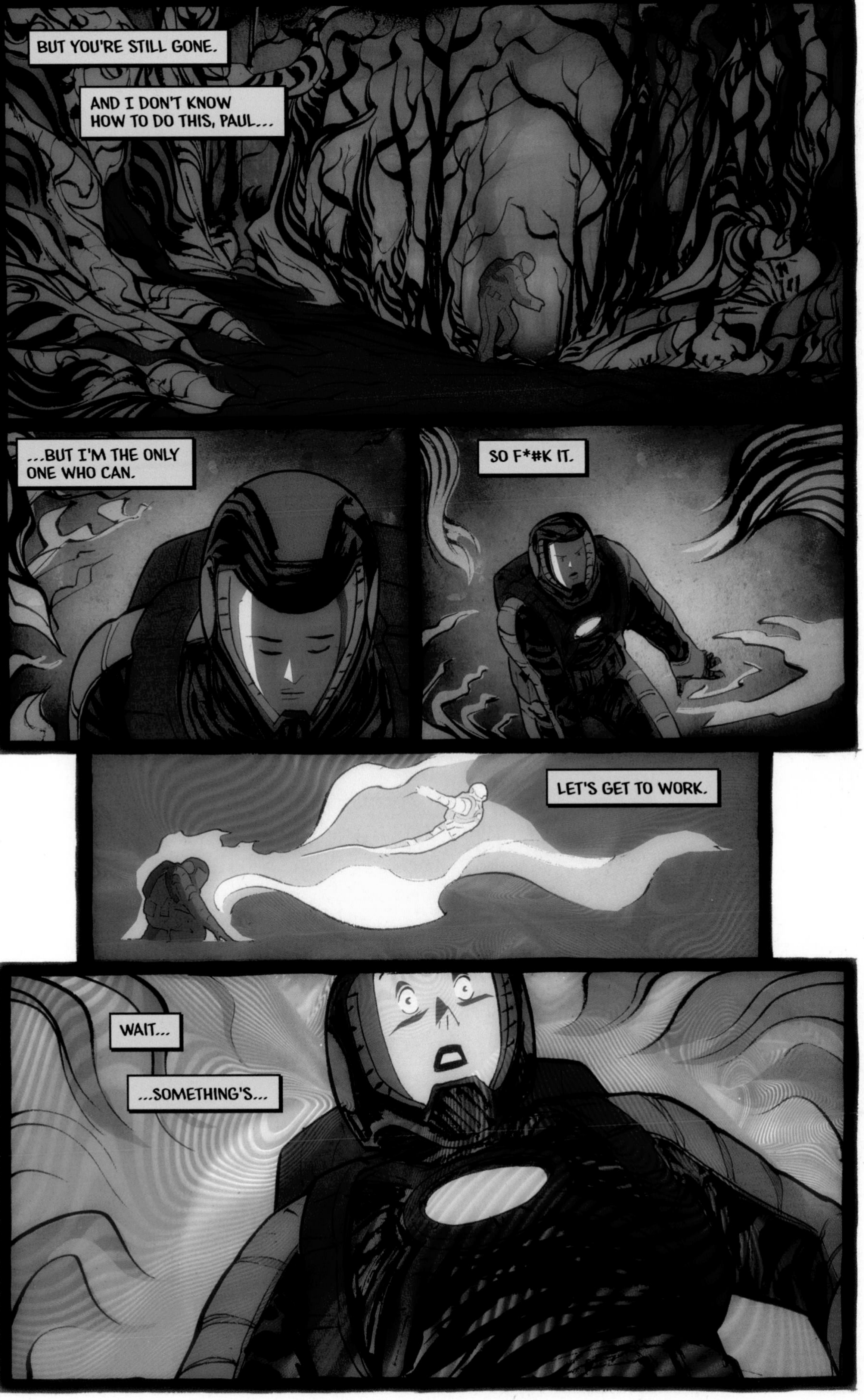
BUT YOU'RE STILL GONE.
AND I DON'T KNOW HOW TO DO THIS, PAUL...
...BUT I'M THE ONLY ONE WHO CAN.
SO F*#K IT.
LET'S GET TO WORK.
WAIT...
...SOMETHING'S...

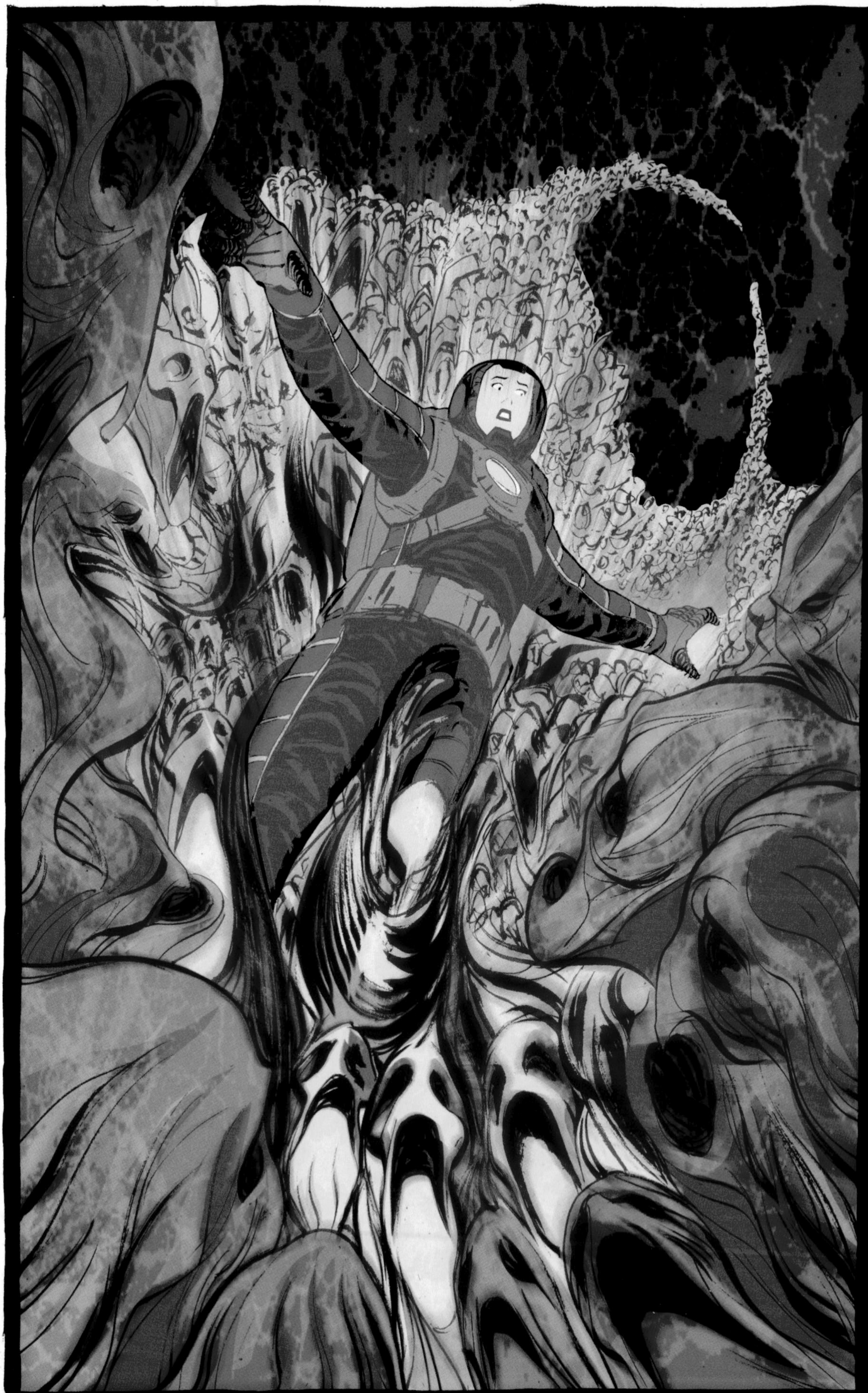

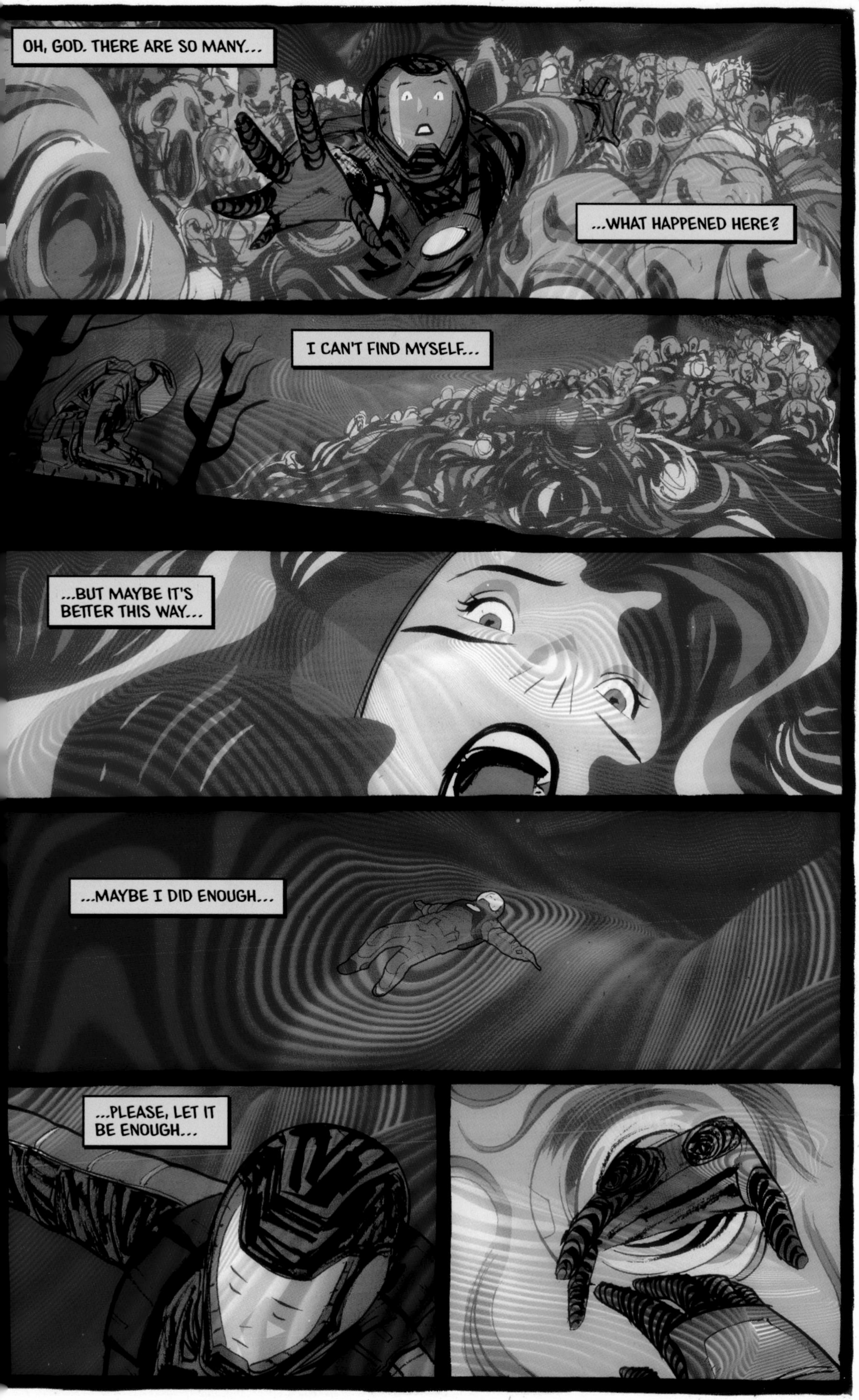
OH, GOD. THERE ARE SO MANY...
...WHAT HAPPENED HERE?
I CAN'T FIND MYSELF...
...BUT MAYBE IT'S BETTER THIS WAY...
...MAYBE I DID ENOUGH...
...PLEASE, LET IT BE ENOUGH...

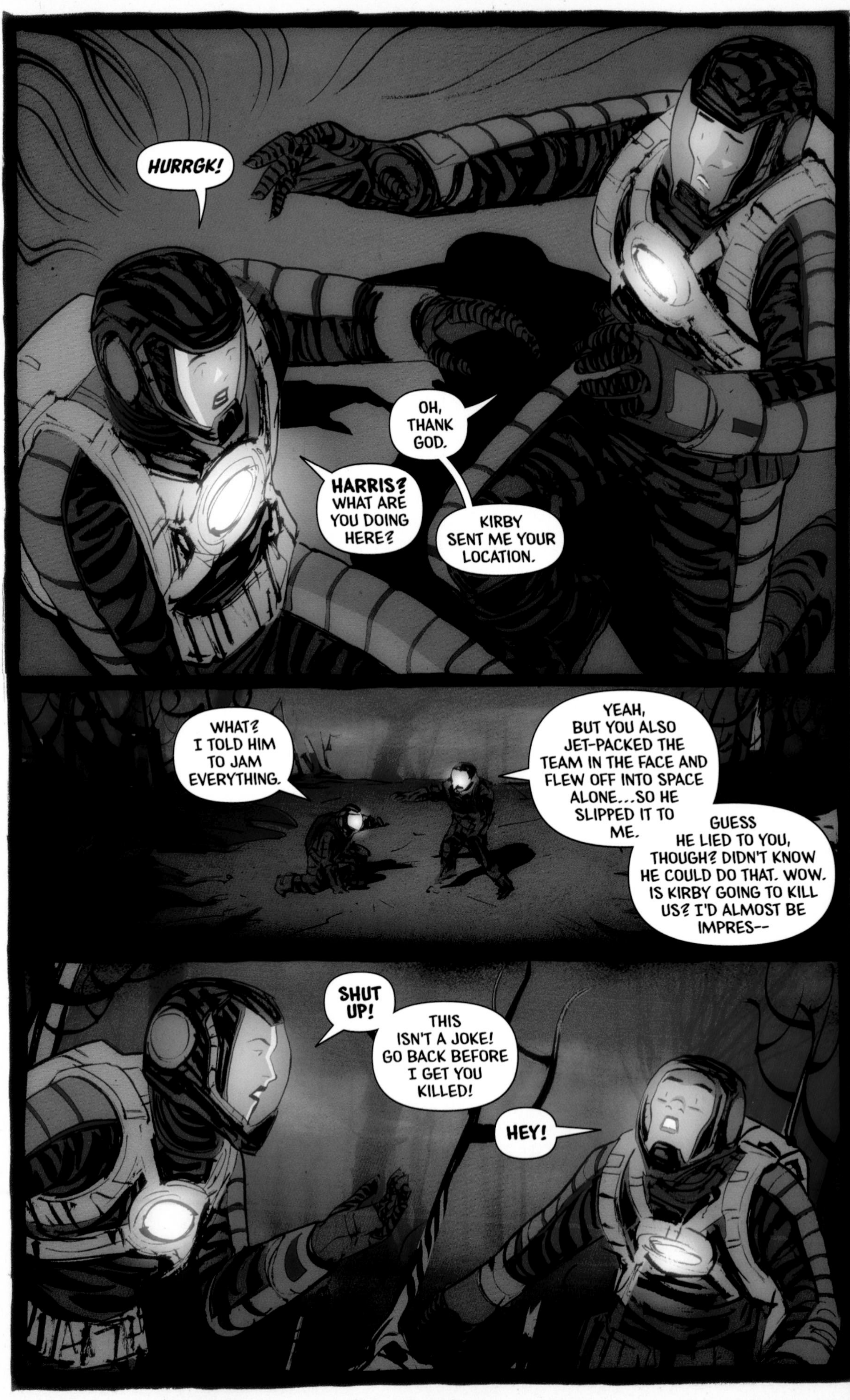
HURRGK!
OH, THANK GOD.
HARRIS? WHAT ARE YOU DOING HERE?
KIRBY SENT ME YOUR LOCATION.
WHAT? I TOLD HIM TO JAM EVERYTHING.
YEAH, BUT YOU ALSO JET-PACKED THE TEAM IN THE FACE AND FLEW OFF INTO SPACE ALONE...SO HE SLIPPED IT TO ME.
GUESS HE LIED TO YOU, THOUGH? DIDN'T KNOW HE COULD DO THAT. WOW. IS KIRBY GOING TO KILL US? I'D ALMOST BE IMPRES--
SHUT UP!
THIS ISN'T A JOKE! GO BACK BEFORE I GET YOU KILLED!
HEY!

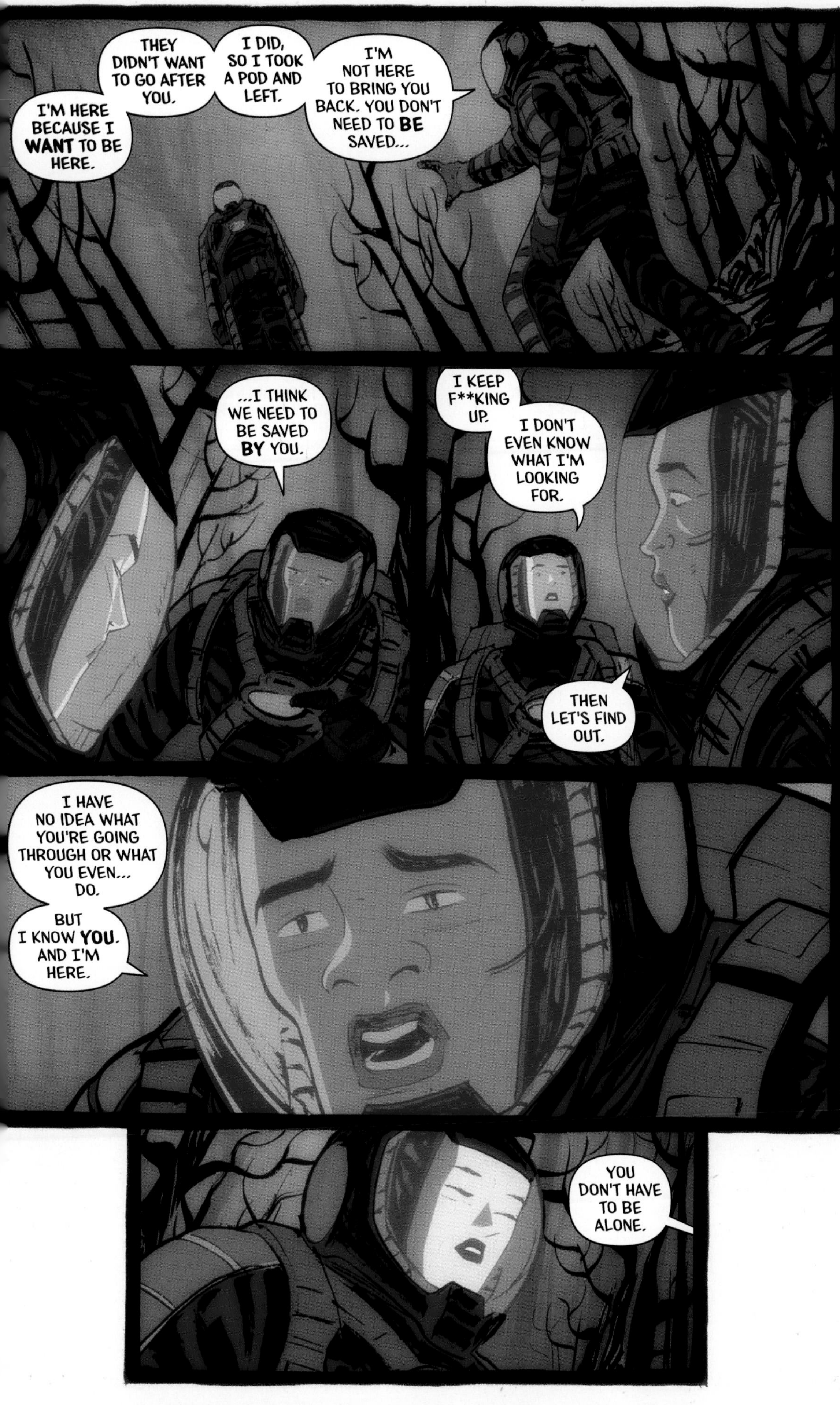
I'M HERE BECAUSE I WANT TO BE HERE.
THEY DIDN'T WANT TO GO AFTER YOU.
I DID, SO I TOOK A POD AND LEFT.
I'M NOT HERE TO BRING YOU BACK. YOU DON'T NEED TO BE SAVED...
...I THINK WE NEED TO BE SAVED BY YOU.
I KEEP F**KING UP.
I DON'T EVEN KNOW WHAT I'M LOOKING FOR.
THEN LET'S FIND OUT.
I HAVE NO IDEA WHAT YOU'RE GOING THROUGH OR WHAT YOU EVEN... DO.
BUT I KNOW YOU. AND I'M HERE.
YOU DON'T HAVE TO BE ALONE.

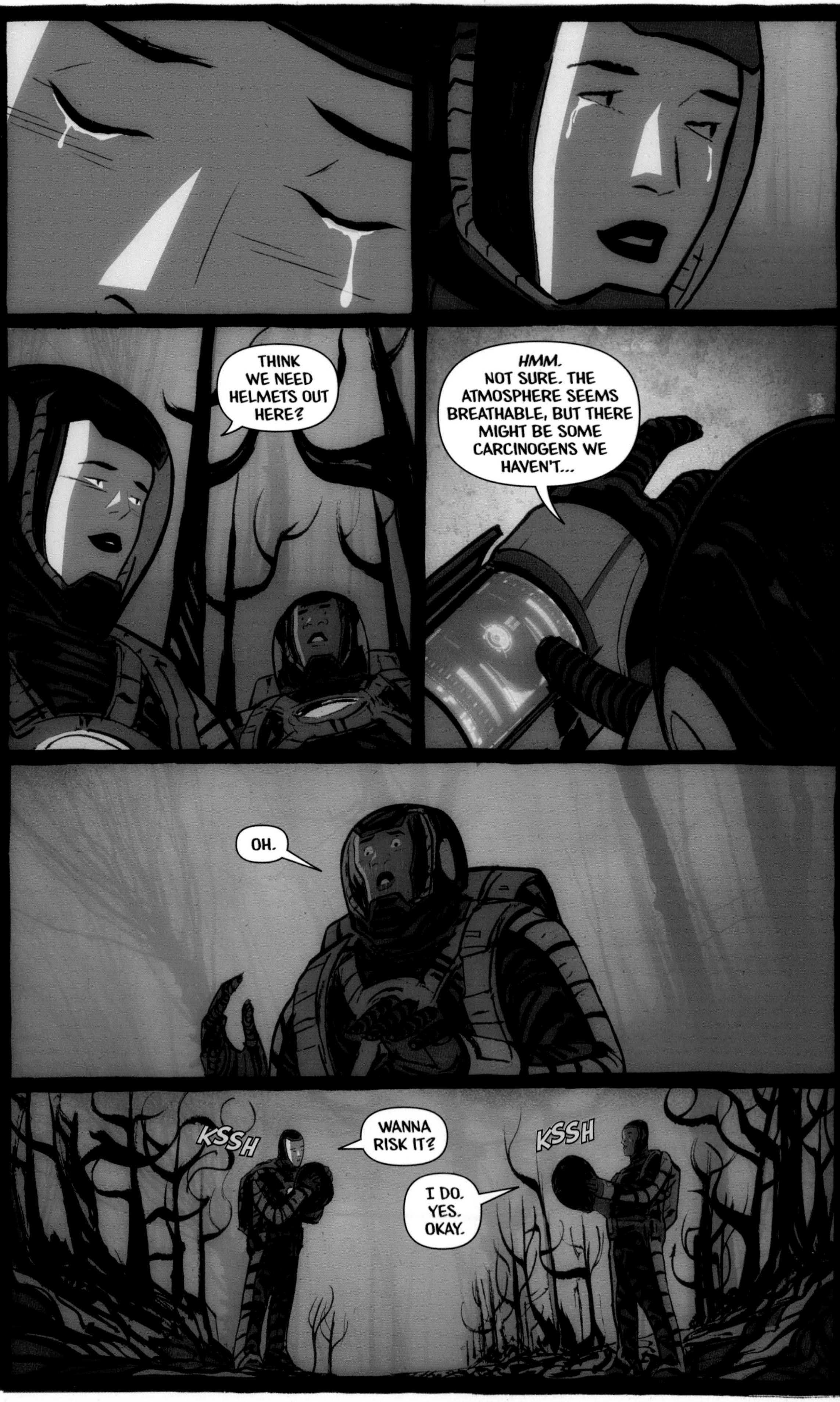
THINK WE NEED HELMETS OUT HERE?
HMM. NOT SURE. THE ATMOSPHERE SEEMS BREATHABLE, BUT THERE MIGHT BE SOME CARCINOGENS WE HAVEN'T...
OH.
KSSH
WANNA RISK IT?
KSSH
I DO. YES. OKAY.

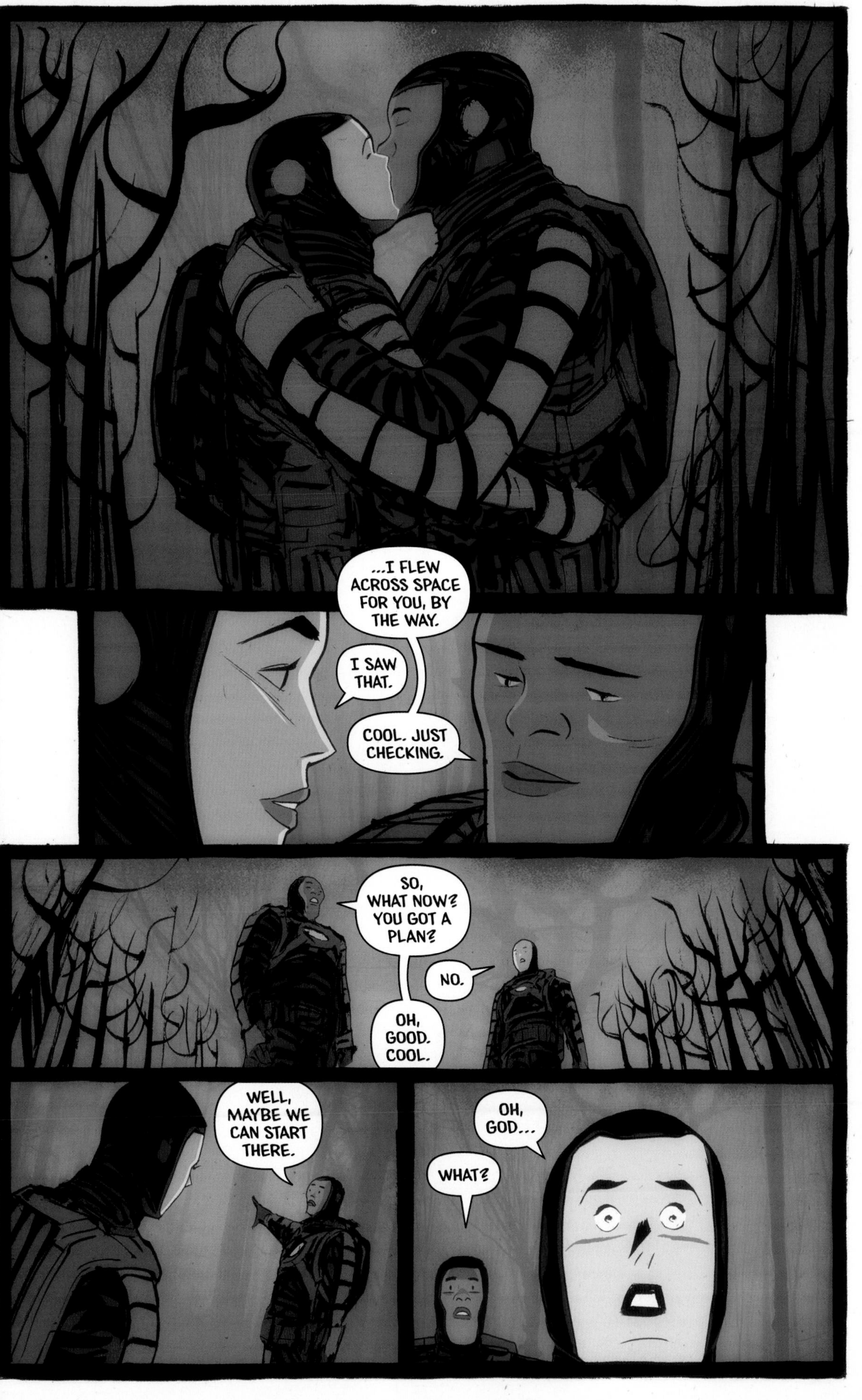
...I FLEW ACROSS SPACE FOR YOU, BY THE WAY.
I SAW THAT.
COOL. JUST CHECKING.
SO, WHAT NOW? YOU GOT A PLAN?
NO.
OH, GOOD. COOL.
WELL, MAYBE WE CAN START THERE.
OH, GOD...
WHAT?

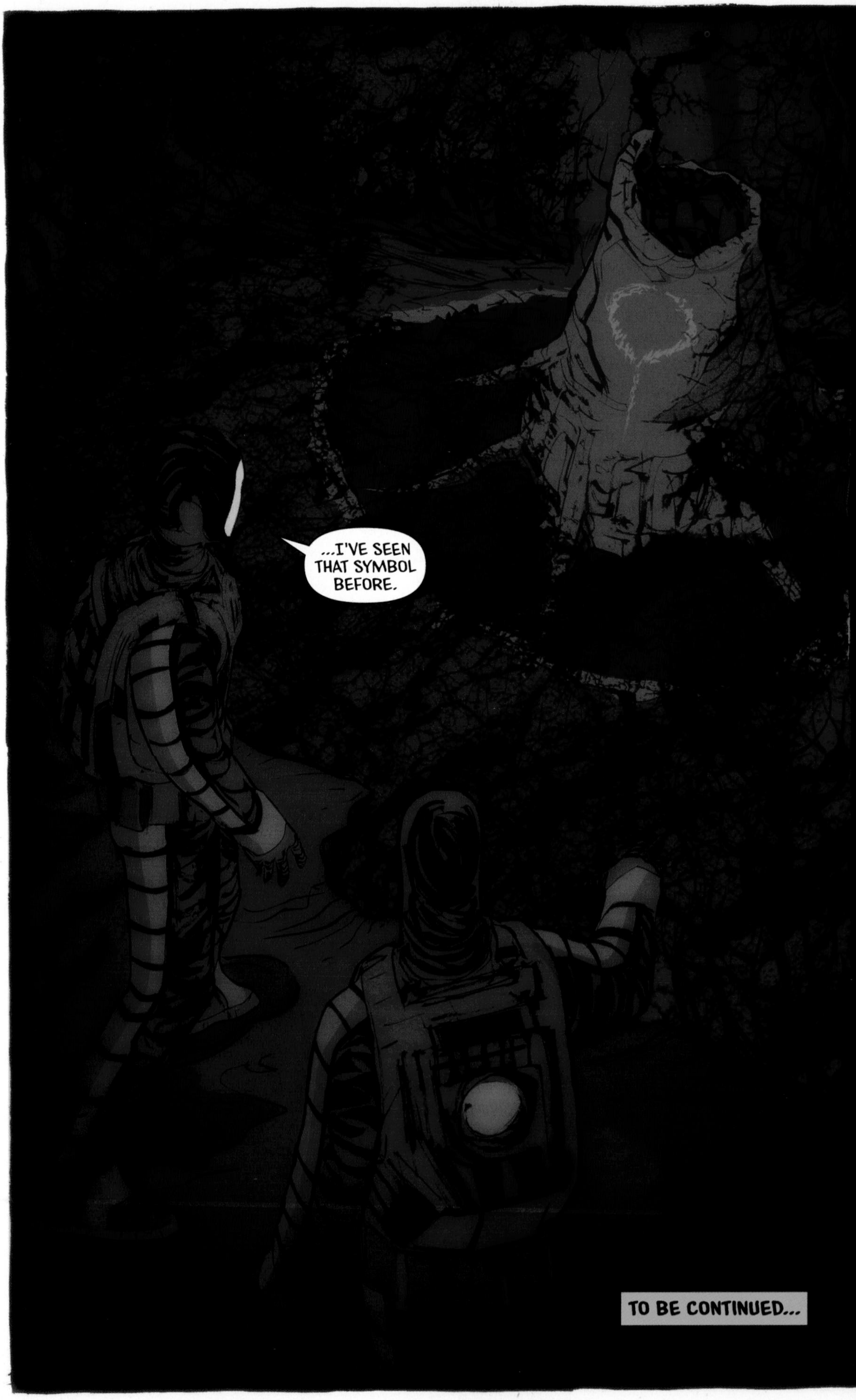
...I'VE SEEN THAT SYMBOL BEFORE.
TO BE CONTINUED...

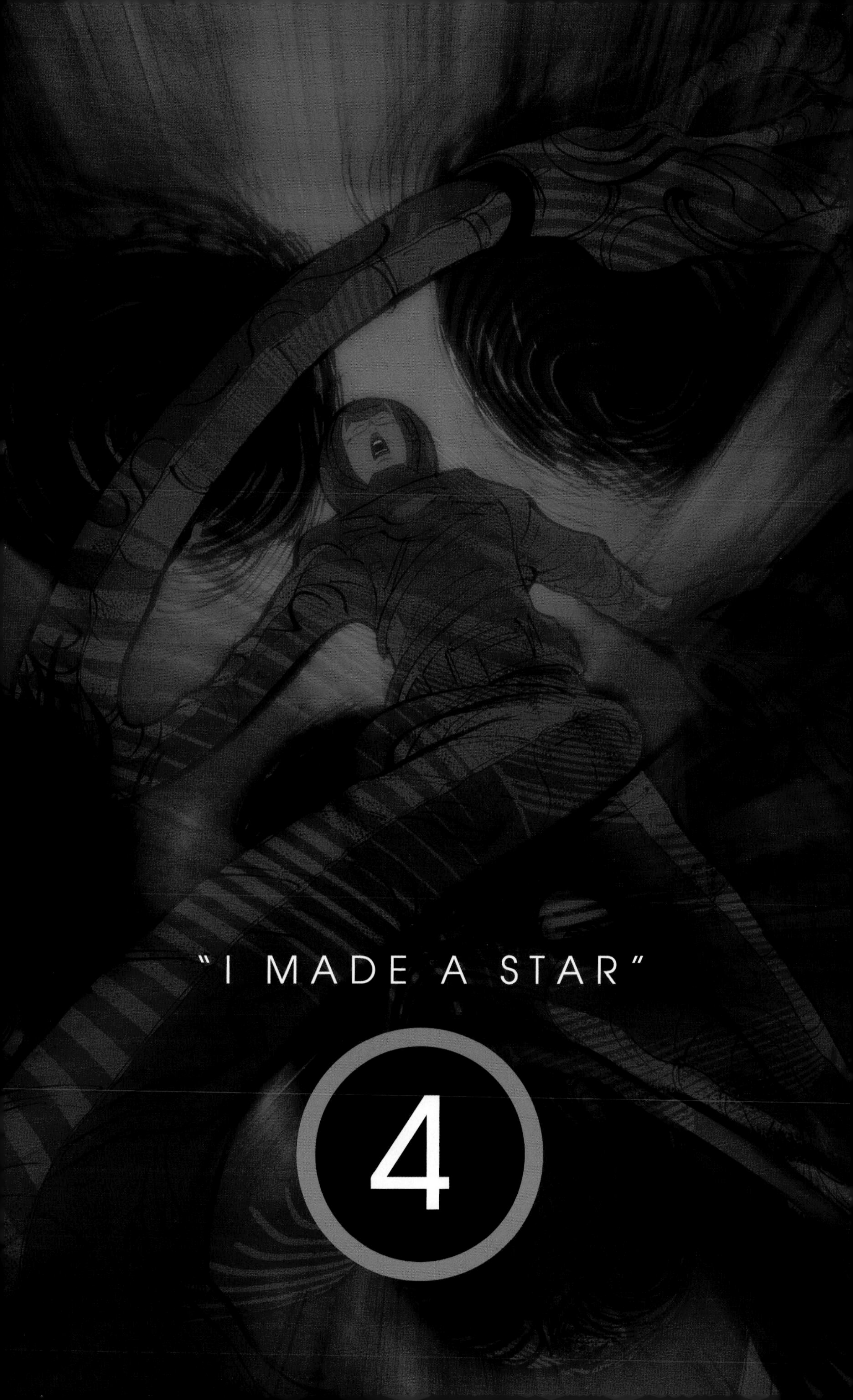

4

"I MADE A STAR"

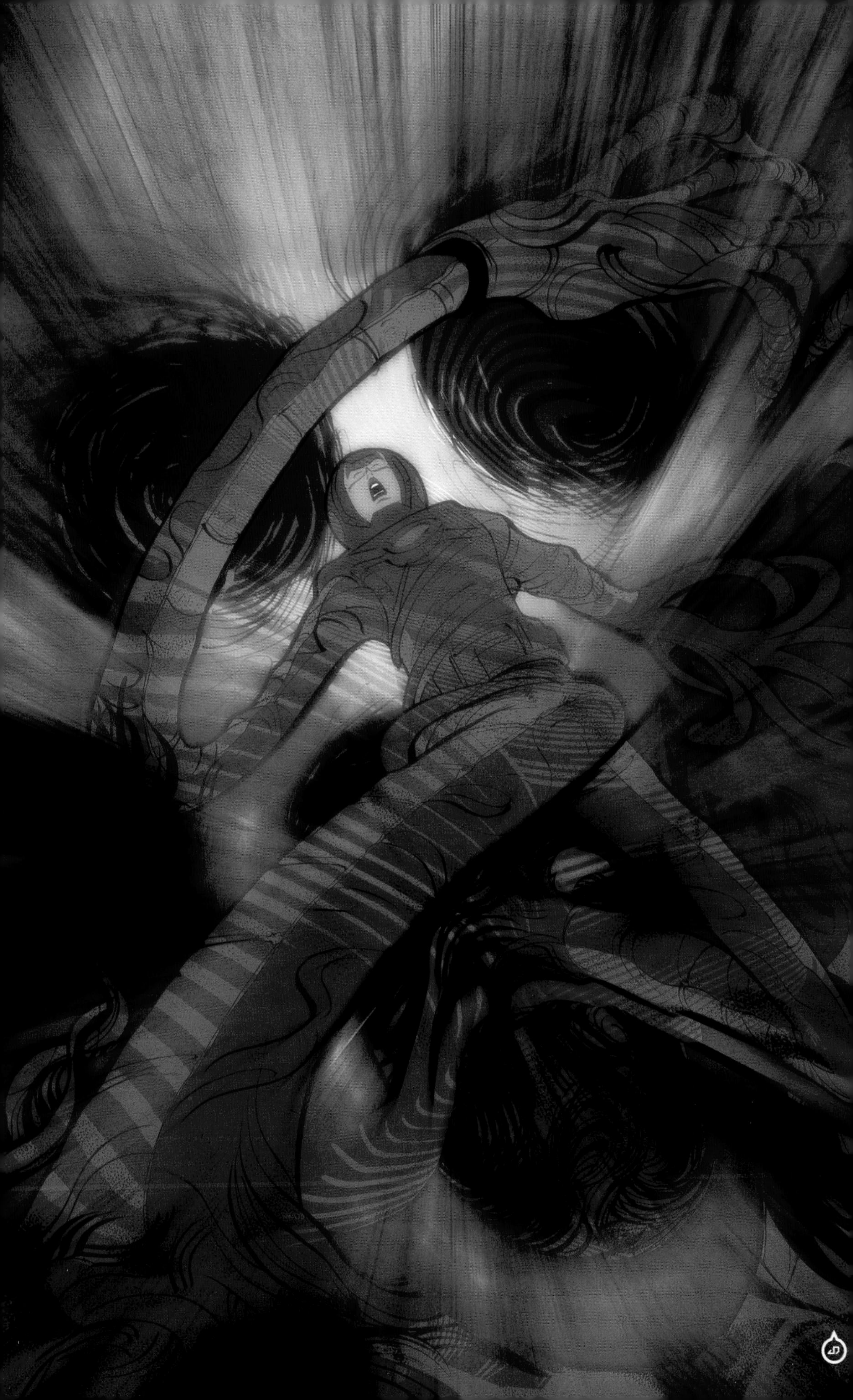

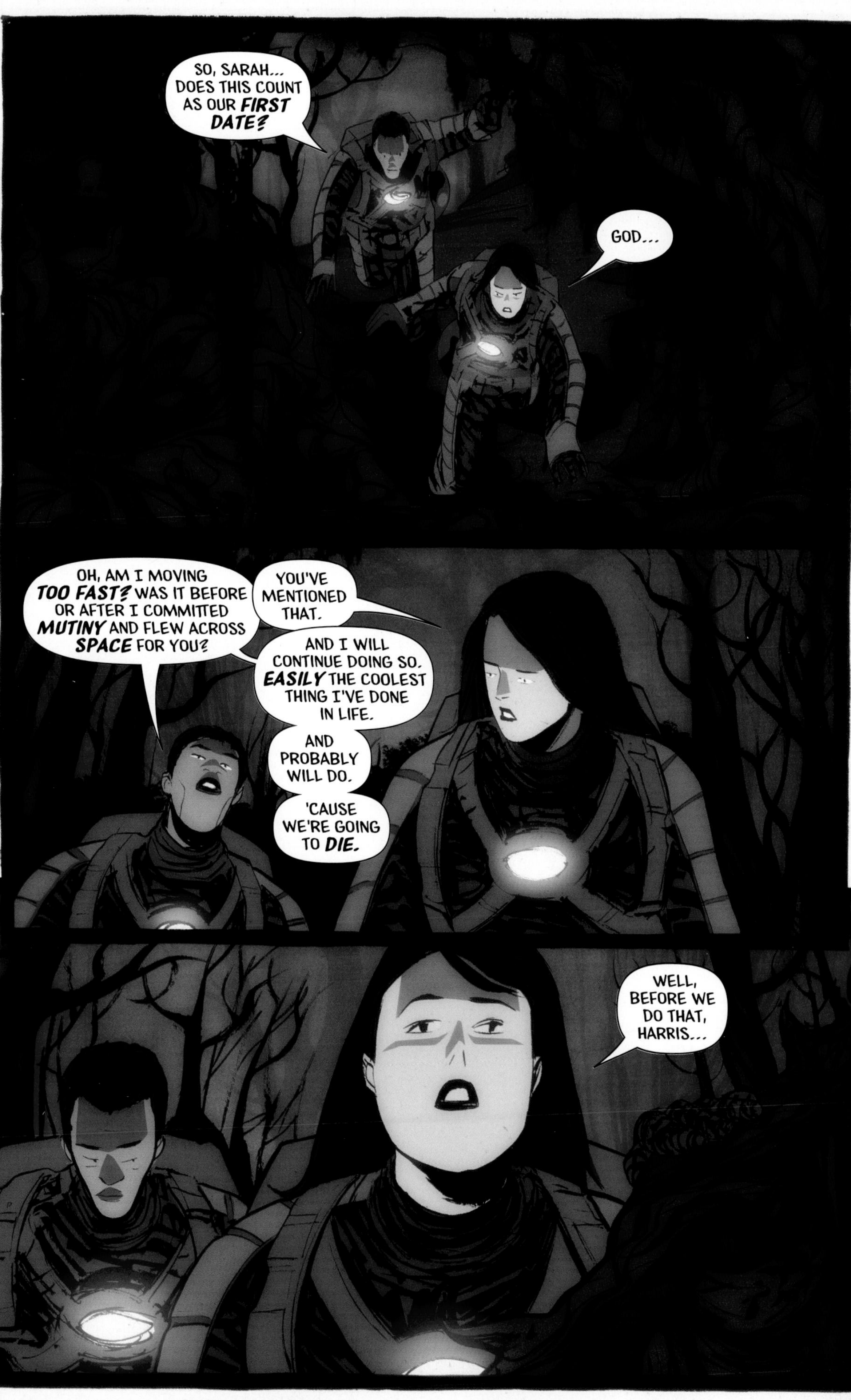
SO, SARAH... DOES THIS COUNT AS OUR FIRST DATE?
GOD...
OH, AM I MOVING TOO FAST? WAS IT BEFORE OR AFTER I COMMITTED MUTINY AND FLEW ACROSS SPACE FOR YOU?
YOU'VE MENTIONED THAT.
AND I WILL CONTINUE DOING SO. EASILY THE COOLEST THING I'VE DONE IN LIFE.
AND PROBABLY WILL DO.
'CAUSE WE'RE GOING TO DIE.
WELL, BEFORE WE DO THAT, HARRIS...

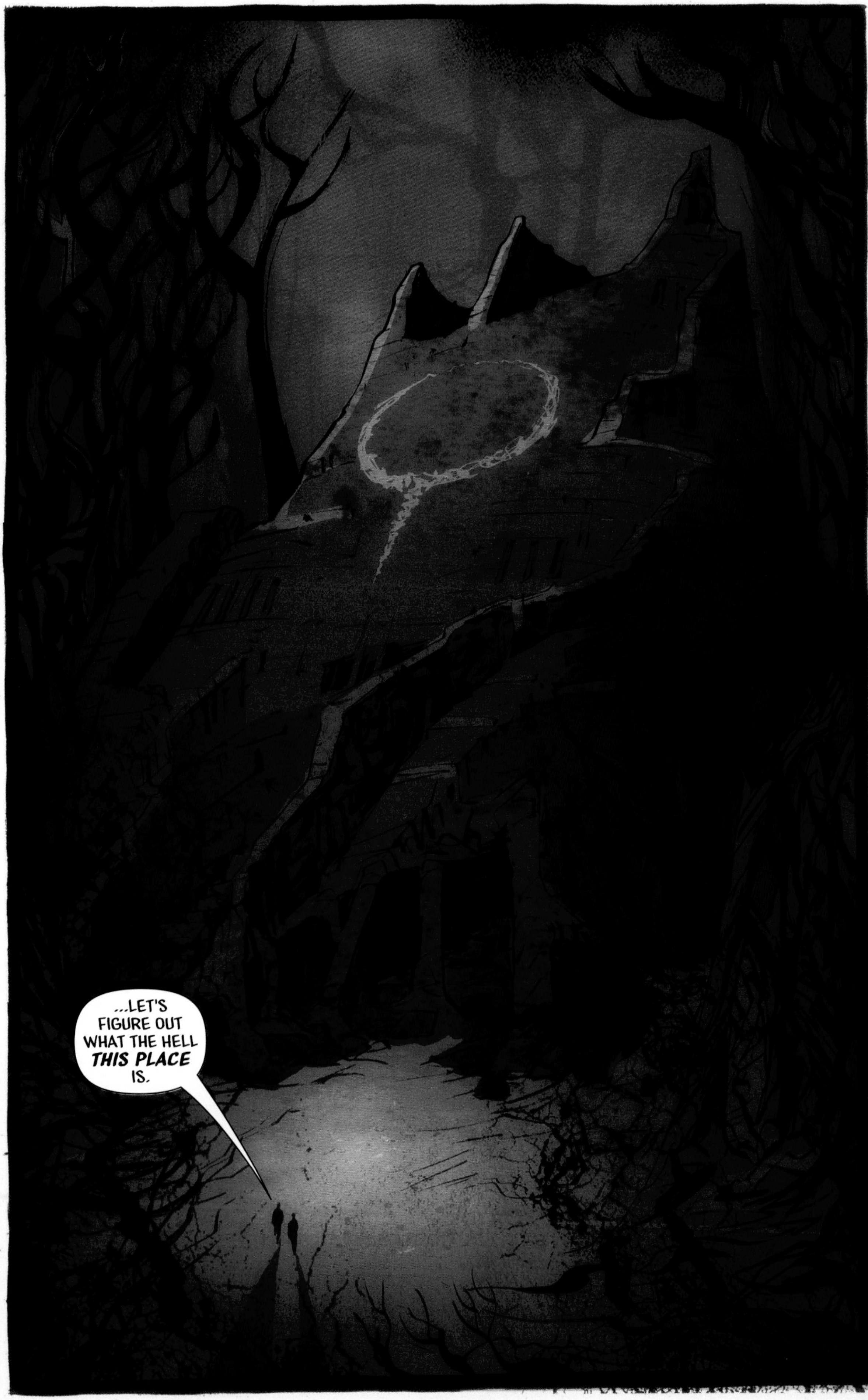
...LET'S FIGURE OUT WHAT THE HELL ***THIS PLACE*** IS.

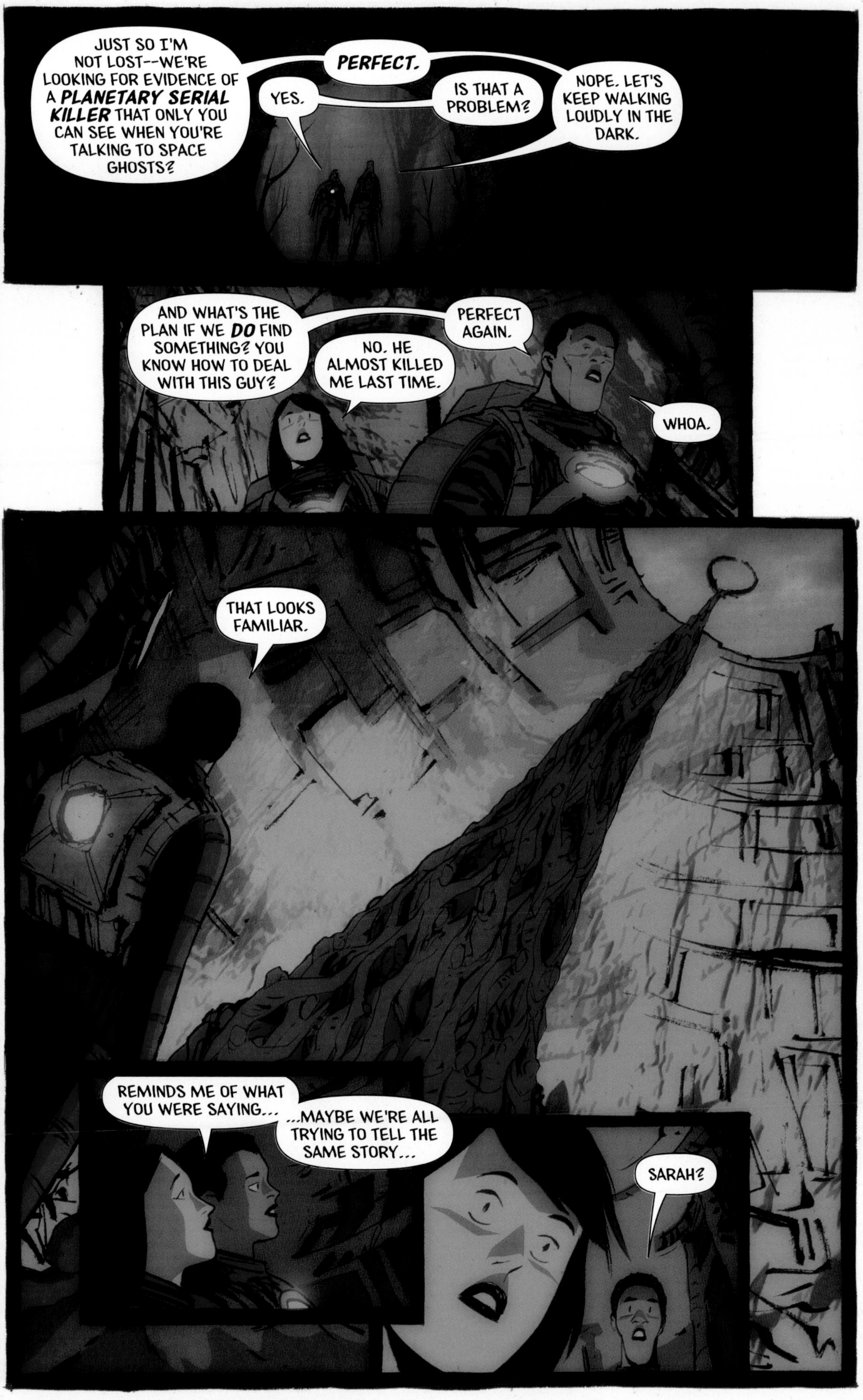
JUST SO I'M NOT LOST--WE'RE LOOKING FOR EVIDENCE OF A PLANETARY SERIAL KILLER THAT ONLY YOU CAN SEE WHEN YOU'RE TALKING TO SPACE GHOSTS?
YES.
PERFECT.
IS THAT A PROBLEM?
NOPE. LET'S KEEP WALKING LOUDLY IN THE DARK.
AND WHAT'S THE PLAN IF WE DO FIND SOMETHING? YOU KNOW HOW TO DEAL WITH THIS GUY?
NO. HE ALMOST KILLED ME LAST TIME.
PERFECT AGAIN.
WHOA.
THAT LOOKS FAMILIAR.
REMINDS ME OF WHAT YOU WERE SAYING...
...MAYBE WE'RE ALL TRYING TO TELL THE SAME STORY...
SARAH?

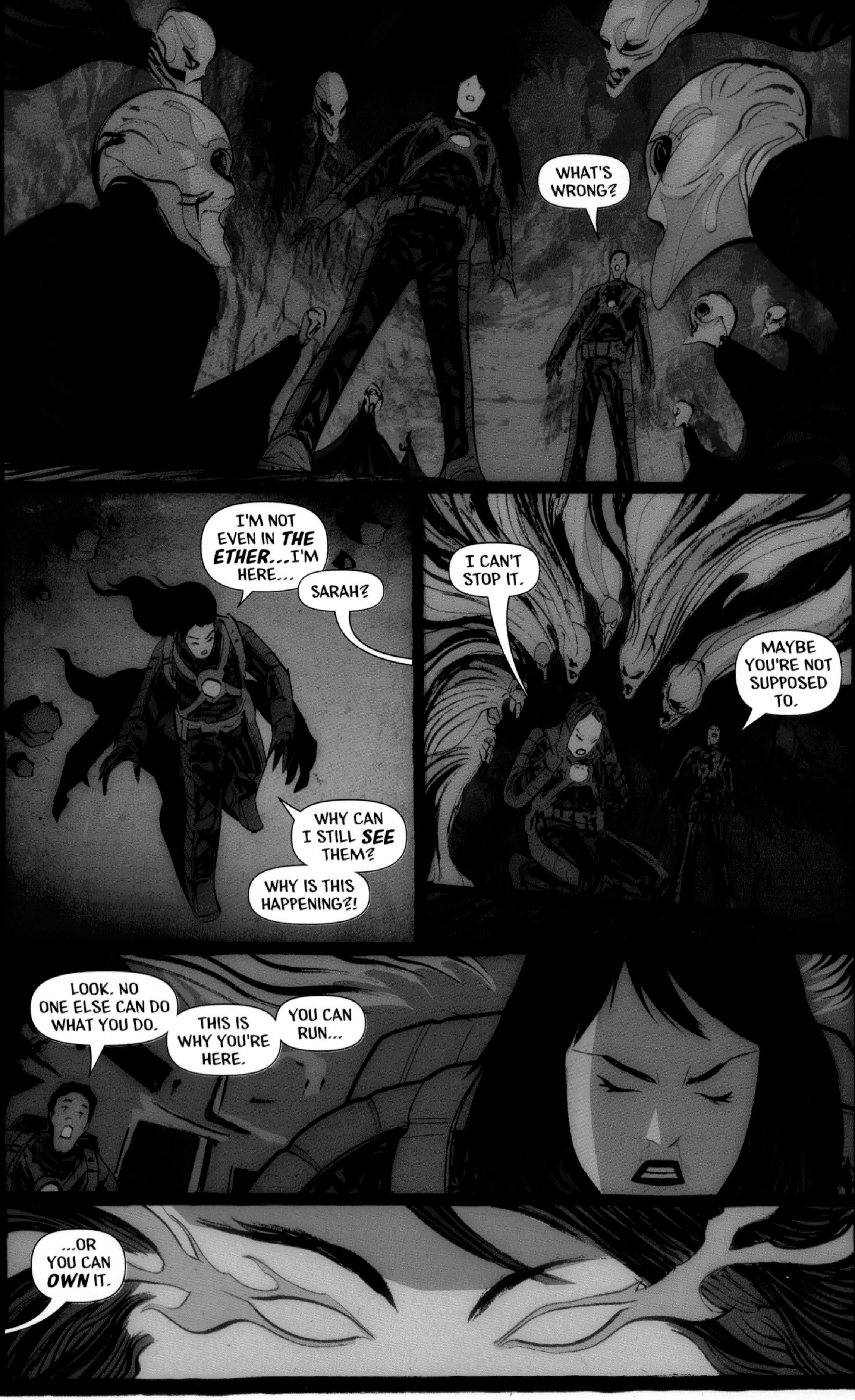
WHAT'S WRONG?
I'M NOT EVEN IN THE ETHER...I'M HERE...
SARAH?
WHY CAN I STILL SEE THEM?
WHY IS THIS HAPPENING?!
I CAN'T STOP IT.
MAYBE YOU'RE NOT SUPPOSED TO.
LOOK. NO ONE ELSE CAN DO WHAT YOU DO.
THIS IS WHY YOU'RE HERE.
YOU CAN RUN...
...OR YOU CAN OWN IT.

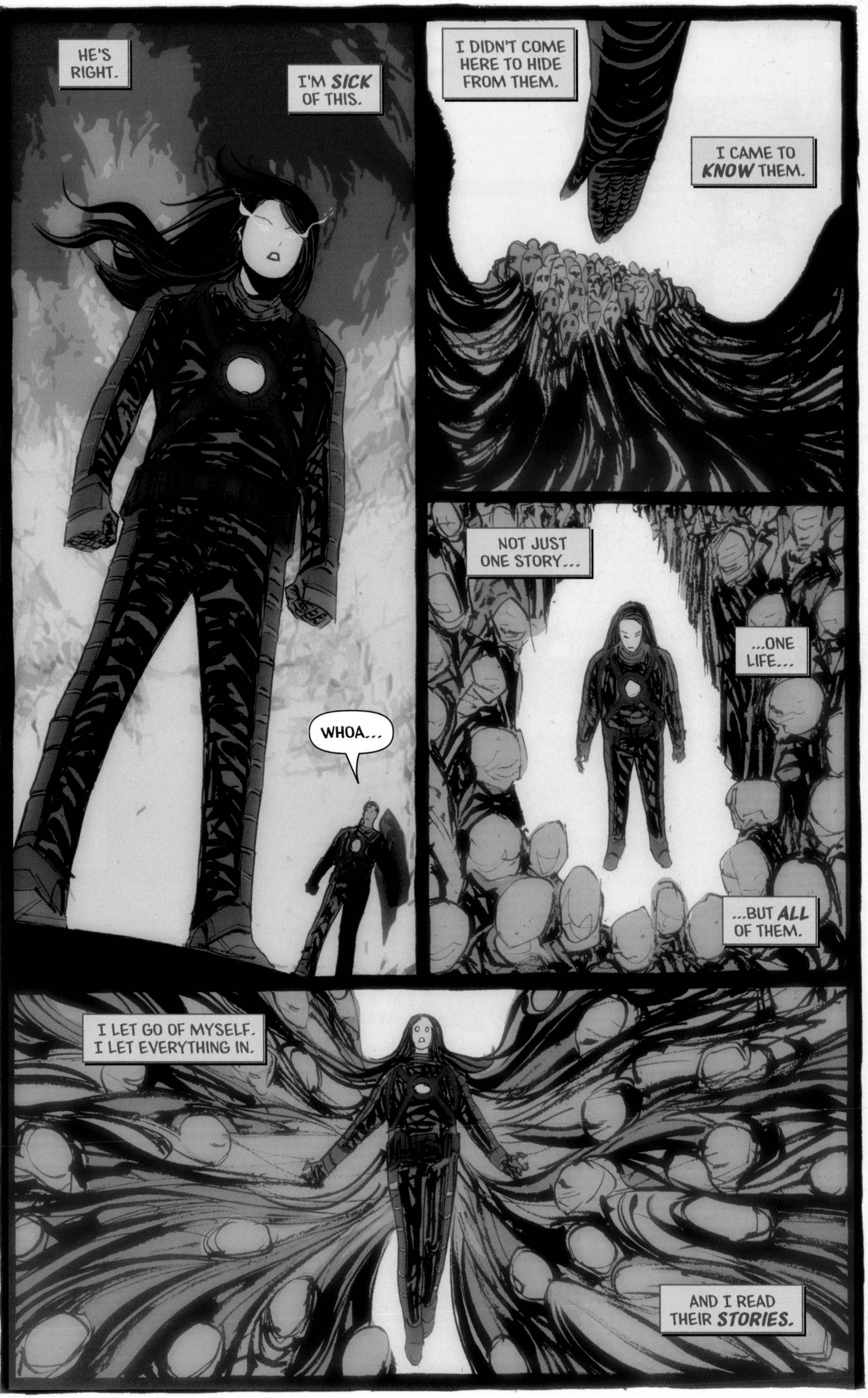
HE'S RIGHT.
I'M SICK OF THIS.
WHOA...
I DIDN'T COME HERE TO HIDE FROM THEM.
I CAME TO KNOW THEM.
NOT JUST ONE STORY...
...ONE LIFE...
...BUT ALL OF THEM.
I LET GO OF MYSELF. I LET EVERYTHING IN.
AND I READ THEIR STORIES.

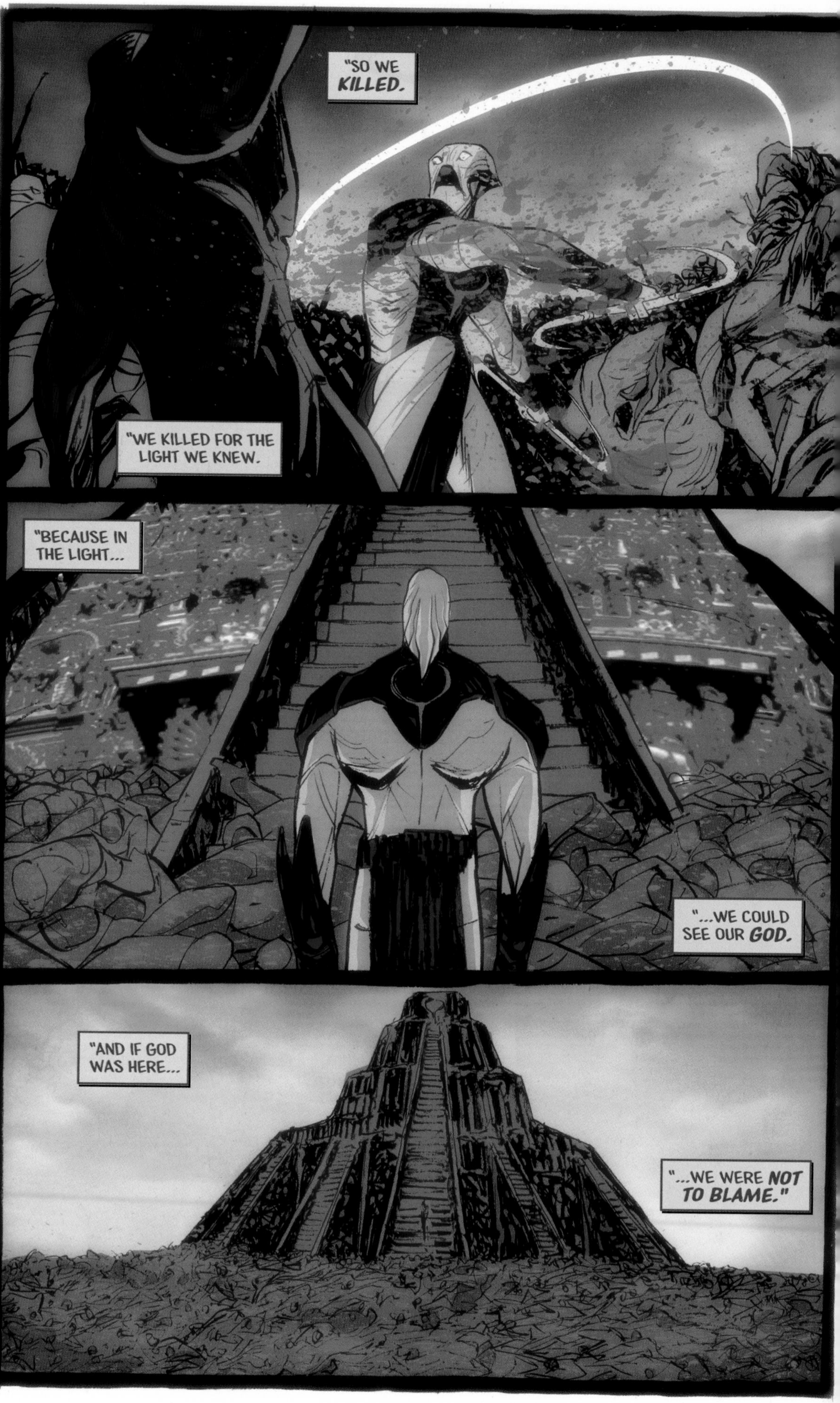
"SO WE KILLED.
"WE KILLED FOR THE LIGHT WE KNEW.
"BECAUSE IN THE LIGHT...
"...WE COULD SEE OUR GOD.
"AND IF GOD WAS HERE...
"...WE WERE NOT TO BLAME."

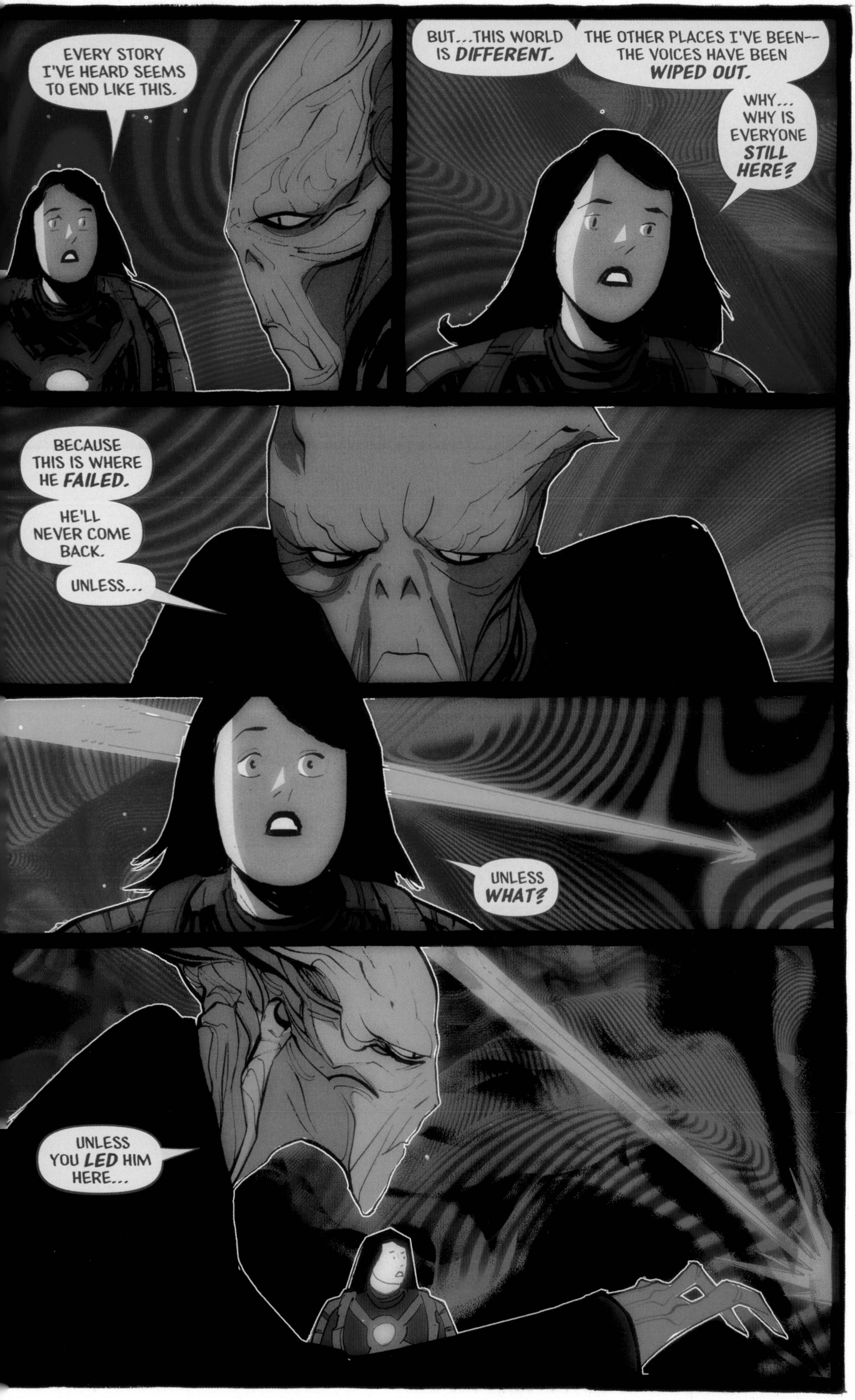
EVERY STORY I'VE HEARD SEEMS TO END LIKE THIS.
BUT...THIS WORLD IS DIFFERENT.
THE OTHER PLACES I'VE BEEN-- THE VOICES HAVE BEEN WIPED OUT.
WHY... WHY IS EVERYONE STILL HERE?
BECAUSE THIS IS WHERE HE FAILED.
HE'LL NEVER COME BACK.
UNLESS...
UNLESS WHAT?
UNLESS YOU LED HIM HERE...

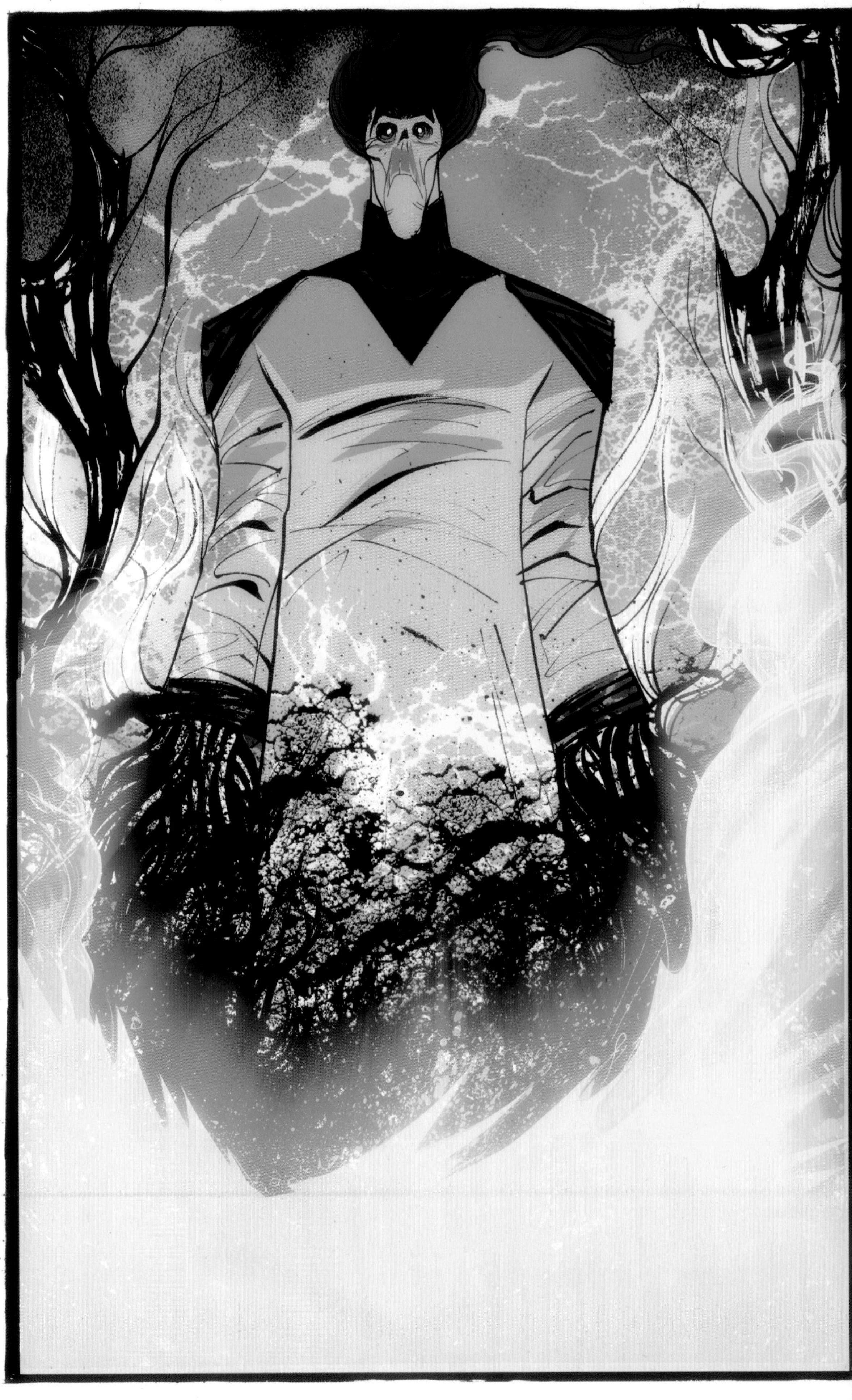

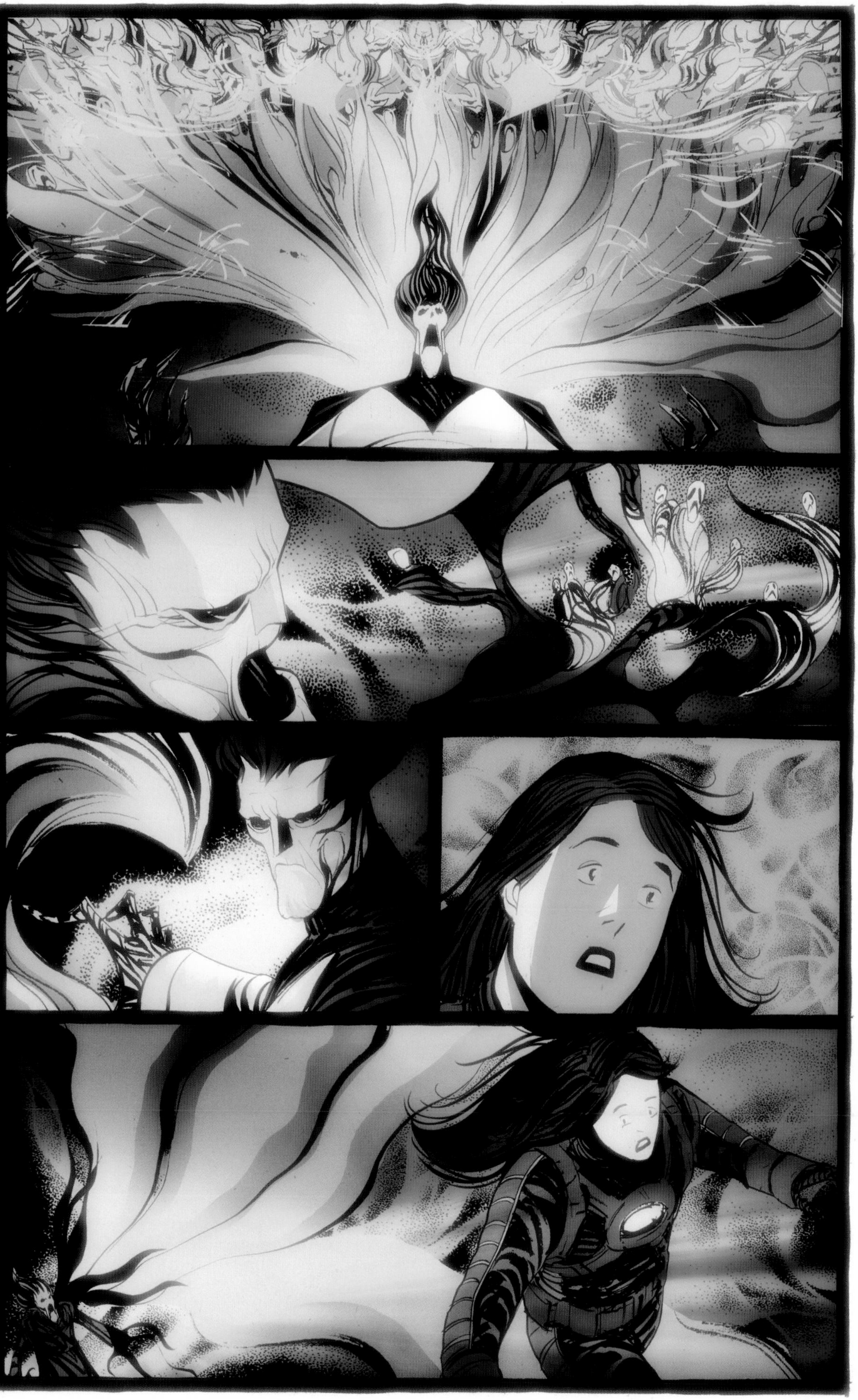

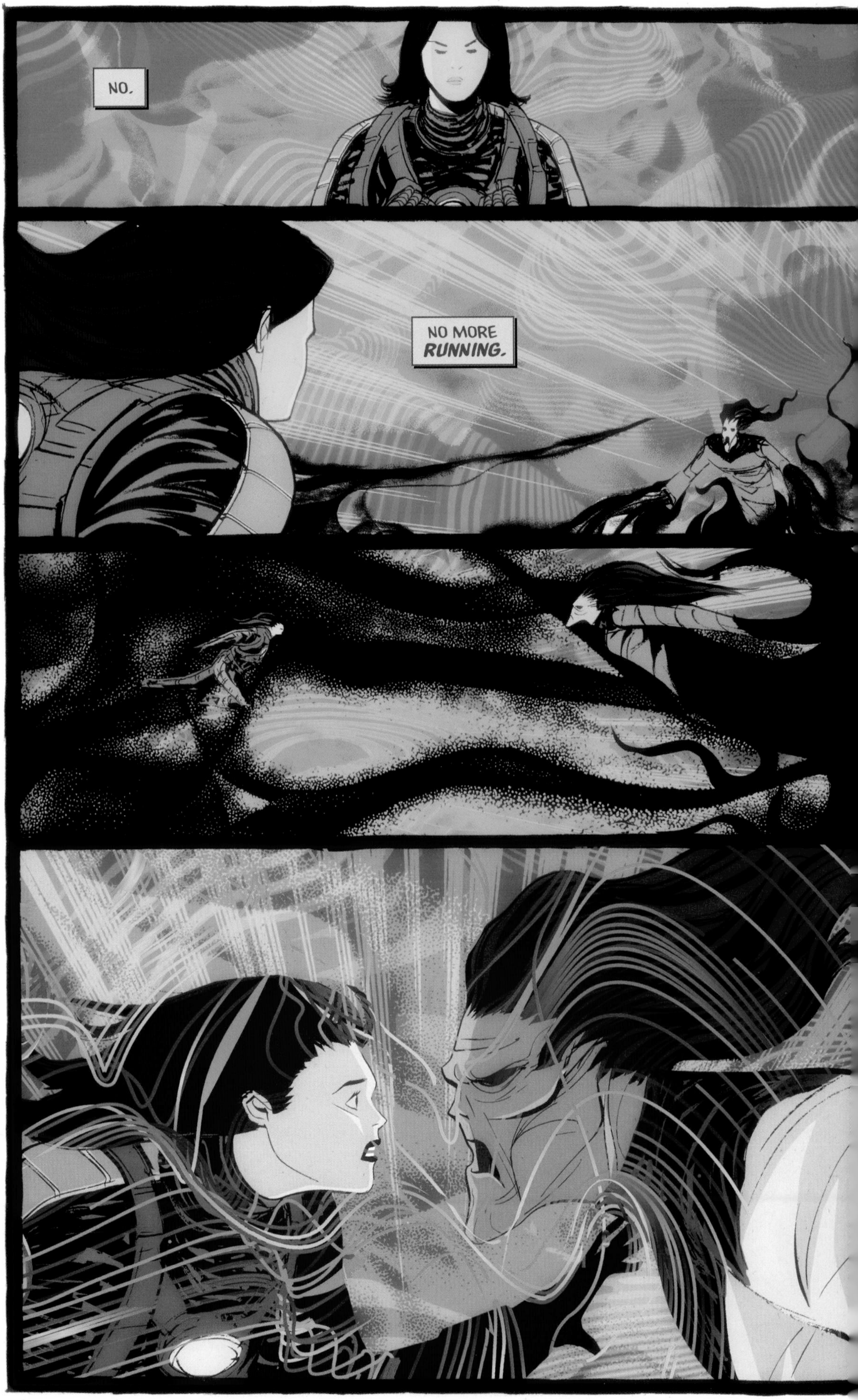
NO.
NO MORE RUNNING.

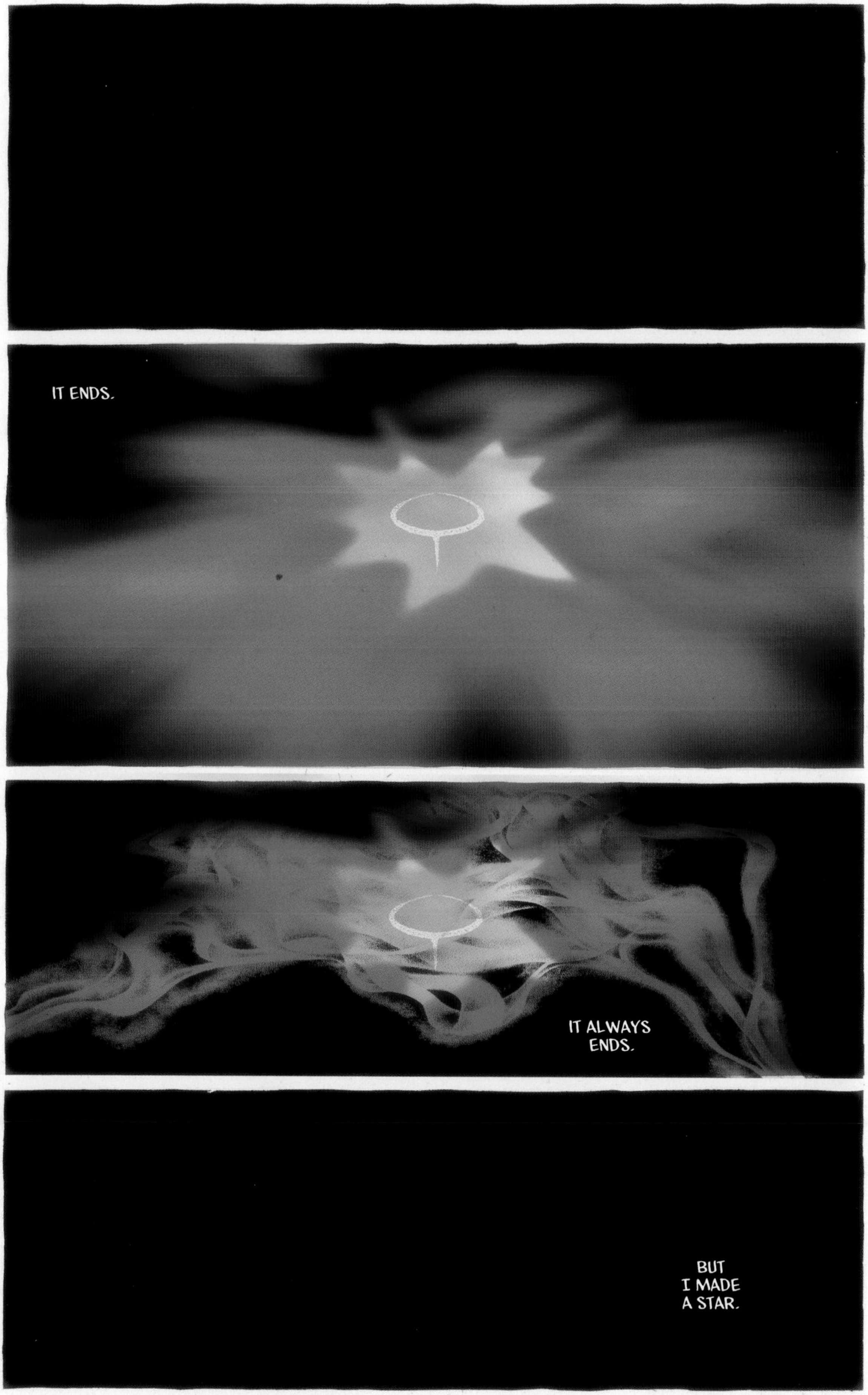
IT ENDS.
IT ALWAYS ENDS.
BUT I MADE A STAR.

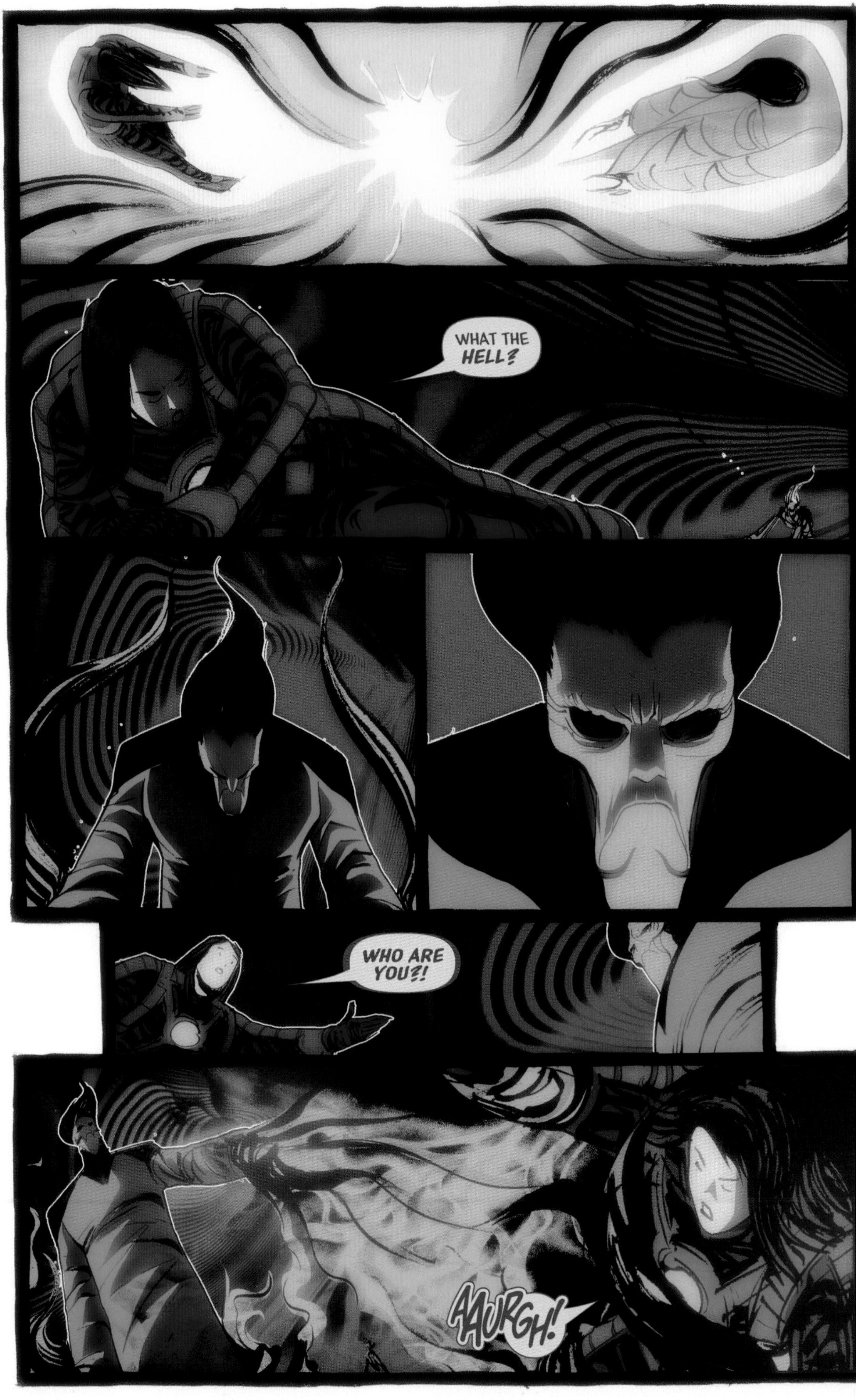
WHAT THE HELL?
WHO ARE YOU?!
AAURGH!

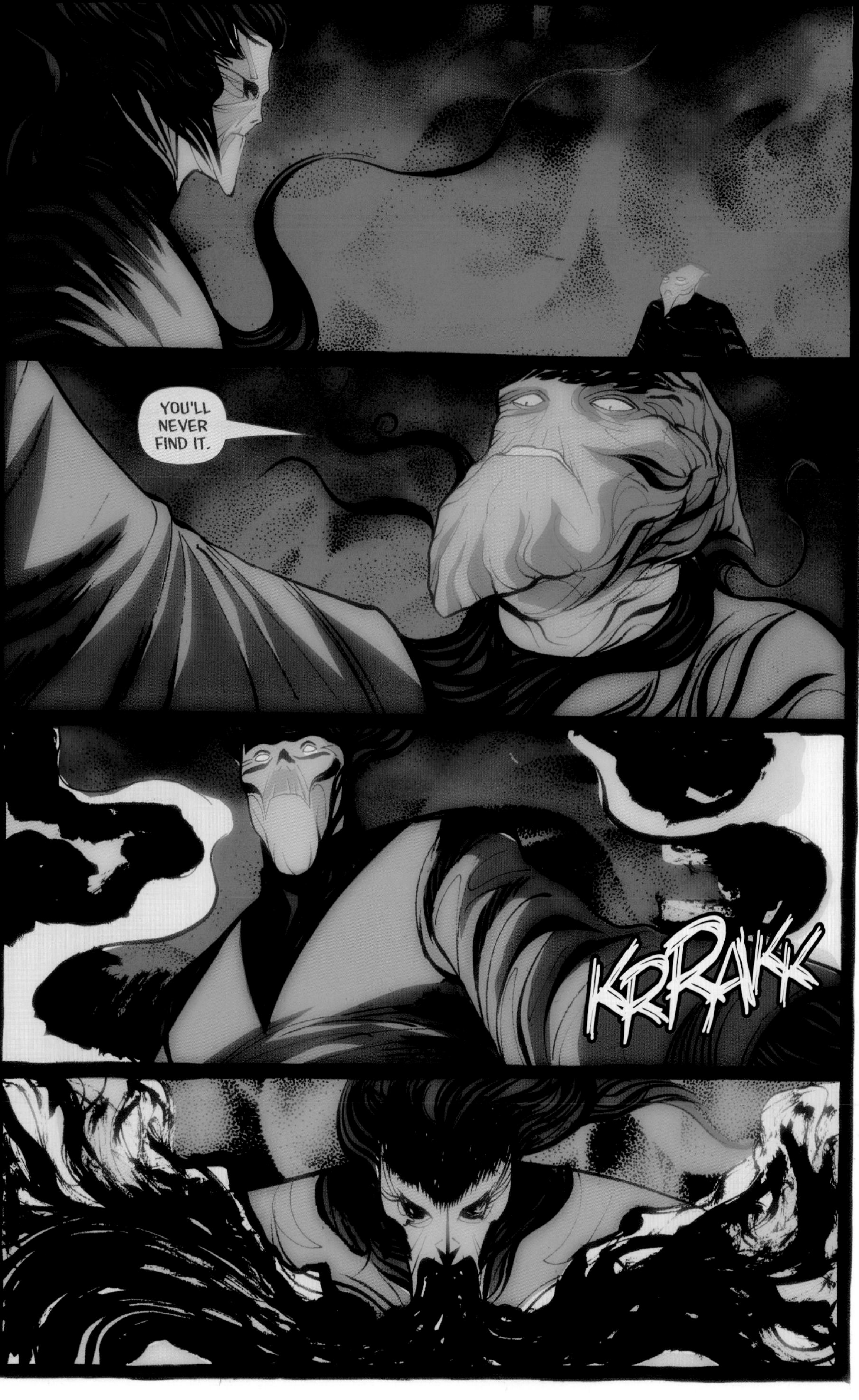
YOU'LL NEVER FIND IT.
KRRAKK

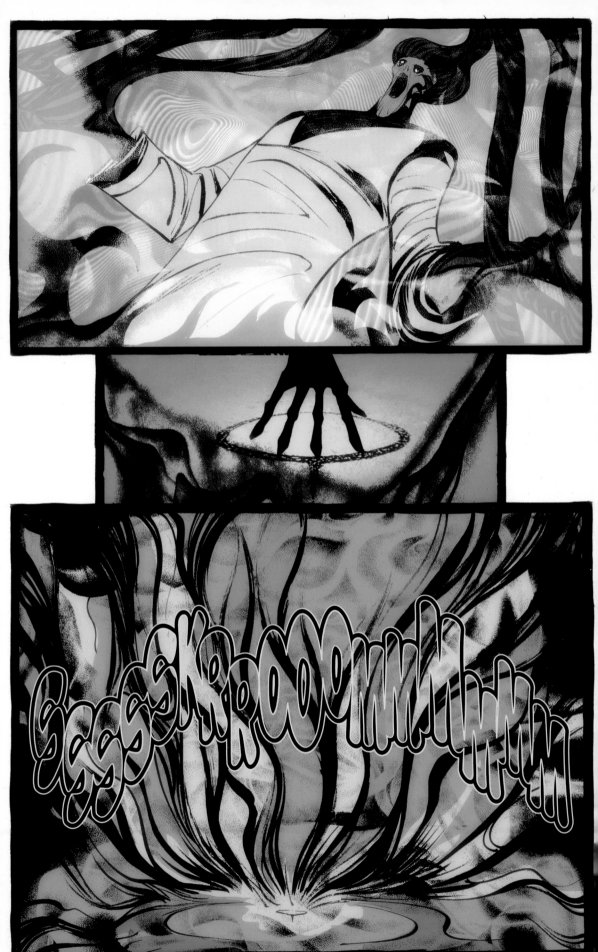

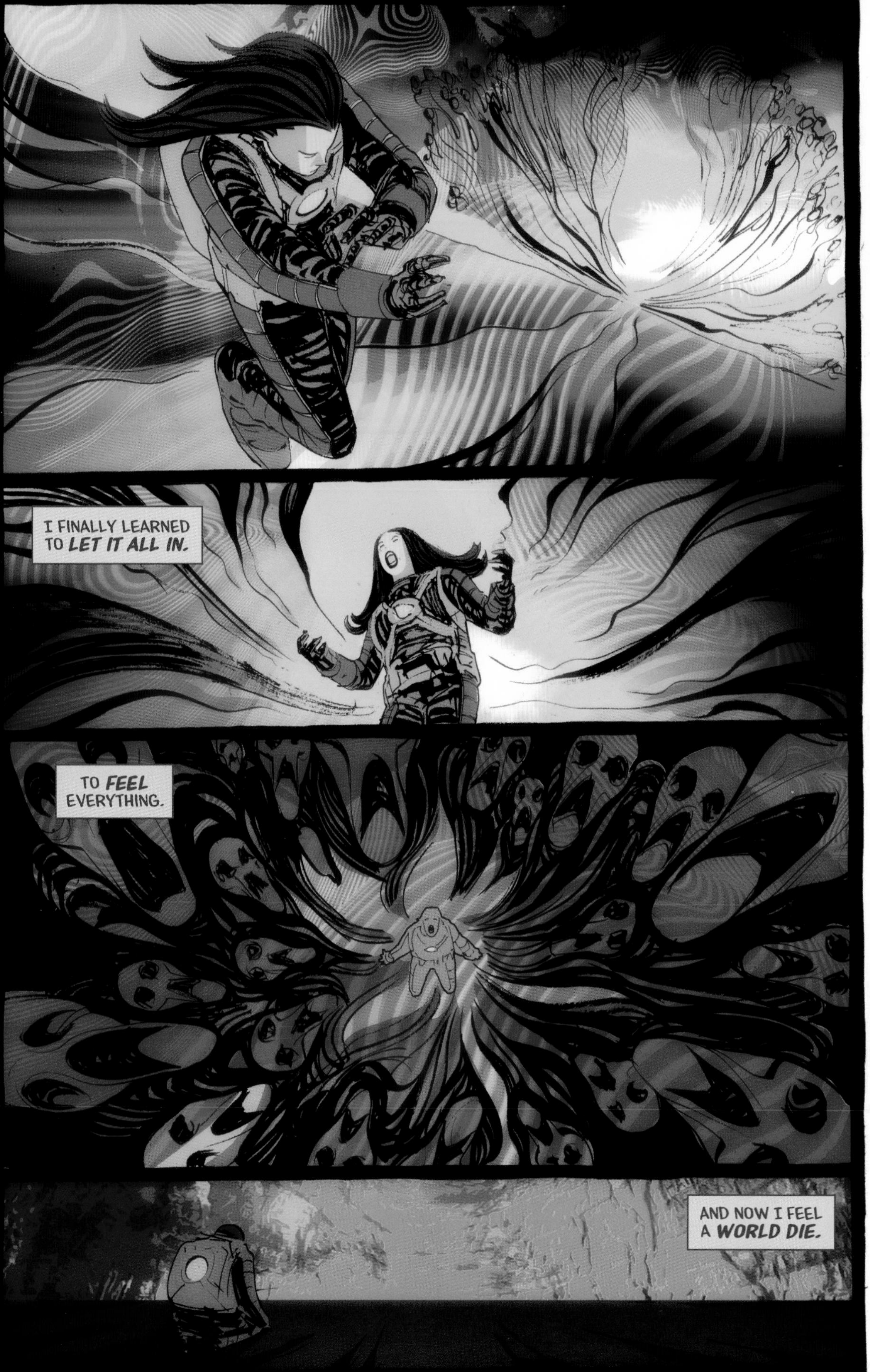
I FINALLY LEARNED TO *LET IT ALL IN.*
TO *FEEL* EVERYTHING.
AND NOW I FEEL A *WORLD DIE.*

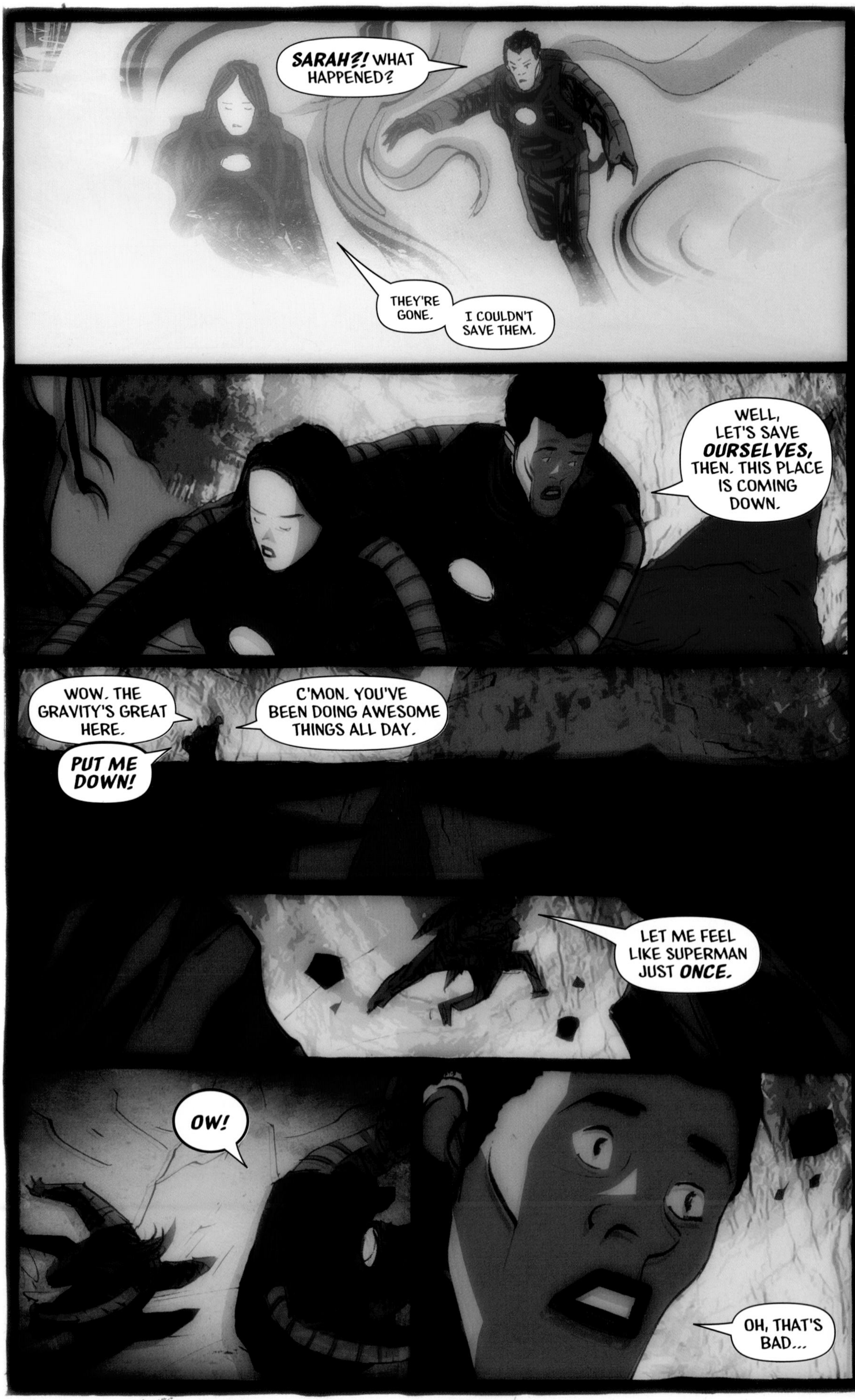

SARAH?! WHAT HAPPENED?
THEY'RE GONE.
I COULDN'T SAVE THEM.
WELL, LET'S SAVE OURSELVES, THEN. THIS PLACE IS COMING DOWN.
WOW. THE GRAVITY'S GREAT HERE.
PUT ME DOWN!
C'MON. YOU'VE BEEN DOING AWESOME THINGS ALL DAY.
LET ME FEEL LIKE SUPERMAN JUST ONCE.
OW!
OH, THAT'S BAD...

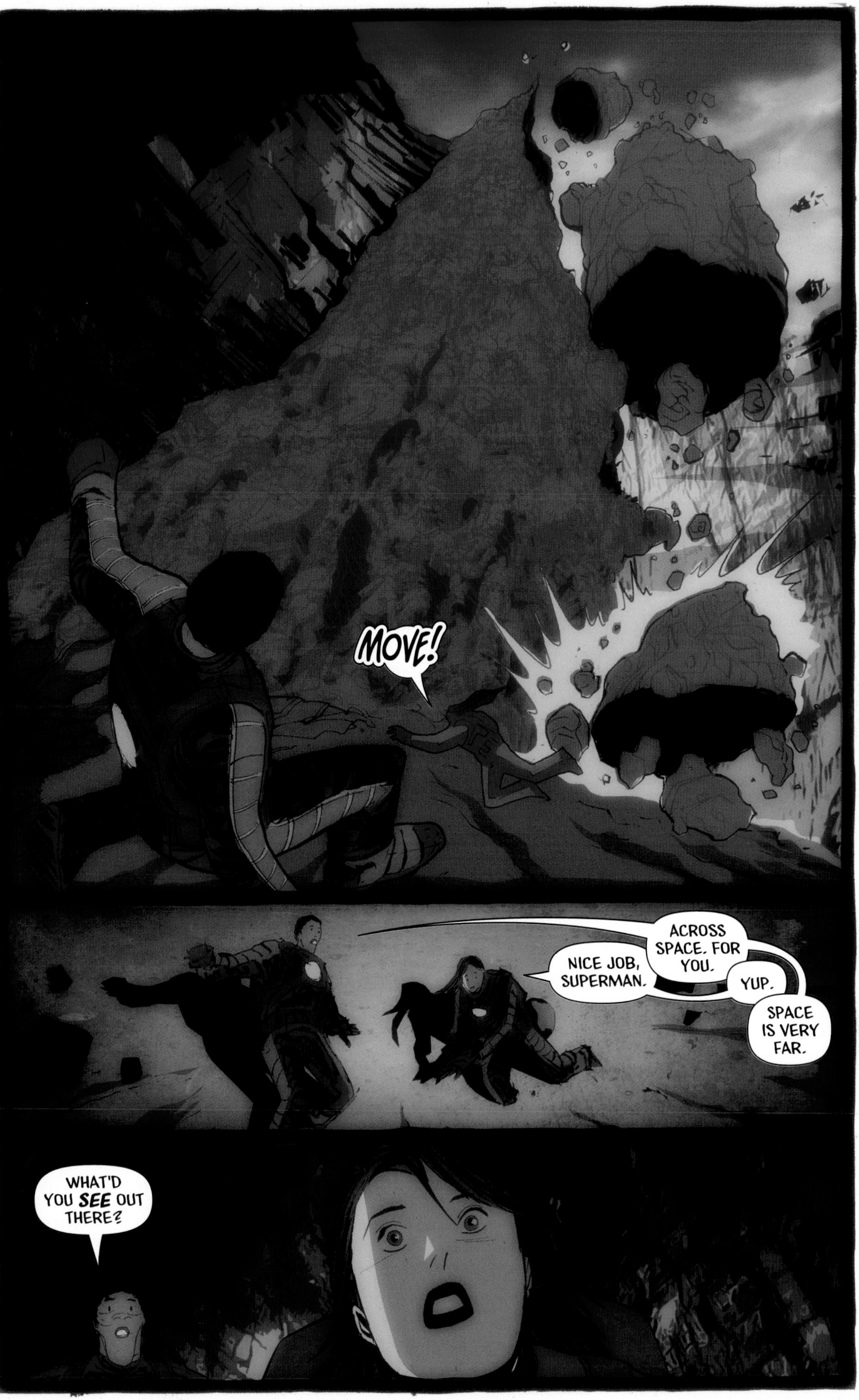
MOVE!
NICE JOB, SUPERMAN.
ACROSS SPACE. FOR YOU.
YUP.
SPACE IS VERY FAR.
WHAT'D YOU SEE OUT THERE?

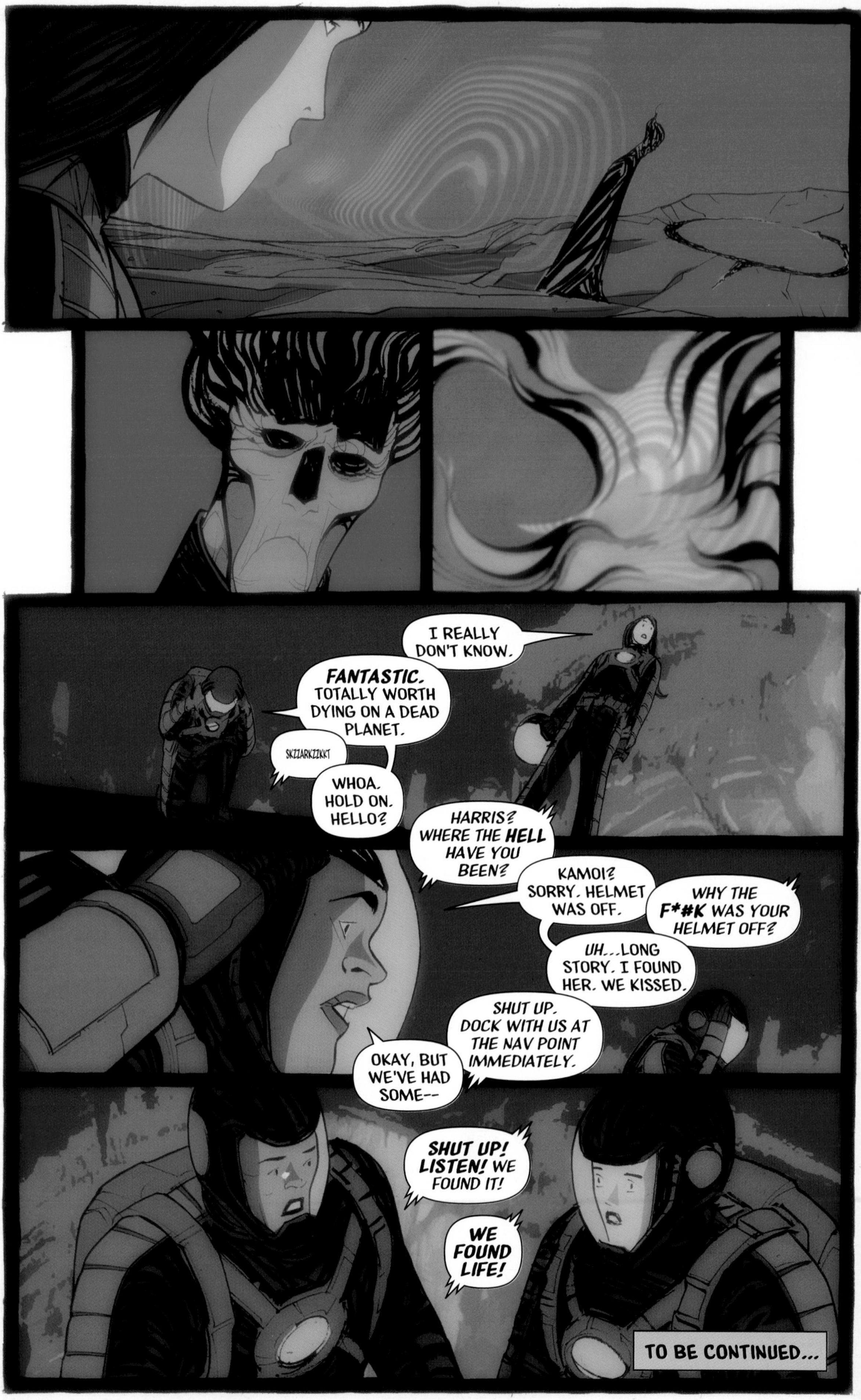
I REALLY DON'T KNOW.
FANTASTIC. TOTALLY WORTH DYING ON A DEAD PLANET.
SKZZARKZZKKT
WHOA. HOLD ON. HELLO?
HARRIS? WHERE THE HELL HAVE YOU BEEN?
KAMOI? SORRY. HELMET WAS OFF.
WHY THE F*#K WAS YOUR HELMET OFF?
UH...LONG STORY. I FOUND HER. WE KISSED.
SHUT UP. DOCK WITH US AT THE NAV POINT IMMEDIATELY.
OKAY, BUT WE'VE HAD SOME--
SHUT UP! LISTEN! WE FOUND IT!
WE FOUND LIFE!
TO BE CONTINUED...

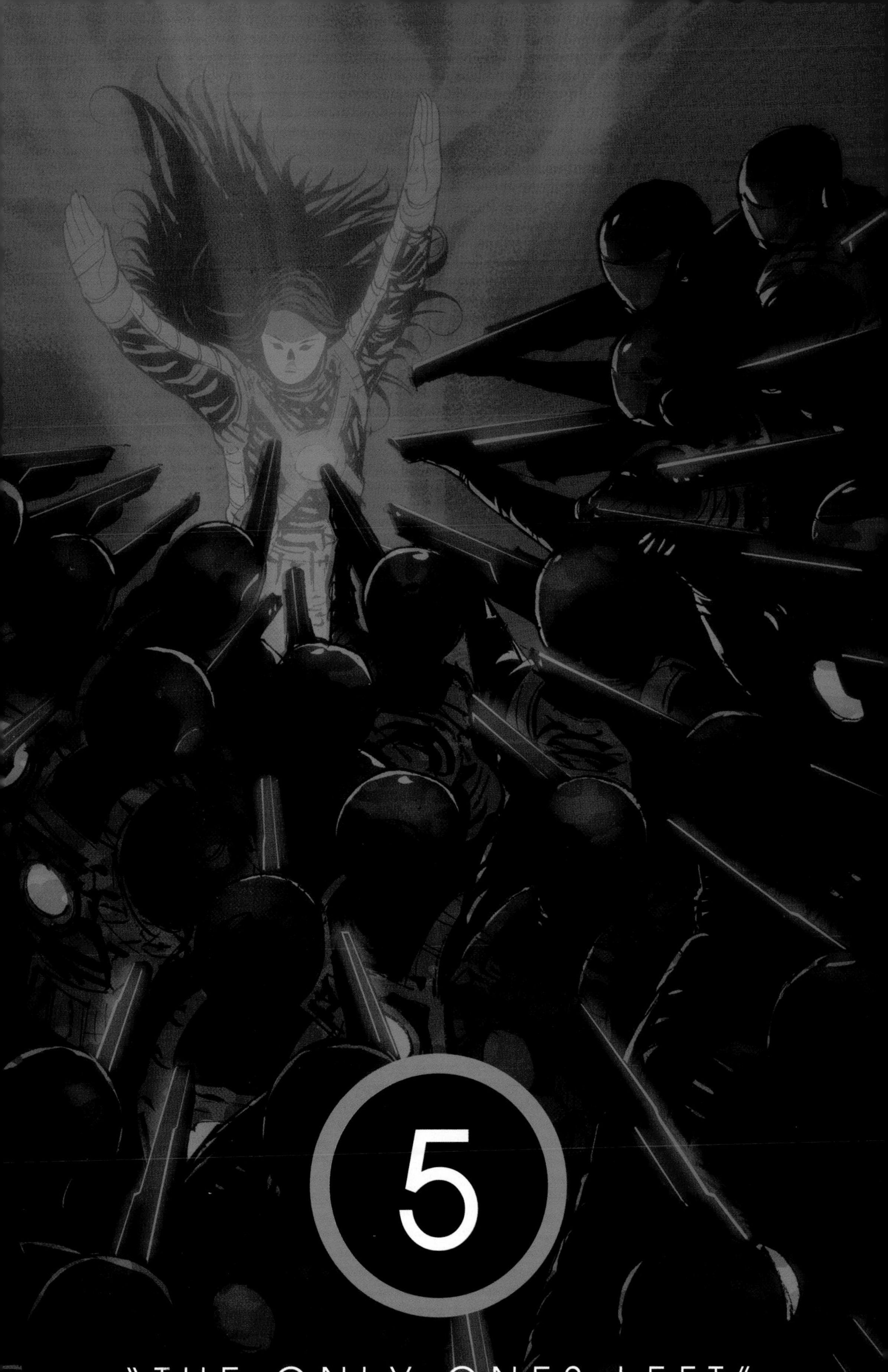
5

“THE ONLY ONES LEFT”

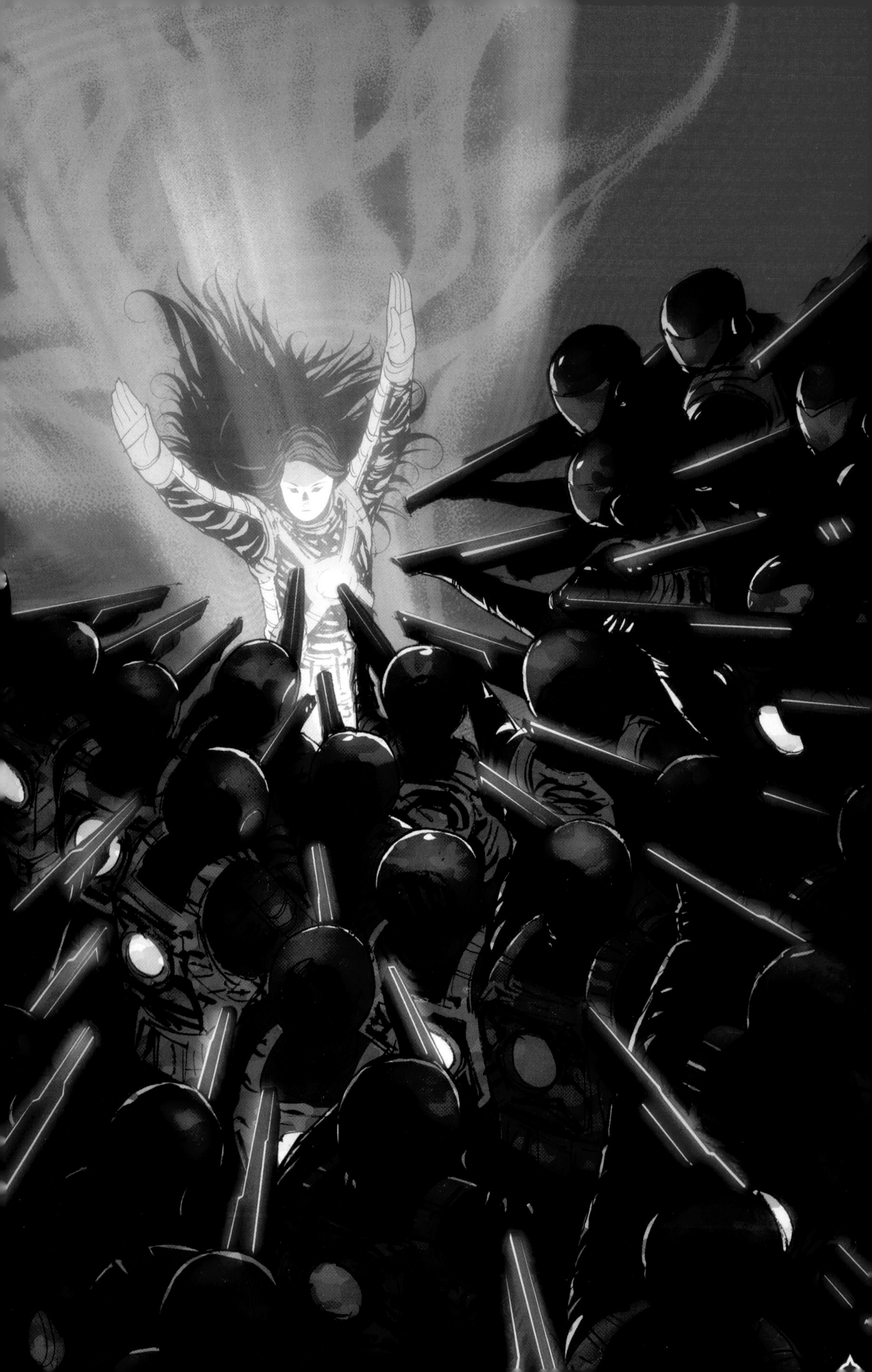

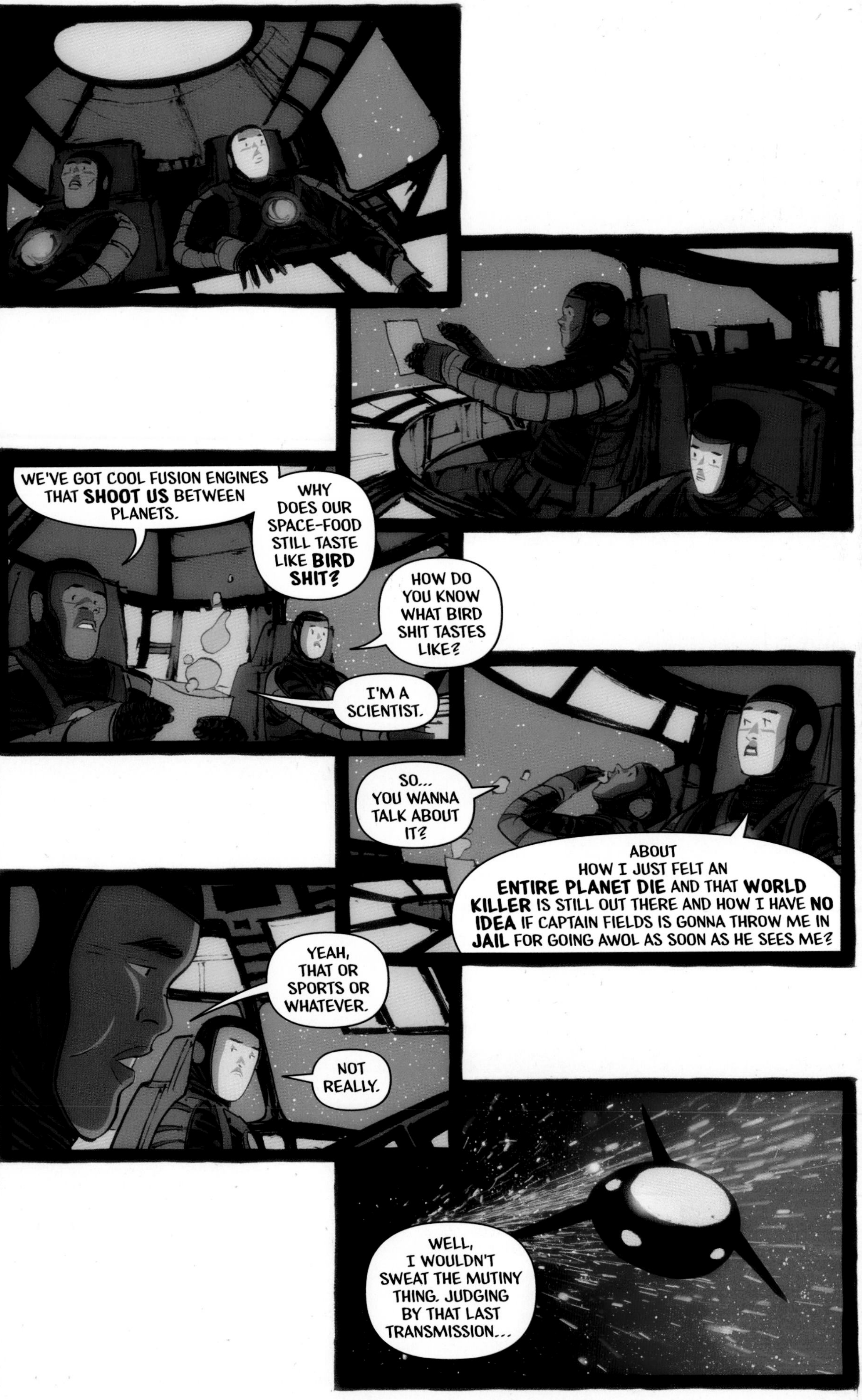

WE'VE GOT COOL FUSION ENGINES THAT **SHOOT US** BETWEEN PLANETS.
WHY DOES OUR SPACE-FOOD STILL TASTE LIKE **BIRD SHIT?**
HOW DO YOU KNOW WHAT BIRD SHIT TASTES LIKE?
I'M A SCIENTIST.
SO... YOU WANNA TALK ABOUT IT?
ABOUT HOW I JUST FELT AN **ENTIRE PLANET DIE** AND THAT **WORLD KILLER** IS STILL OUT THERE AND HOW I HAVE **NO IDEA** IF CAPTAIN FIELDS IS GONNA THROW ME IN **JAIL** FOR GOING AWOL AS SOON AS HE SEES ME?
YEAH, THAT OR SPORTS OR WHATEVER.
NOT REALLY.
WELL, I WOULDN'T SWEAT THE MUTINY THING. JUDGING BY THAT LAST TRANSMISSION...

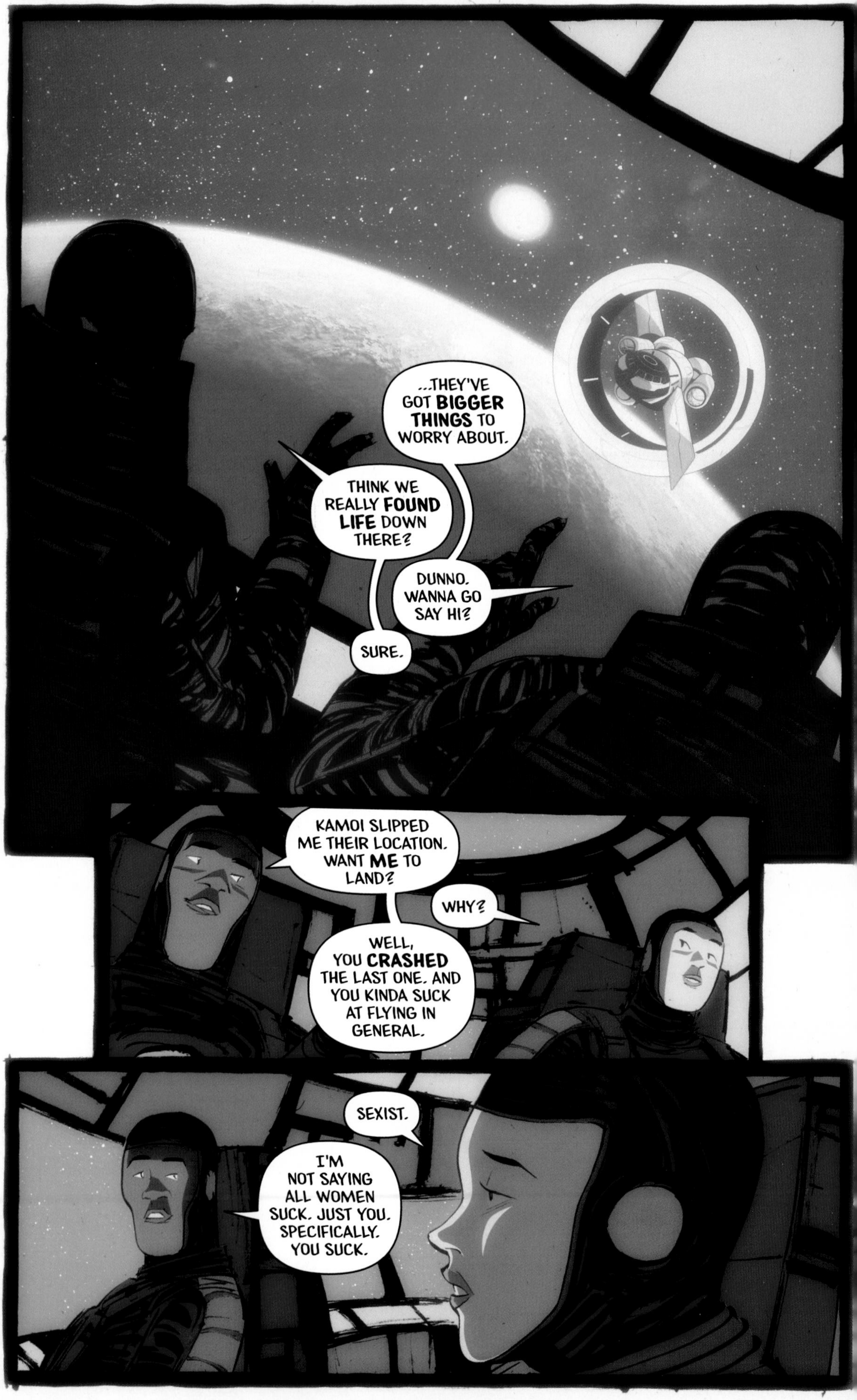

...THEY'VE GOT BIGGER THINGS TO WORRY ABOUT.
THINK WE REALLY FOUND LIFE DOWN THERE?
DUNNO. WANNA GO SAY HI?
SURE.
KAMOI SLIPPED ME THEIR LOCATION. WANT ME TO LAND?
WHY?
WELL, YOU CRASHED THE LAST ONE. AND YOU KINDA SUCK AT FLYING IN GENERAL.
SEXIST.
I'M NOT SAYING ALL WOMEN SUCK. JUST YOU. SPECIFICALLY. YOU SUCK.

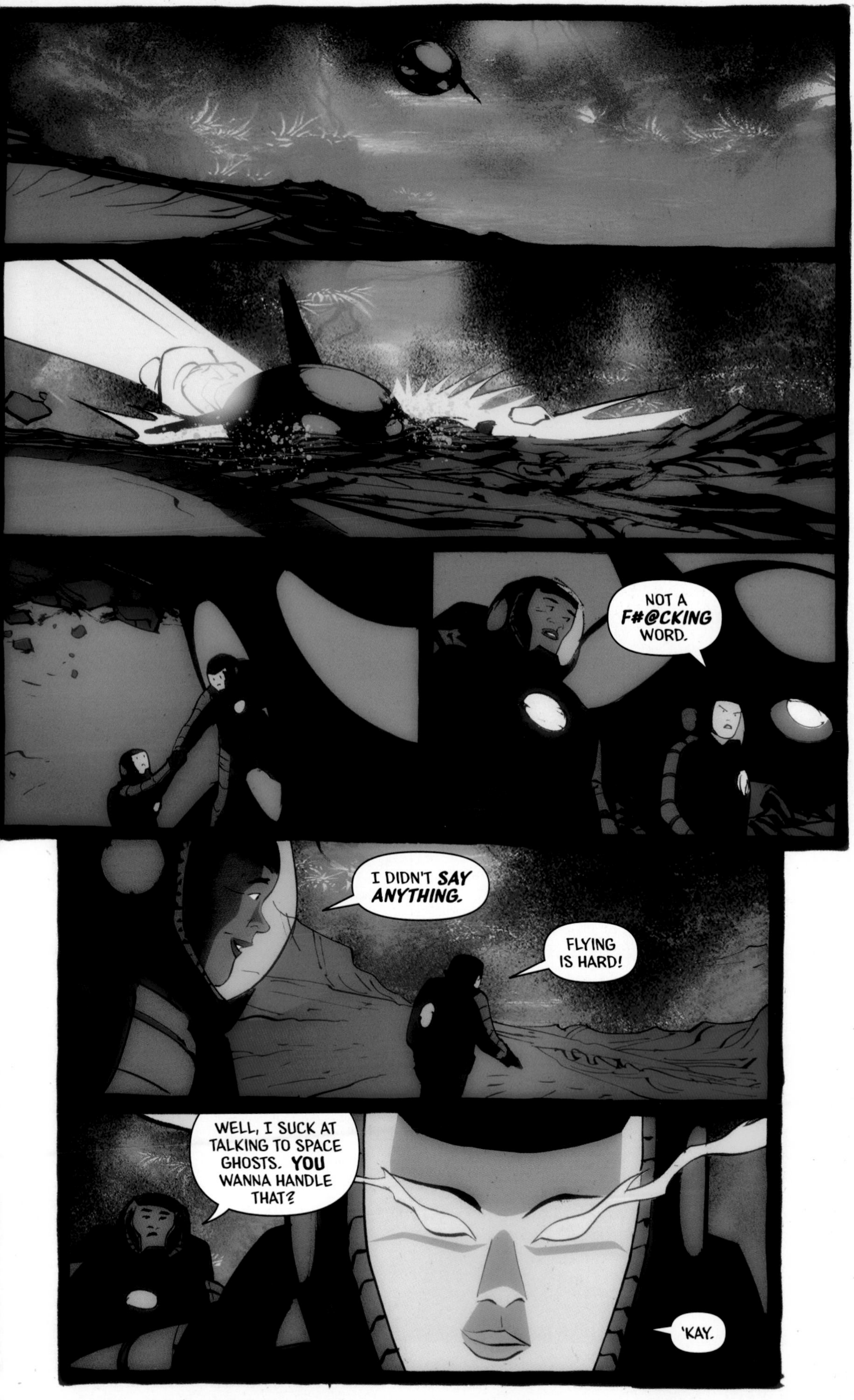
NOT A F#@CKING WORD.
I DIDN'T SAY ANYTHING.
FLYING IS HARD!
WELL, I SUCK AT TALKING TO SPACE GHOSTS. YOU WANNA HANDLE THAT?
'KAY.

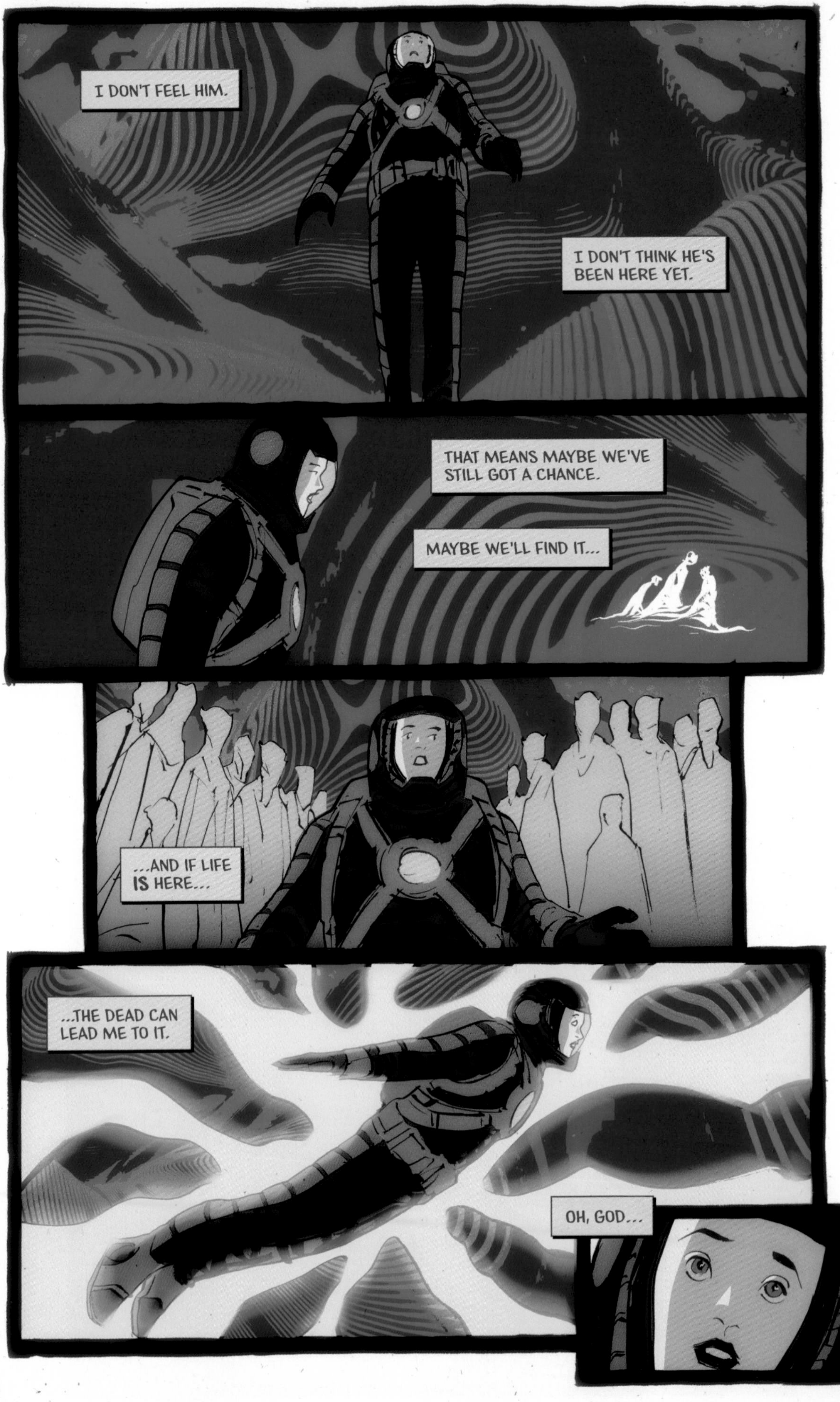
I DON'T FEEL HIM.
I DON'T THINK HE'S BEEN HERE YET.
THAT MEANS MAYBE WE'VE STILL GOT A CHANCE.
MAYBE WE'LL FIND IT...
...AND IF LIFE IS HERE...
...THE DEAD CAN LEAD ME TO IT.
OH, GOD...

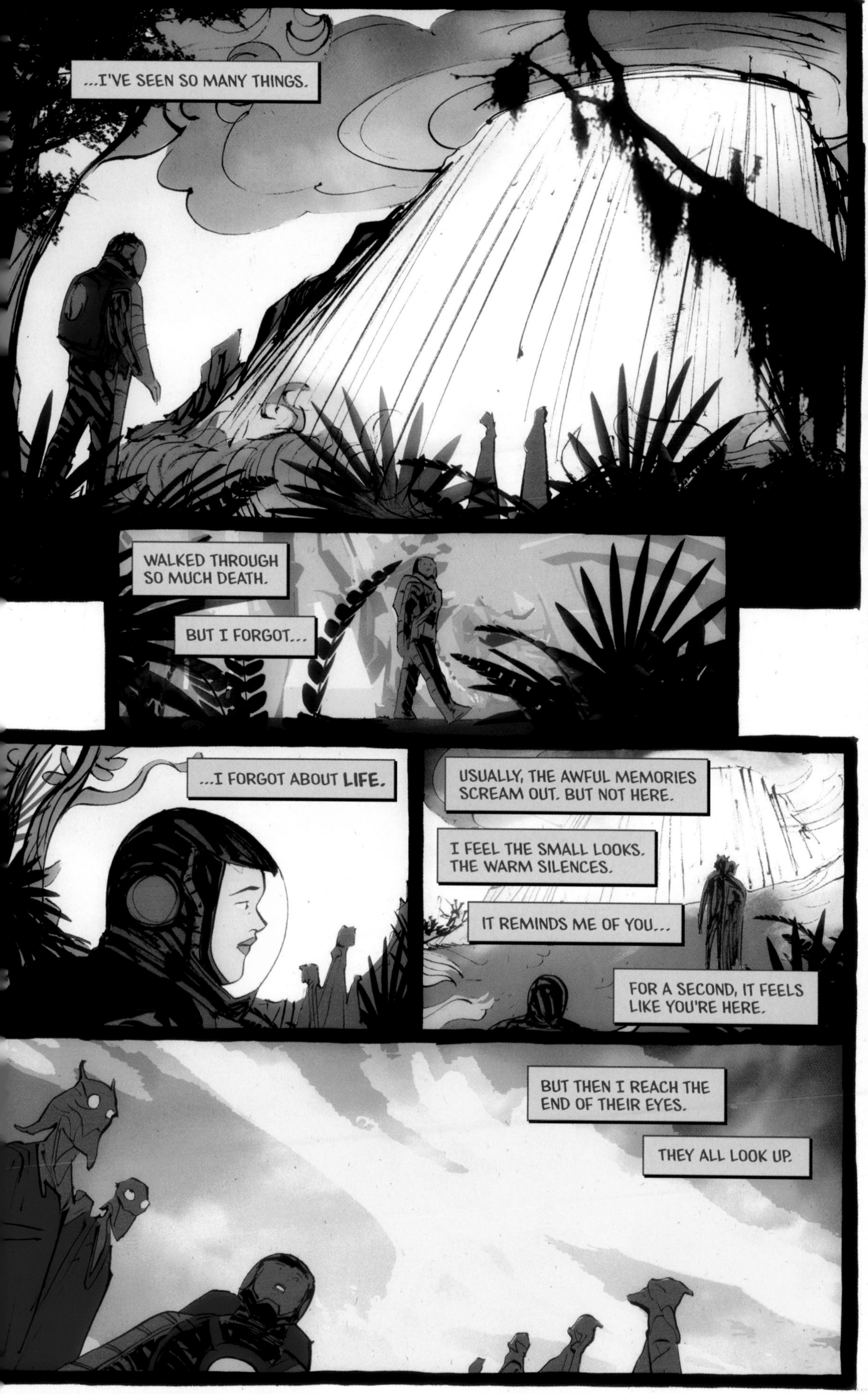
...I'VE SEEN SO MANY THINGS.
WALKED THROUGH SO MUCH DEATH.
BUT I FORGOT...
...I FORGOT ABOUT LIFE.
USUALLY, THE AWFUL MEMORIES SCREAM OUT. BUT NOT HERE.
I FEEL THE SMALL LOOKS. THE WARM SILENCES.
IT REMINDS ME OF YOU...
FOR A SECOND, IT FEELS LIKE YOU'RE HERE.
BUT THEN I REACH THE END OF THEIR EYES.
THEY ALL LOOK UP.

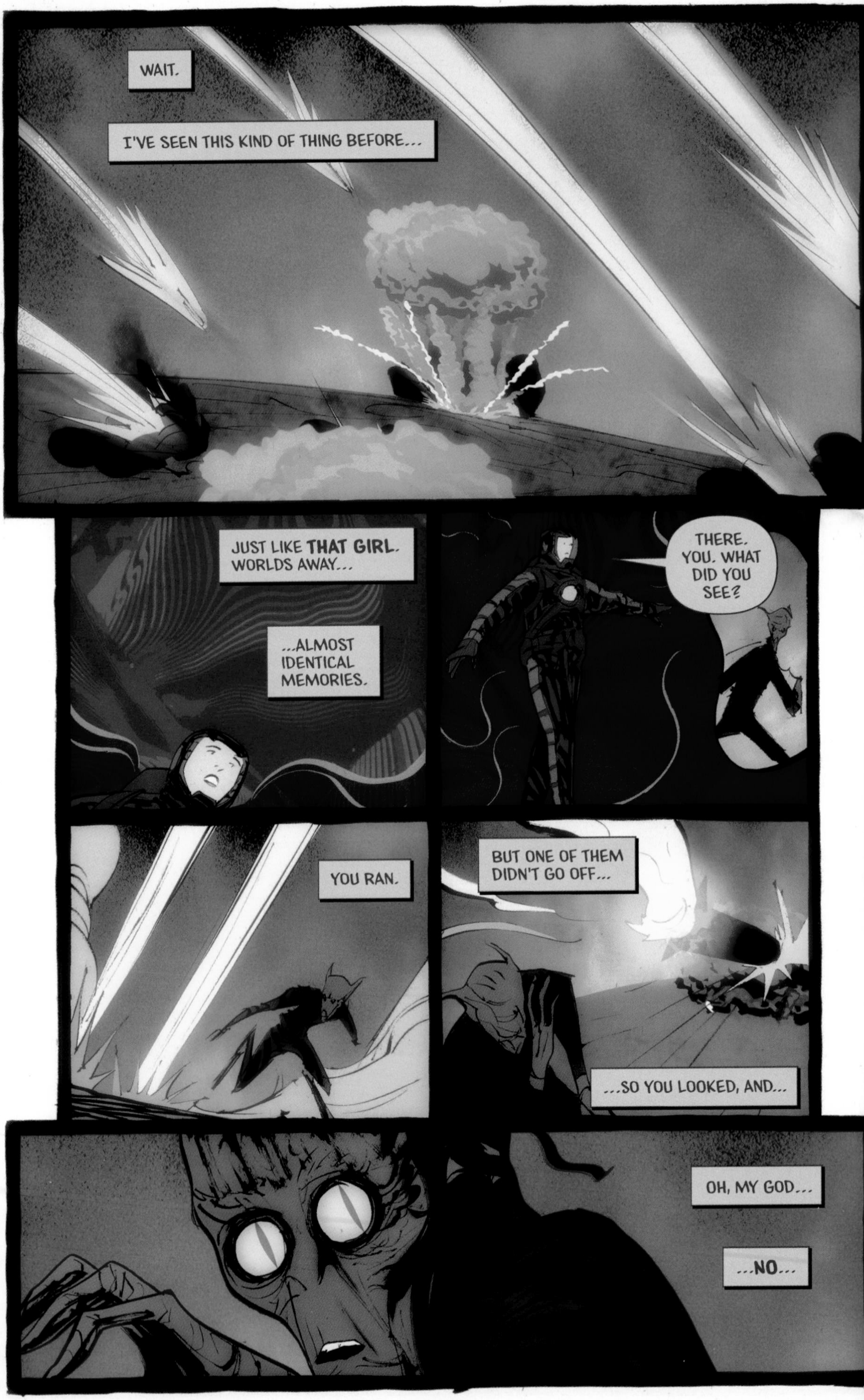
WAIT.
I'VE SEEN THIS KIND OF THING BEFORE...
JUST LIKE THAT GIRL. WORLDS AWAY...
...ALMOST IDENTICAL MEMORIES.
THERE. YOU. WHAT DID YOU SEE?
YOU RAN.
BUT ONE OF THEM DIDN'T GO OFF...
...SO YOU LOOKED, AND...
OH, MY GOD...
...NO...

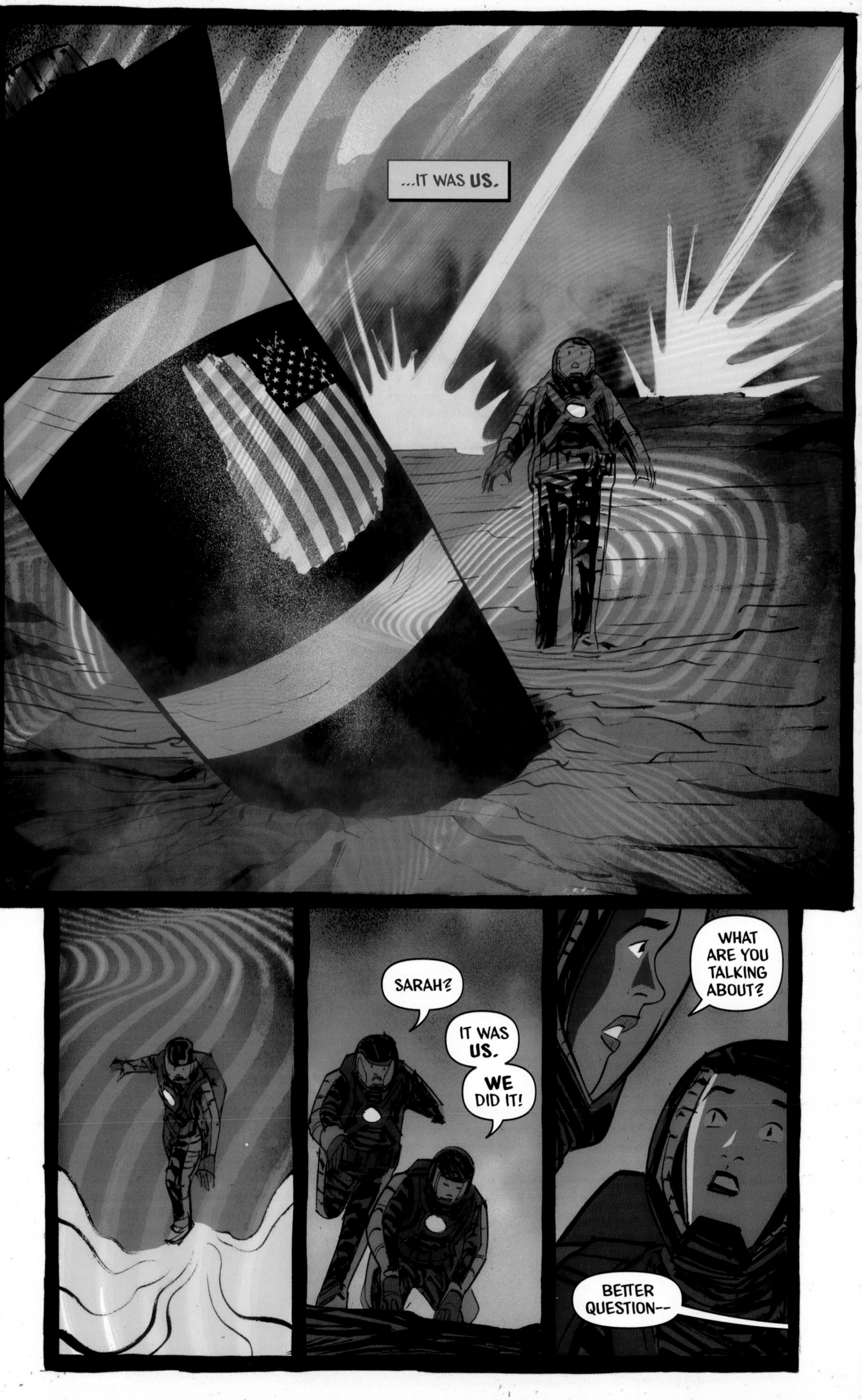
...IT WAS US.
SARAH?
IT WAS US.
WE DID IT!
WHAT ARE YOU TALKING ABOUT?
BETTER QUESTION--

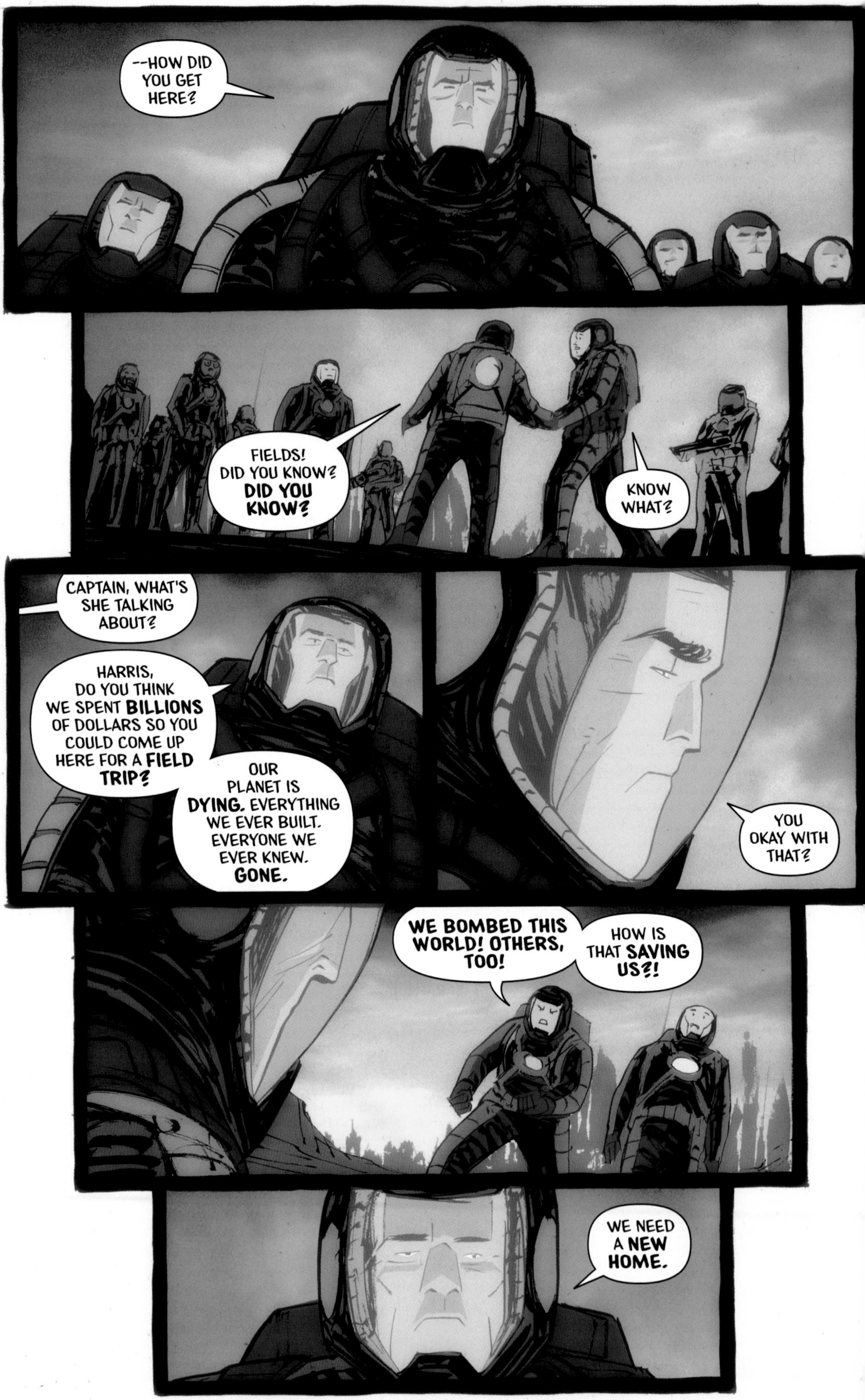
--HOW DID YOU GET HERE?
FIELDS! DID YOU KNOW? DID YOU KNOW?
KNOW WHAT?
CAPTAIN, WHAT'S SHE TALKING ABOUT?
HARRIS, DO YOU THINK WE SPENT BILLIONS OF DOLLARS SO YOU COULD COME UP HERE FOR A FIELD TRIP?
OUR PLANET IS DYING. EVERYTHING WE EVER BUILT. EVERYONE WE EVER KNEW. GONE.
YOU OKAY WITH THAT?
WE BOMBED THIS WORLD! OTHERS, TOO!
HOW IS THAT SAVING US?!
WE NEED A NEW HOME.

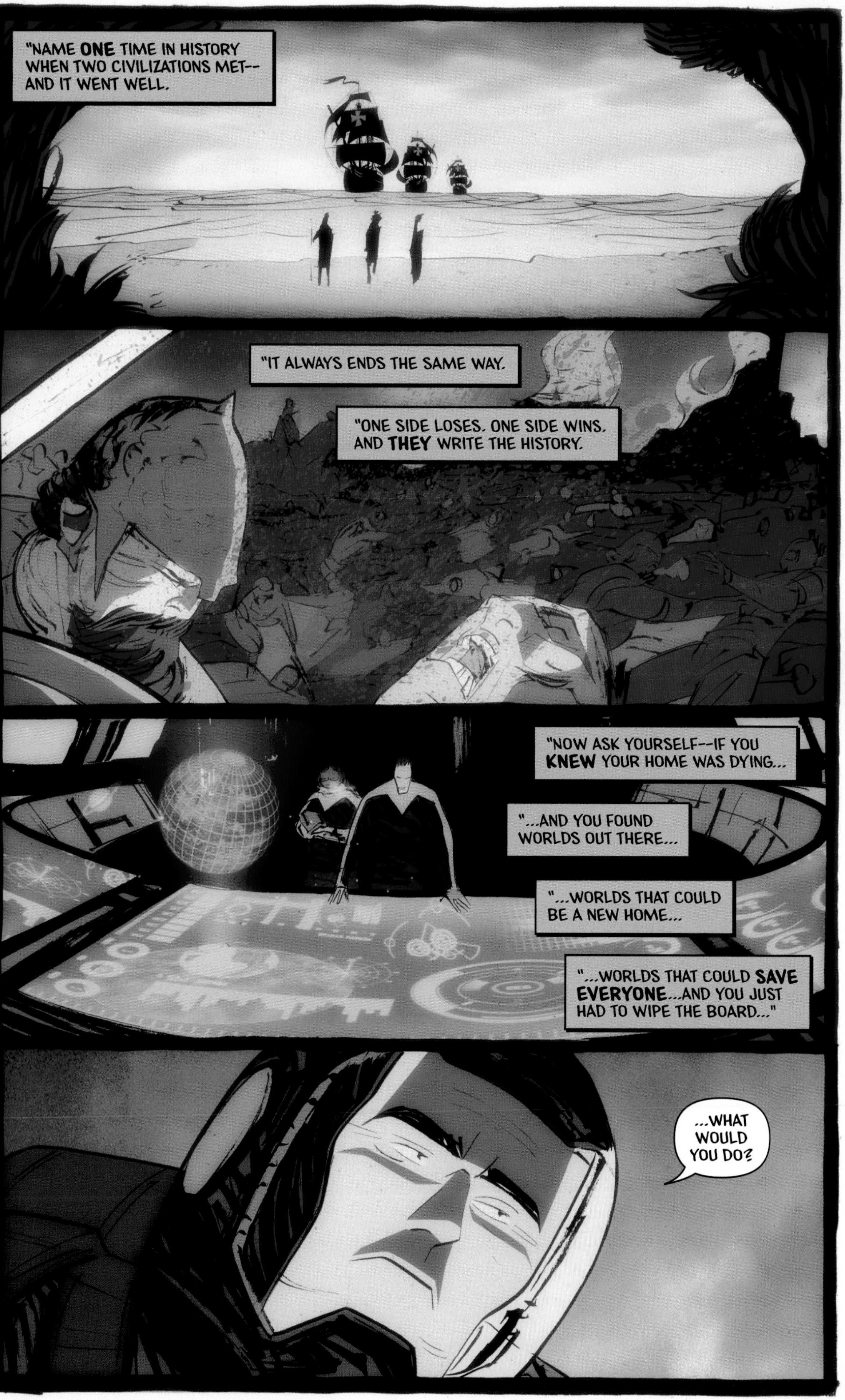
"NAME ONE TIME IN HISTORY WHEN TWO CIVILIZATIONS MET--AND IT WENT WELL.
"IT ALWAYS ENDS THE SAME WAY.
"ONE SIDE LOSES. ONE SIDE WINS. AND THEY WRITE THE HISTORY.
"NOW ASK YOURSELF--IF YOU KNEW YOUR HOME WAS DYING...
"...AND YOU FOUND WORLDS OUT THERE...
"...WORLDS THAT COULD BE A NEW HOME...
"...WORLDS THAT COULD SAVE EVERYONE...AND YOU JUST HAD TO WIPE THE BOARD..."
...WHAT WOULD YOU DO?

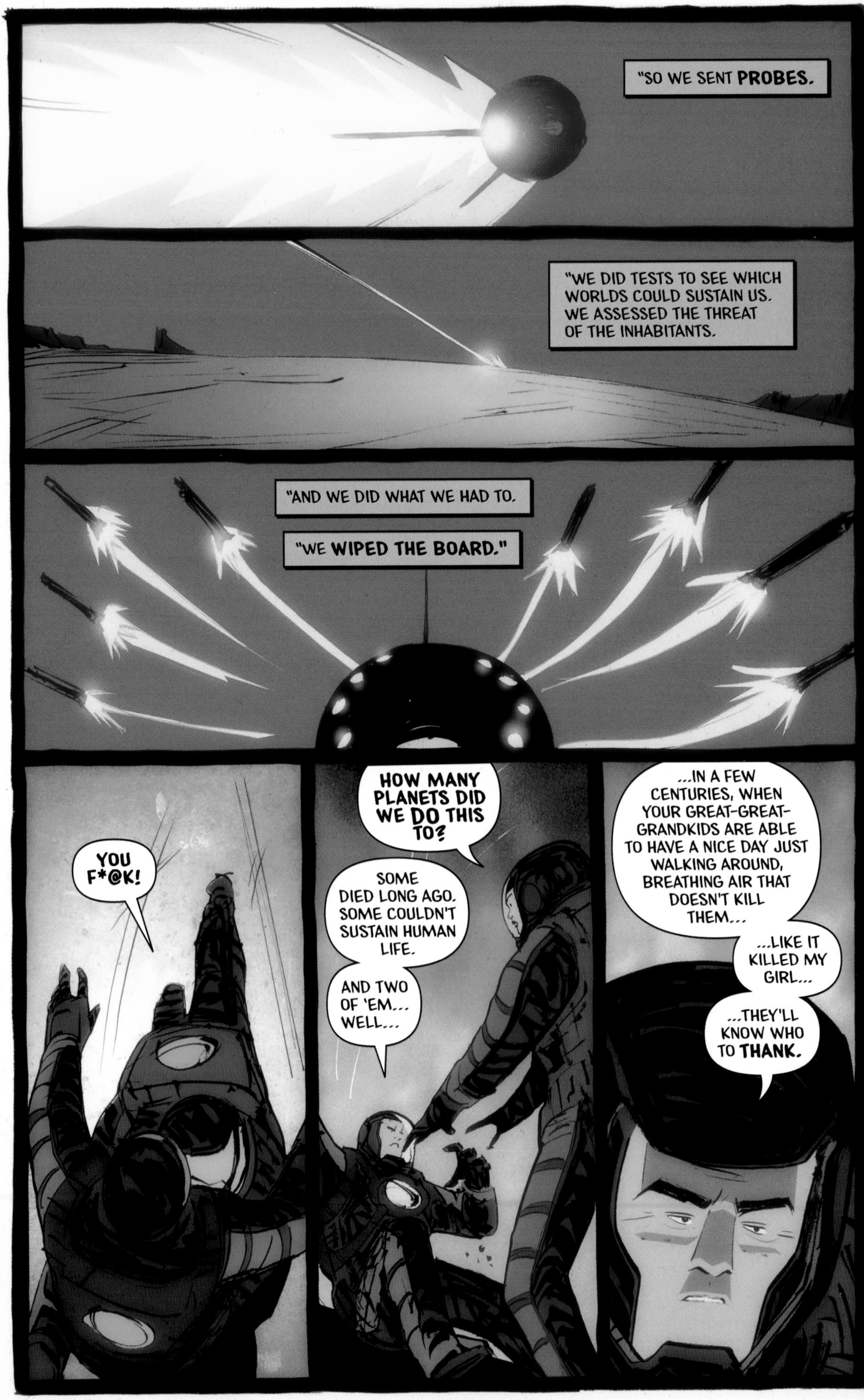

"SO WE SENT **PROBES.**
"WE DID TESTS TO SEE WHICH WORLDS COULD SUSTAIN US. WE ASSESSED THE THREAT OF THE INHABITANTS.
"AND WE DID WHAT WE HAD TO.
"WE **WIPED THE BOARD.**"
YOU F*@K!
HOW MANY PLANETS DID WE **DO** THIS TO?
SOME DIED LONG AGO. SOME COULDN'T SUSTAIN HUMAN LIFE.
AND TWO OF 'EM... WELL...
...IN A FEW CENTURIES, WHEN YOUR GREAT-GREAT-GRANDKIDS ARE ABLE TO HAVE A NICE DAY JUST WALKING AROUND, BREATHING AIR THAT DOESN'T KILL THEM...
...LIKE IT KILLED MY GIRL...
...THEY'LL KNOW WHO TO **THANK.**

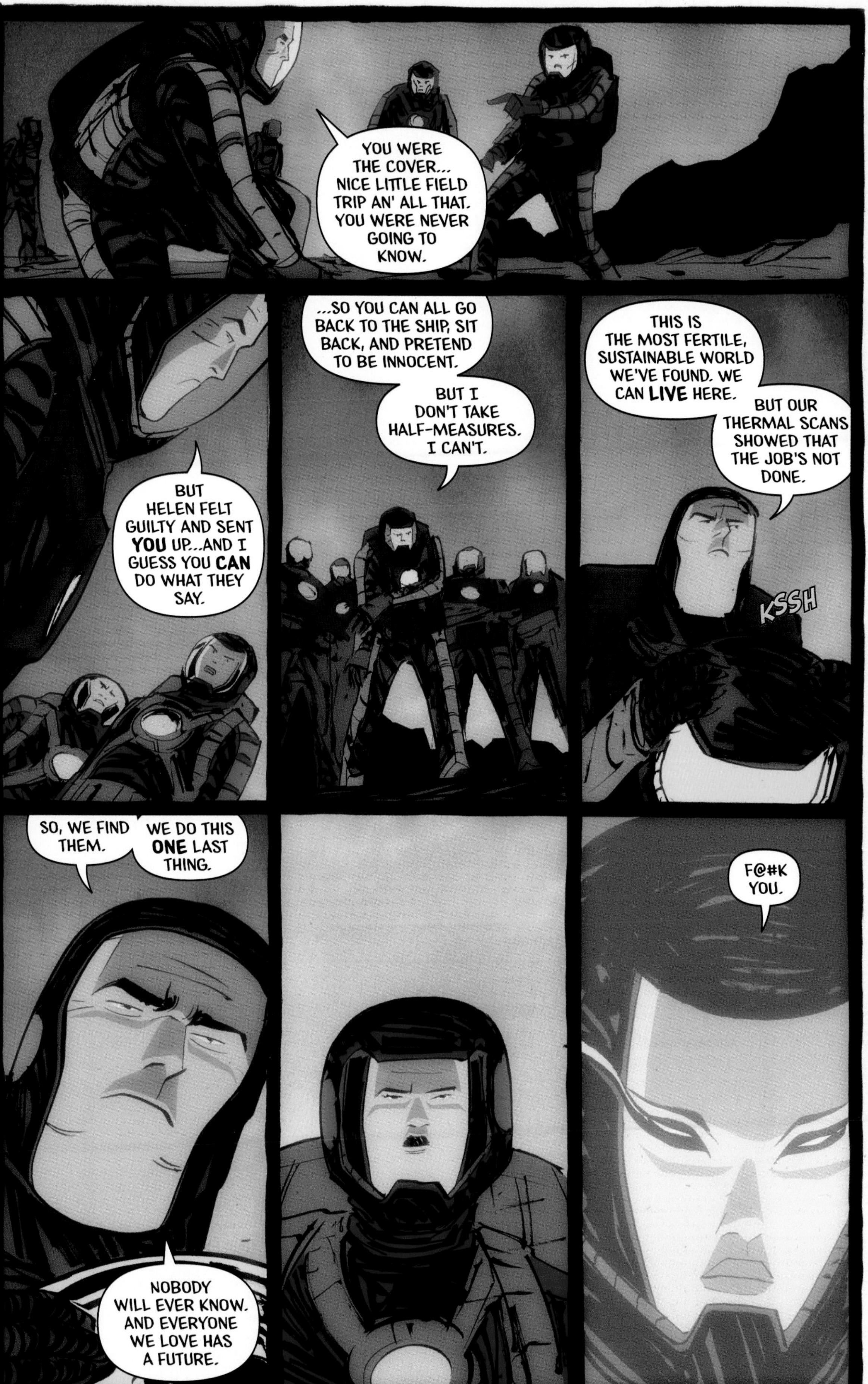
YOU WERE THE COVER... NICE LITTLE FIELD TRIP AN' ALL THAT. YOU WERE NEVER GOING TO KNOW.
BUT HELEN FELT GUILTY AND SENT YOU UP...AND I GUESS YOU CAN DO WHAT THEY SAY.
...SO YOU CAN ALL GO BACK TO THE SHIP, SIT BACK, AND PRETEND TO BE INNOCENT.
BUT I DON'T TAKE HALF-MEASURES. I CAN'T.
THIS IS THE MOST FERTILE, SUSTAINABLE WORLD WE'VE FOUND. WE CAN LIVE HERE.
BUT OUR THERMAL SCANS SHOWED THAT THE JOB'S NOT DONE.
KSSH
SO, WE FIND THEM.
WE DO THIS ONE LAST THING.
NOBODY WILL EVER KNOW. AND EVERYONE WE LOVE HAS A FUTURE.
F@#K YOU.

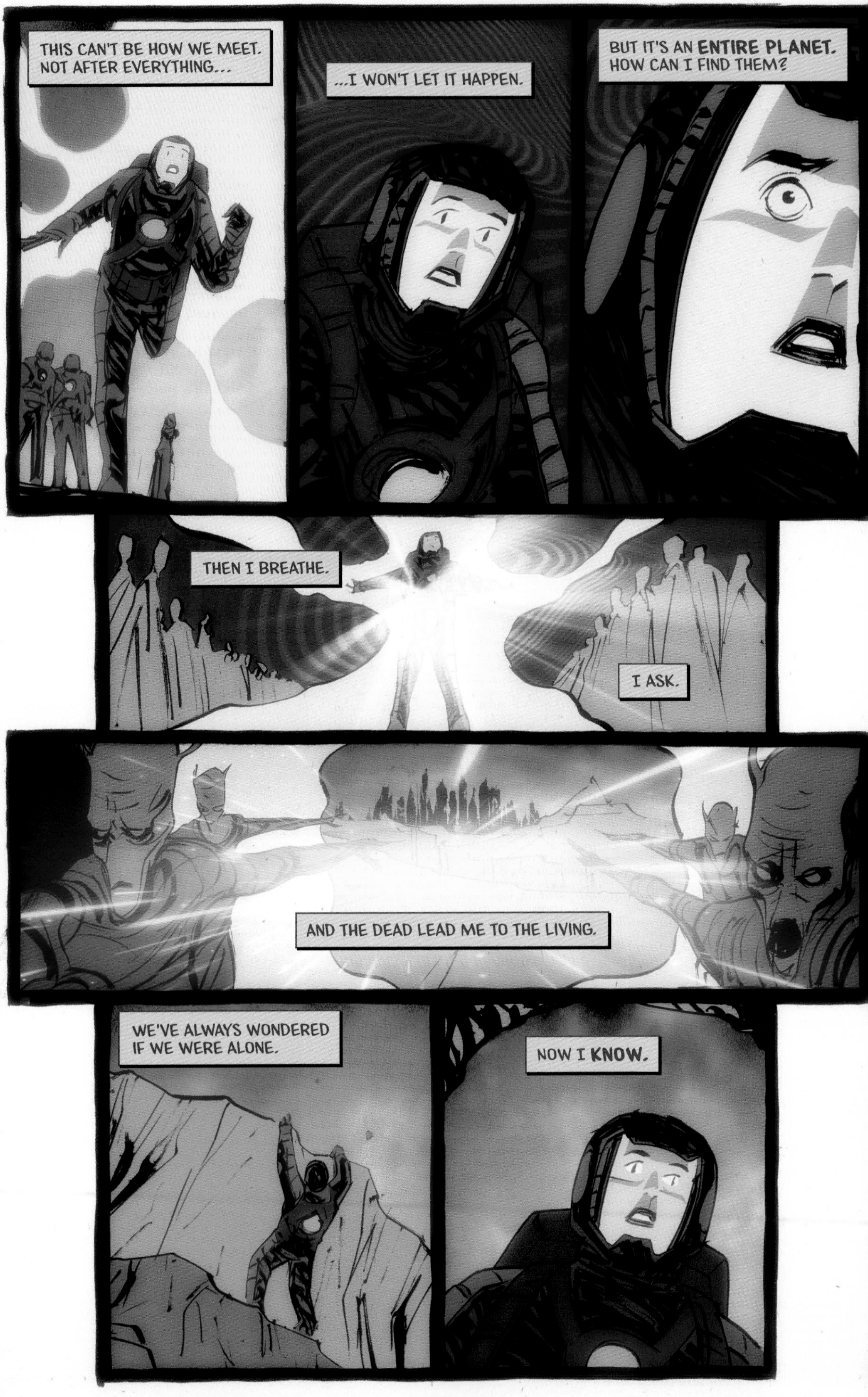
THIS CAN'T BE HOW WE MEET. NOT AFTER EVERYTHING...
...I WON'T LET IT HAPPEN.
BUT IT'S AN **ENTIRE PLANET.** HOW CAN I FIND THEM?
THEN I BREATHE.
I ASK.
AND THE DEAD LEAD ME TO THE LIVING.
WE'VE ALWAYS WONDERED IF WE WERE ALONE.
NOW I **KNOW.**

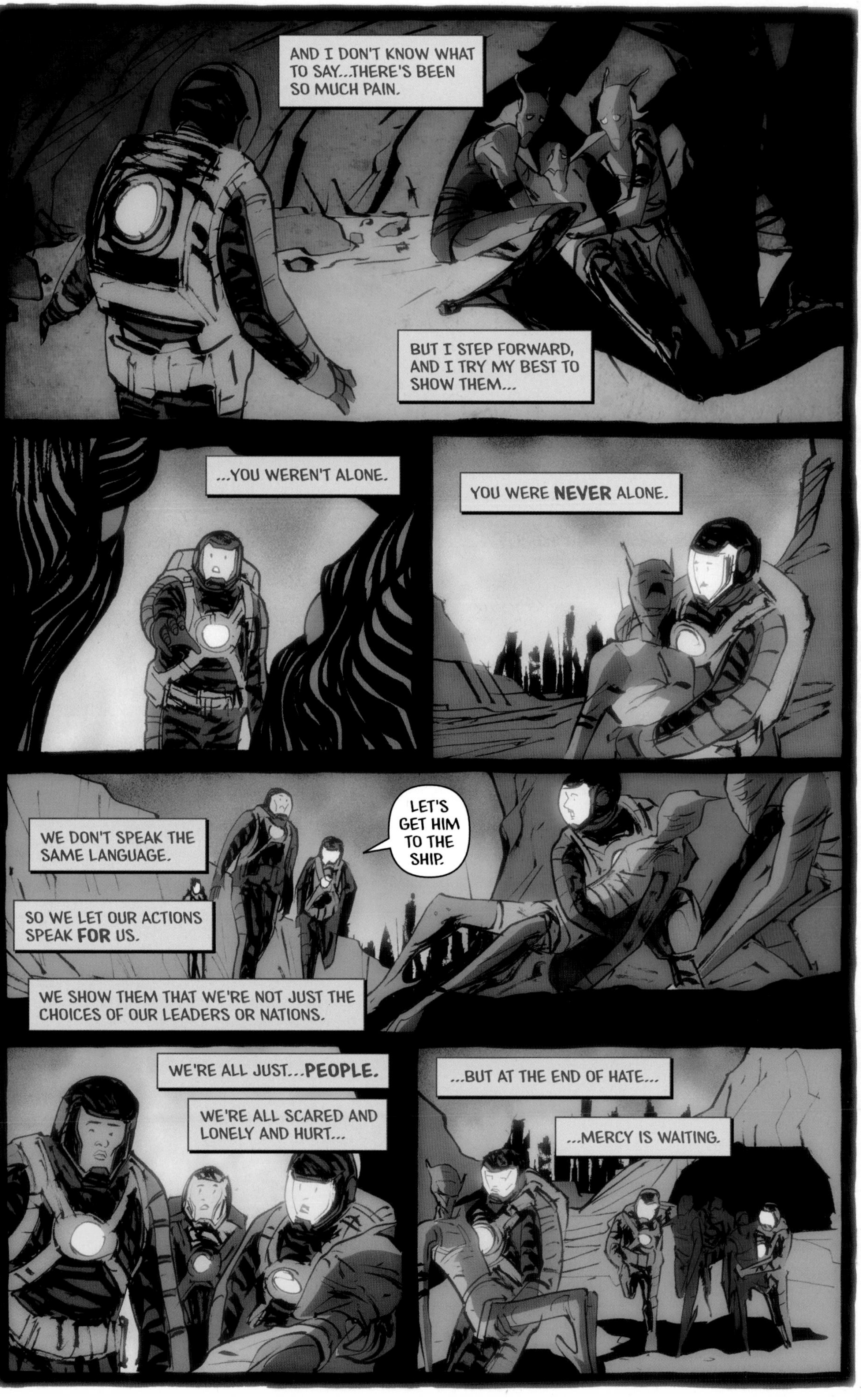
AND I DON'T KNOW WHAT TO SAY...THERE'S BEEN SO MUCH PAIN.
BUT I STEP FORWARD, AND I TRY MY BEST TO SHOW THEM...
...YOU WEREN'T ALONE.
YOU WERE NEVER ALONE.
WE DON'T SPEAK THE SAME LANGUAGE.
SO WE LET OUR ACTIONS SPEAK FOR US.
WE SHOW THEM THAT WE'RE NOT JUST THE CHOICES OF OUR LEADERS OR NATIONS.
LET'S GET HIM TO THE SHIP.
WE'RE ALL JUST...PEOPLE.
WE'RE ALL SCARED AND LONELY AND HURT...
...BUT AT THE END OF HATE...
...MERCY IS WAITING.

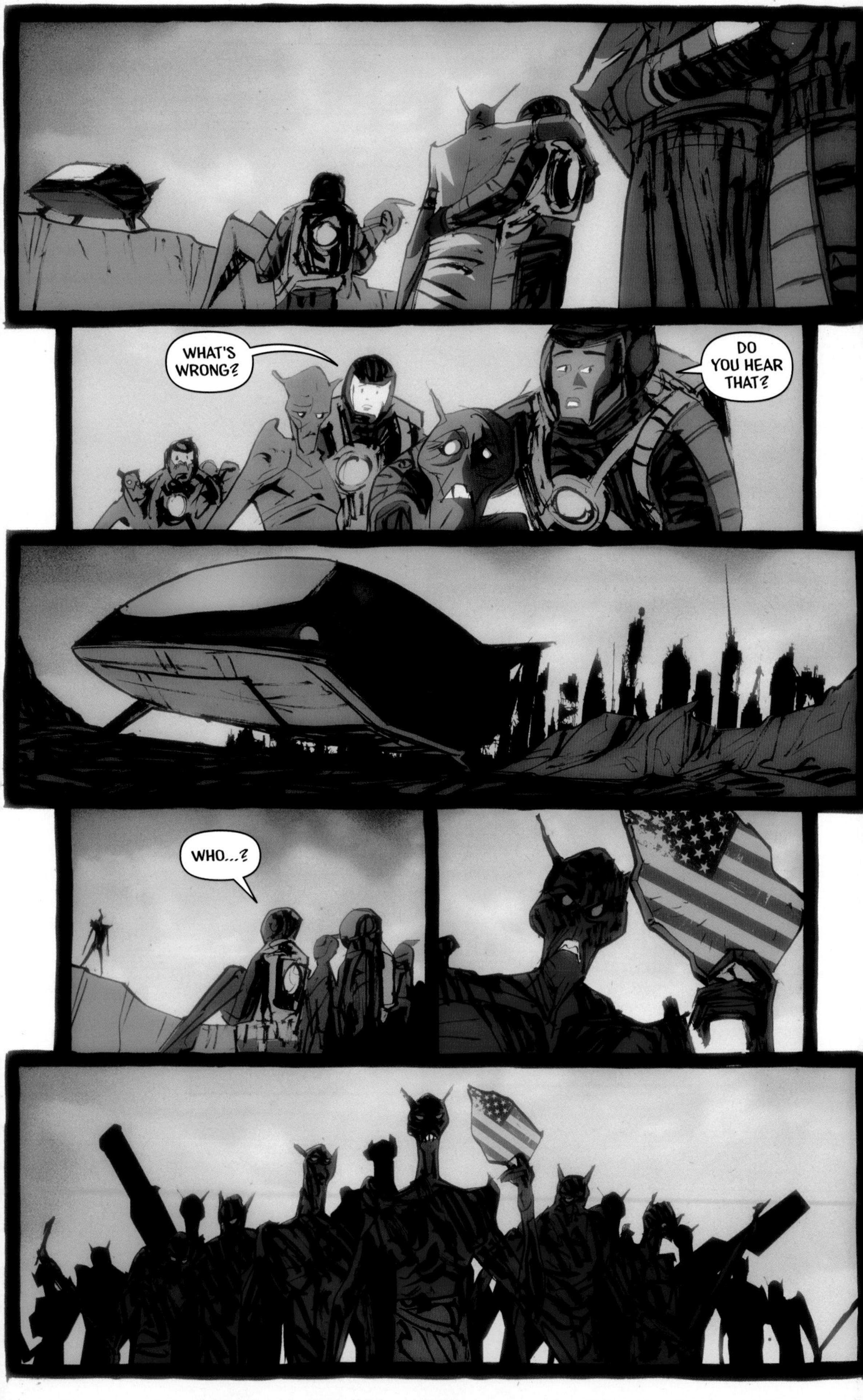
WHAT'S WRONG?
DO YOU HEAR THAT?
WHO...?

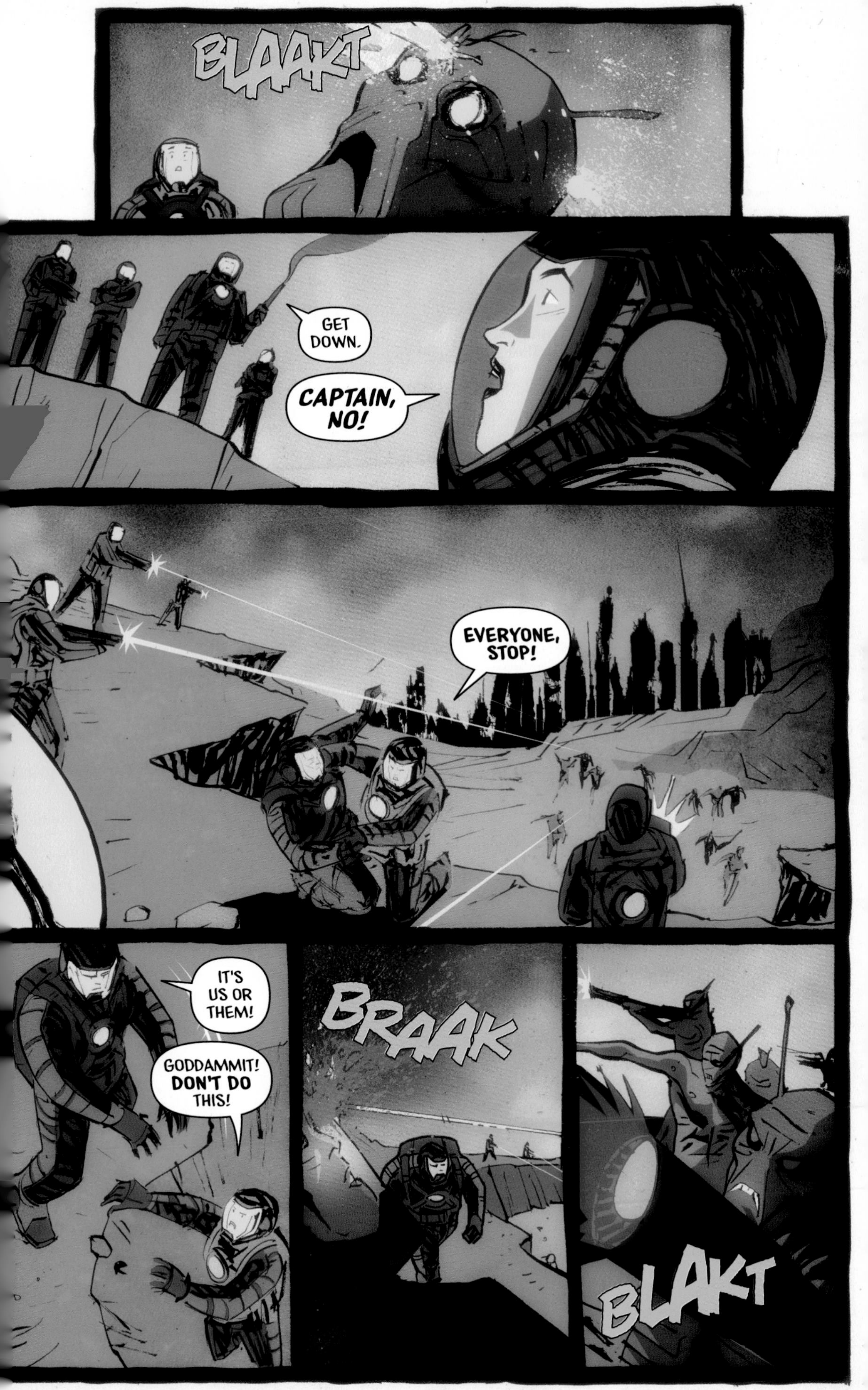
BLAAKT
GET DOWN.
CAPTAIN, NO!
EVERYONE, STOP!
IT'S US OR THEM!
GODDAMMIT! DON'T DO THIS!
BRAAK
BLAKT

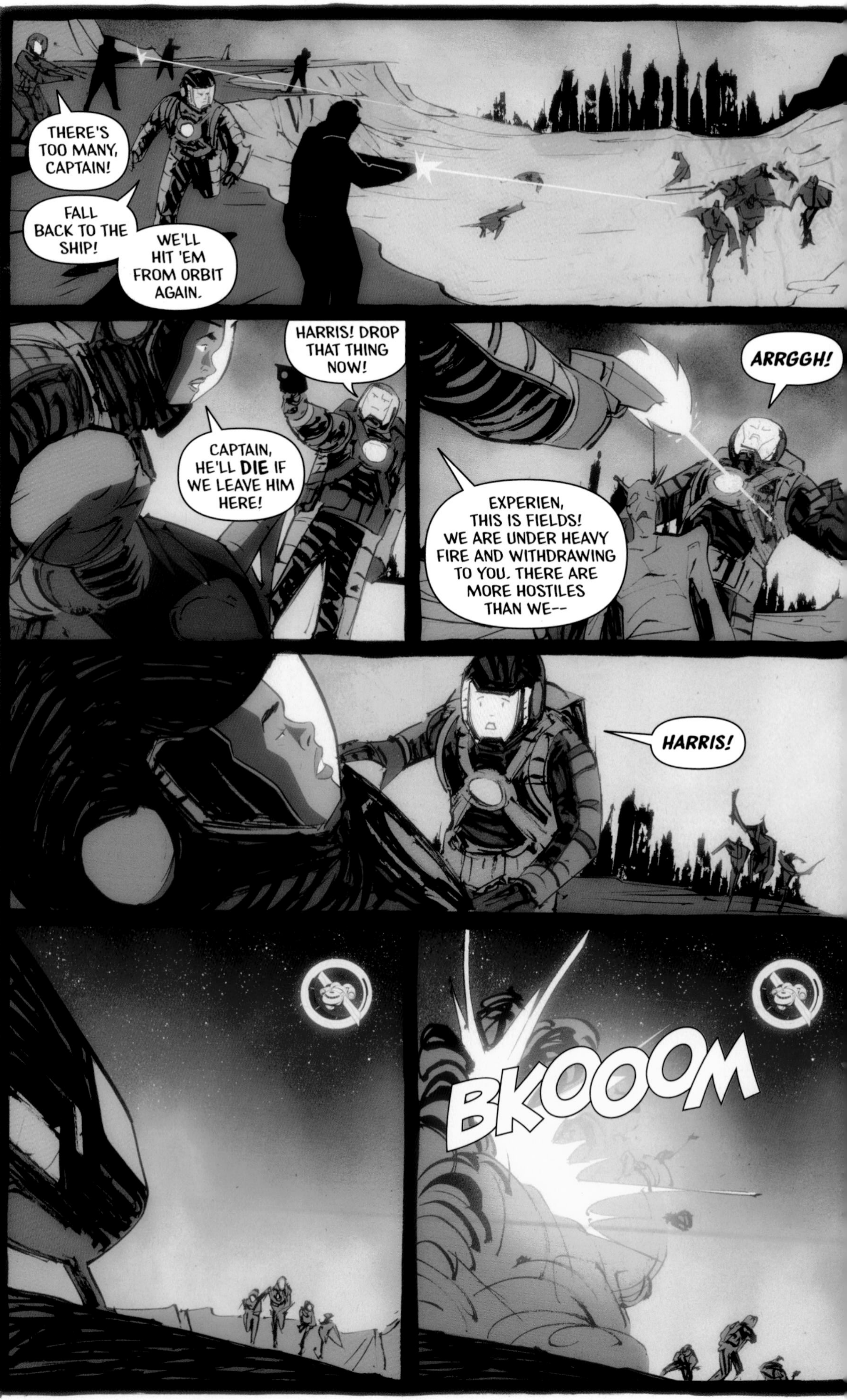
THERE'S TOO MANY, CAPTAIN!
FALL BACK TO THE SHIP!
WE'LL HIT 'EM FROM ORBIT AGAIN.
HARRIS! DROP THAT THING NOW!
CAPTAIN, HE'LL DIE IF WE LEAVE HIM HERE!
ARRGGH!
EXPERIEN, THIS IS FIELDS! WE ARE UNDER HEAVY FIRE AND WITHDRAWING TO YOU. THERE ARE MORE HOSTILES THAN WE--
HARRIS!
BKOOOM

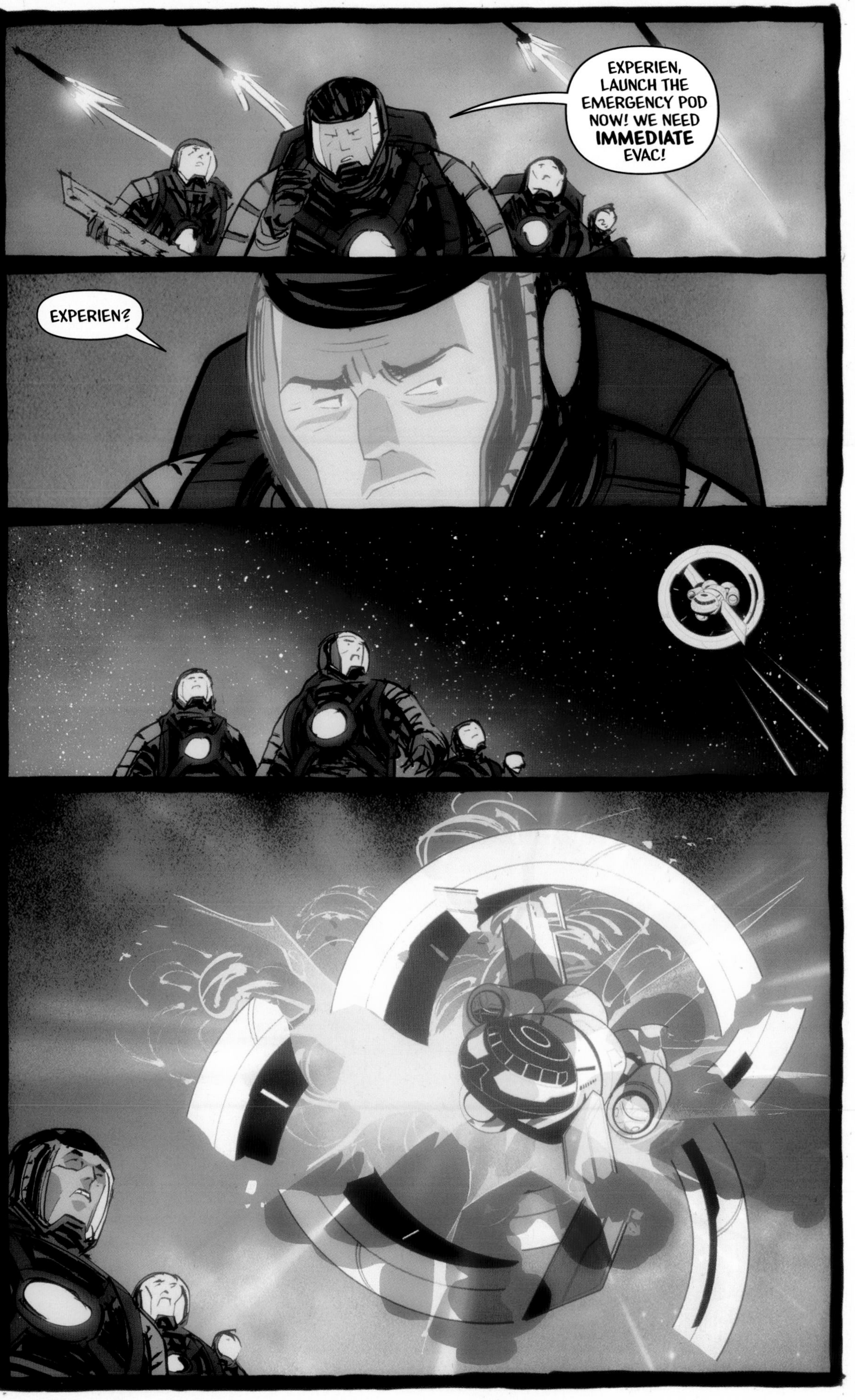
EXPERIEN, LAUNCH THE EMERGENCY POD NOW! WE NEED **IMMEDIATE** EVAC!
EXPERIEN?

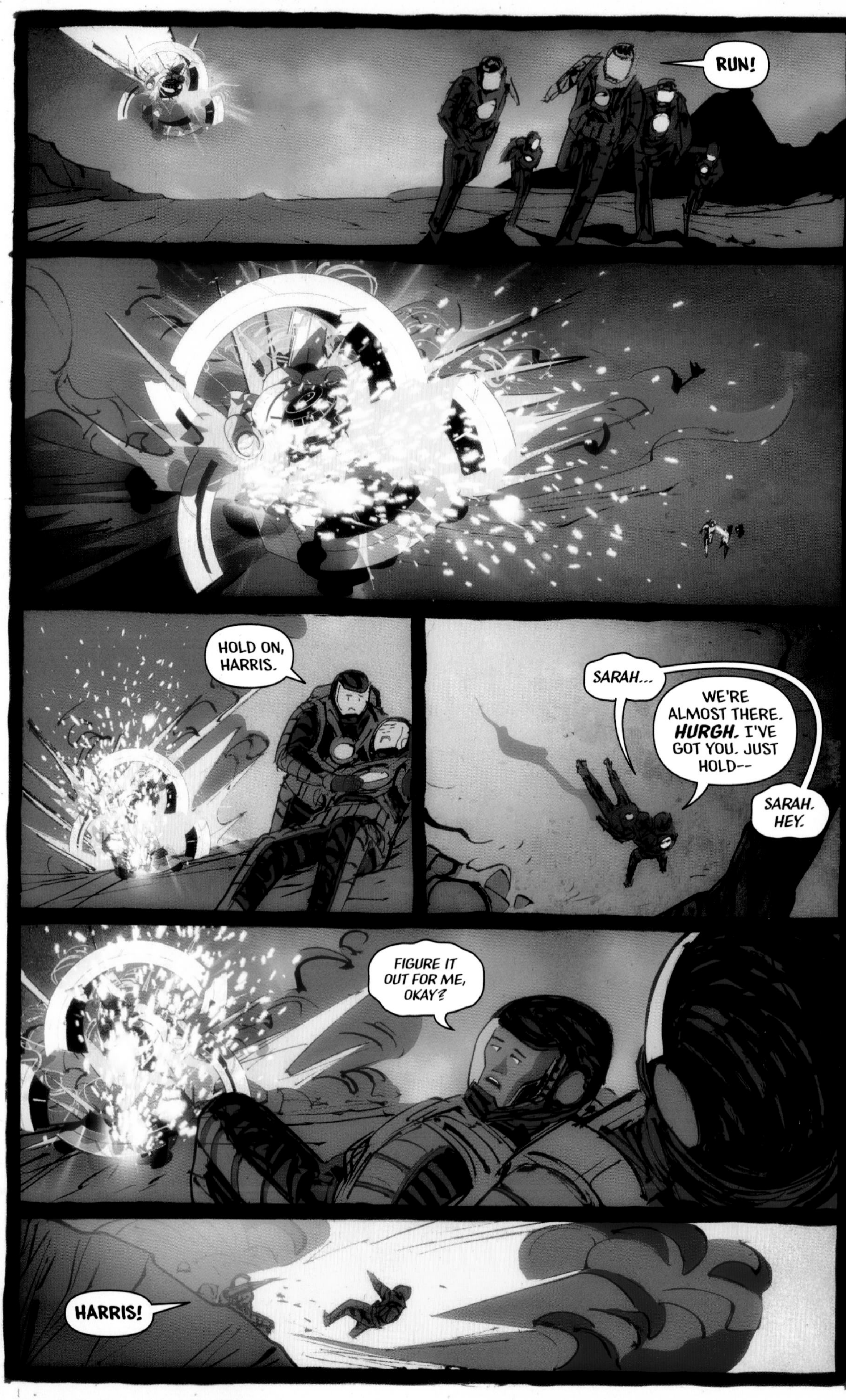
RUN!
HOLD ON, HARRIS.
SARAH...
WE'RE ALMOST THERE. **HURGH.** I'VE GOT YOU. JUST HOLD--
SARAH. HEY.
FIGURE IT OUT FOR ME, OKAY?
HARRIS!

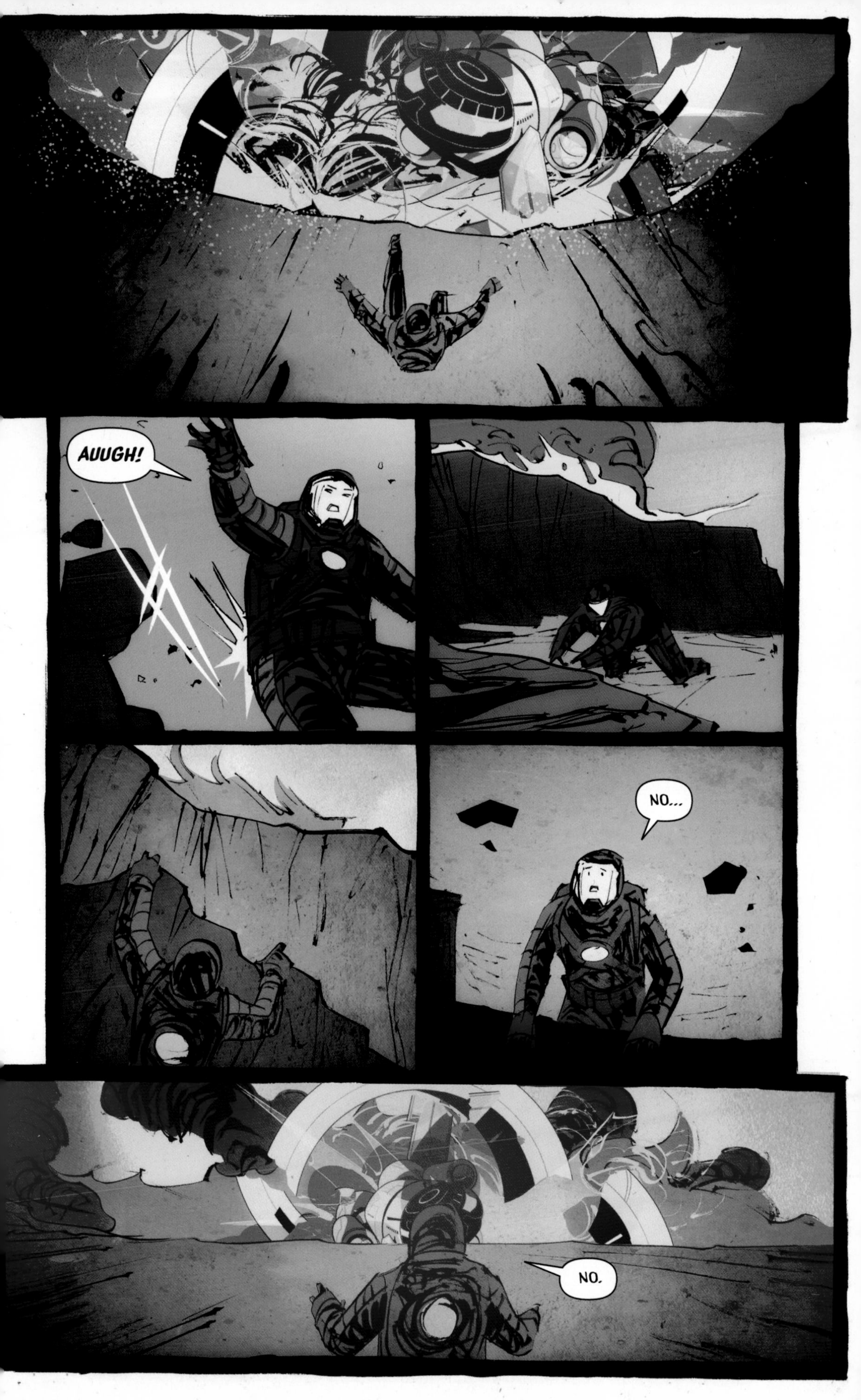
AUUGH!
NO...
NO.

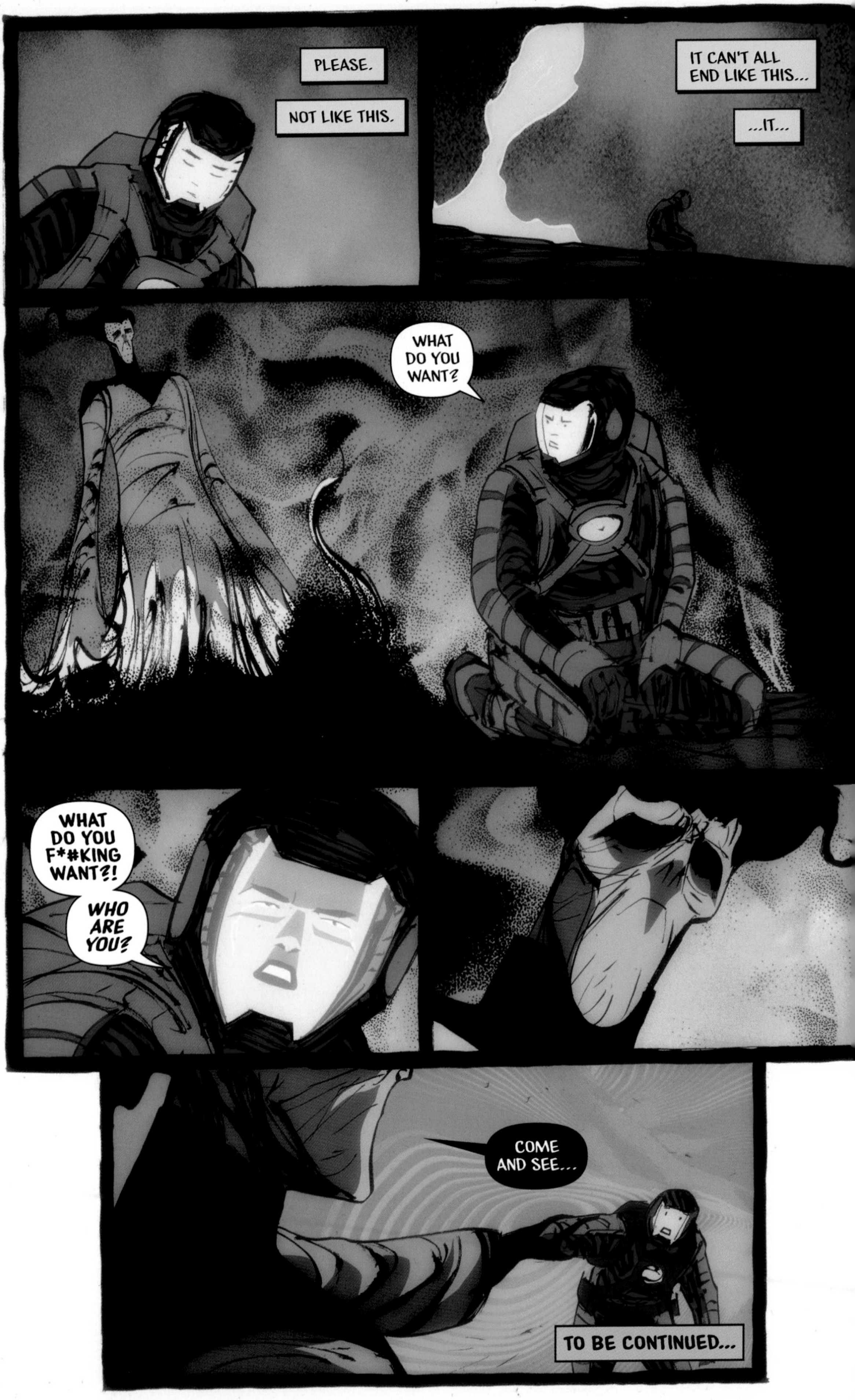
PLEASE.
NOT LIKE THIS.
IT CAN'T ALL END LIKE THIS...
...IT...
WHAT DO YOU WANT?
WHAT DO YOU F*#KING WANT?!
WHO ARE YOU?
COME AND SEE...
TO BE CONTINUED...

6

"SOMETHING NEW"

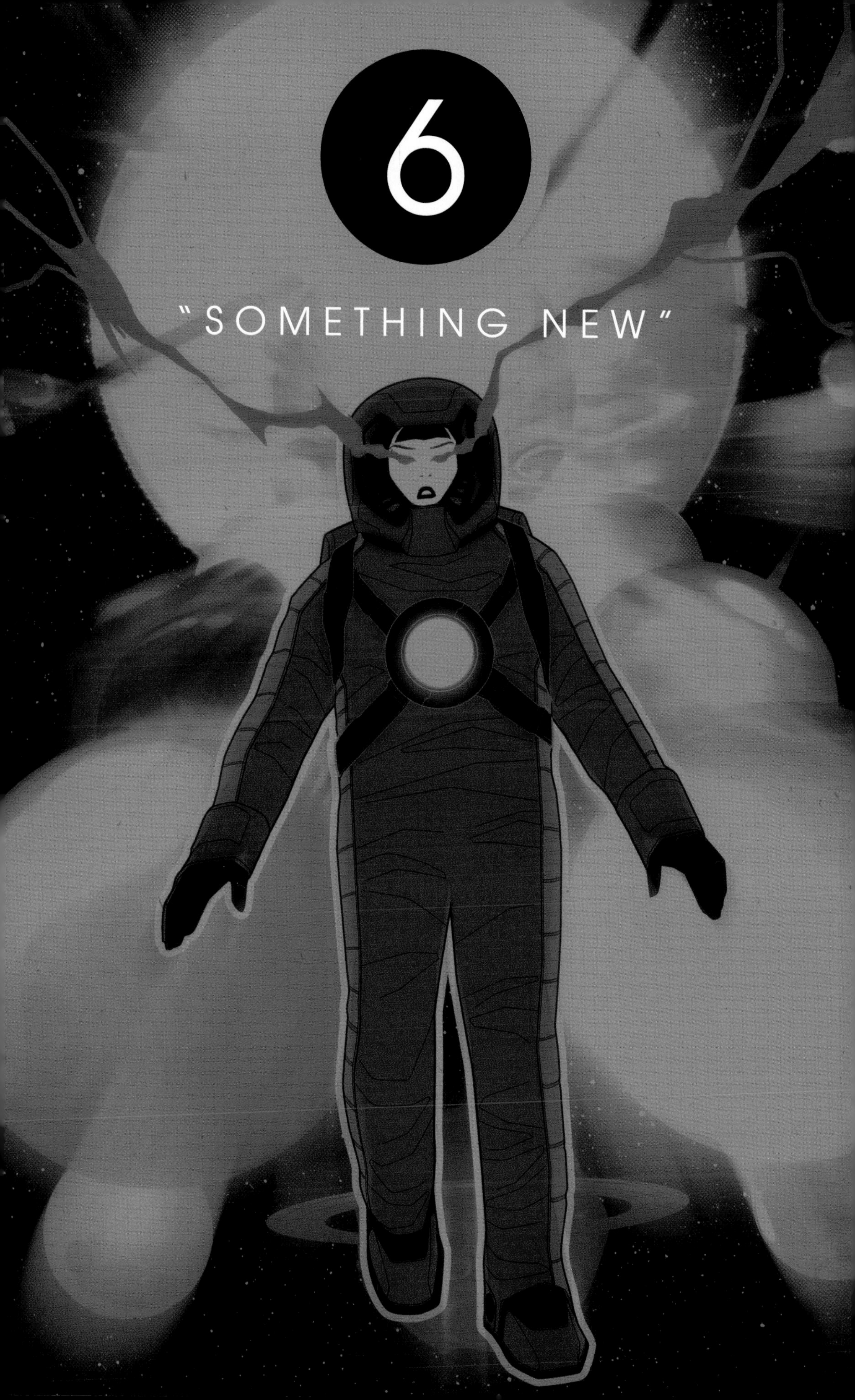

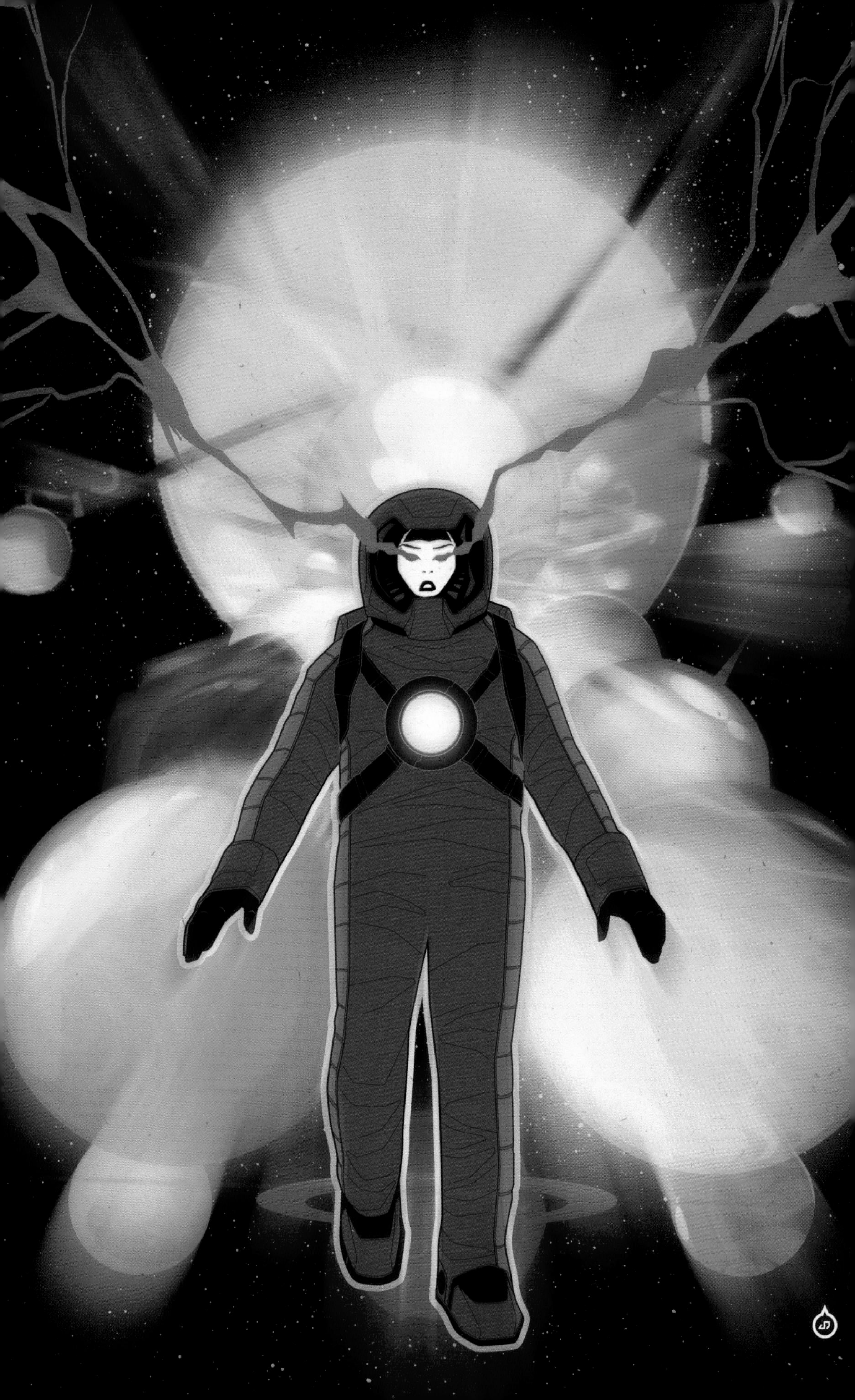

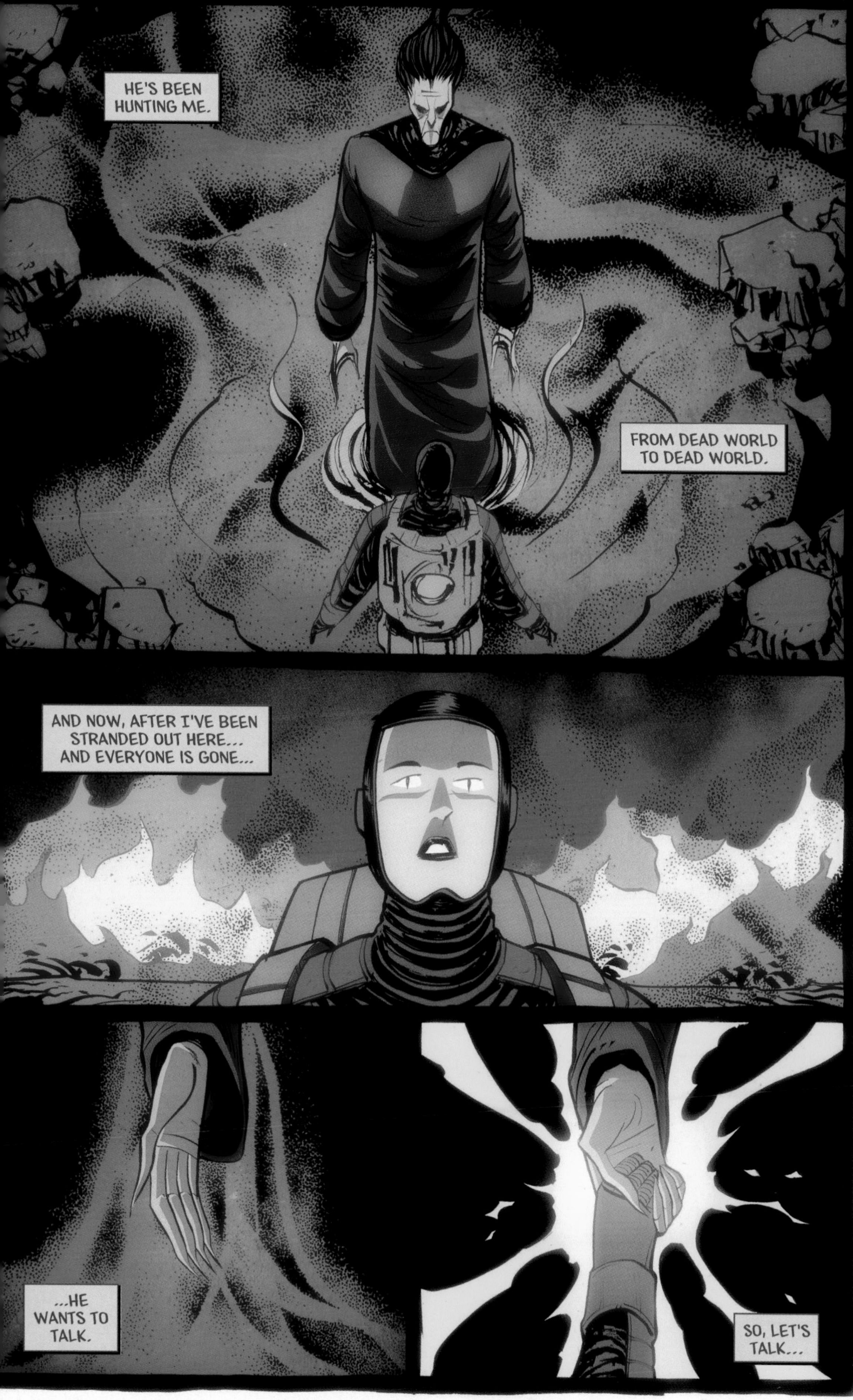
HE'S BEEN HUNTING ME.
FROM DEAD WORLD TO DEAD WORLD.
AND NOW, AFTER I'VE BEEN STRANDED OUT HERE... AND EVERYONE IS GONE...
...HE WANTS TO TALK.
SO, LET'S TALK...

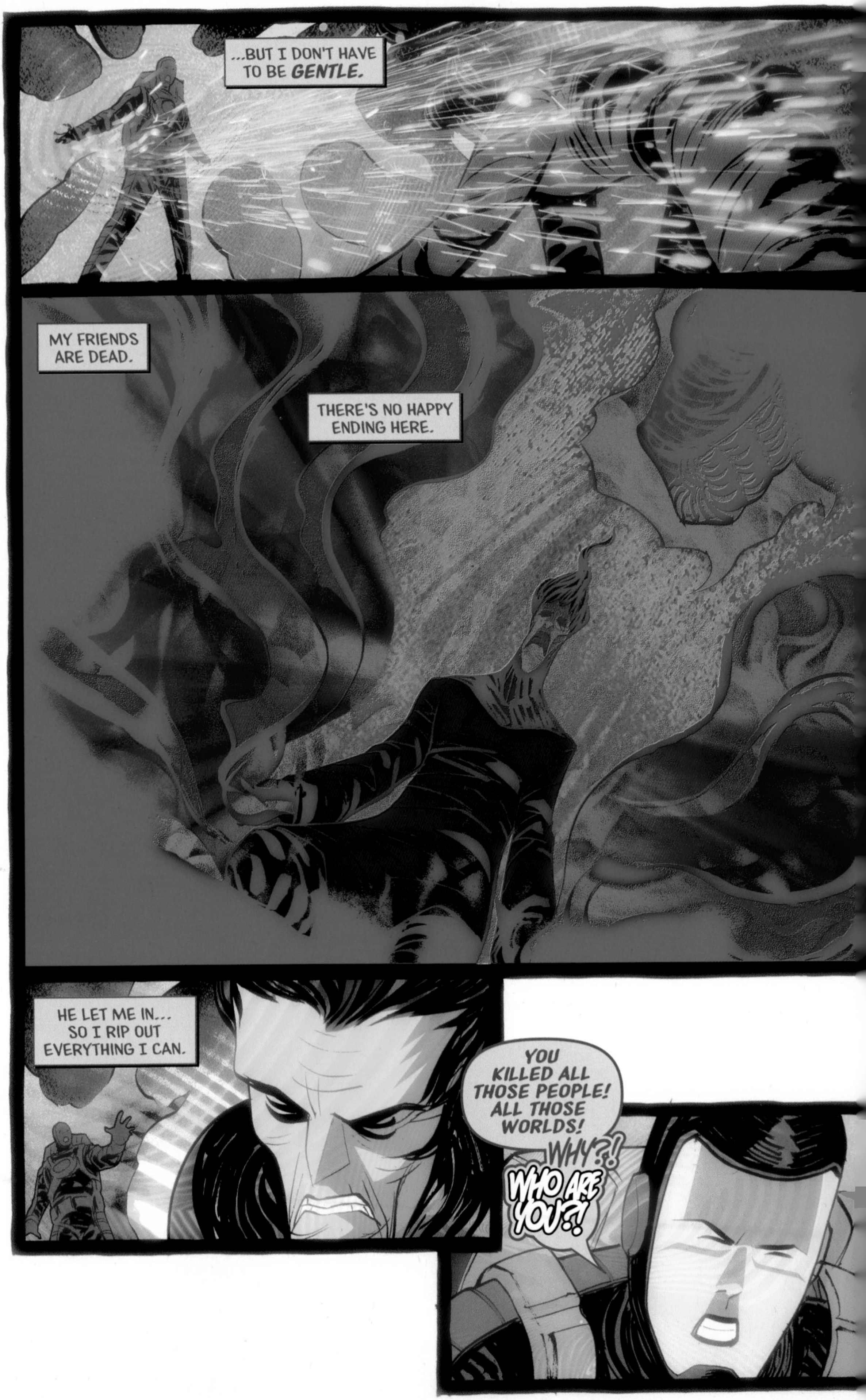
...BUT I DON'T HAVE TO BE GENTLE.
MY FRIENDS ARE DEAD.
THERE'S NO HAPPY ENDING HERE.
HE LET ME IN... SO I RIP OUT EVERYTHING I CAN.
YOU KILLED ALL THOSE PEOPLE! ALL THOSE WORLDS! WHY?!
WHO ARE YOU?!

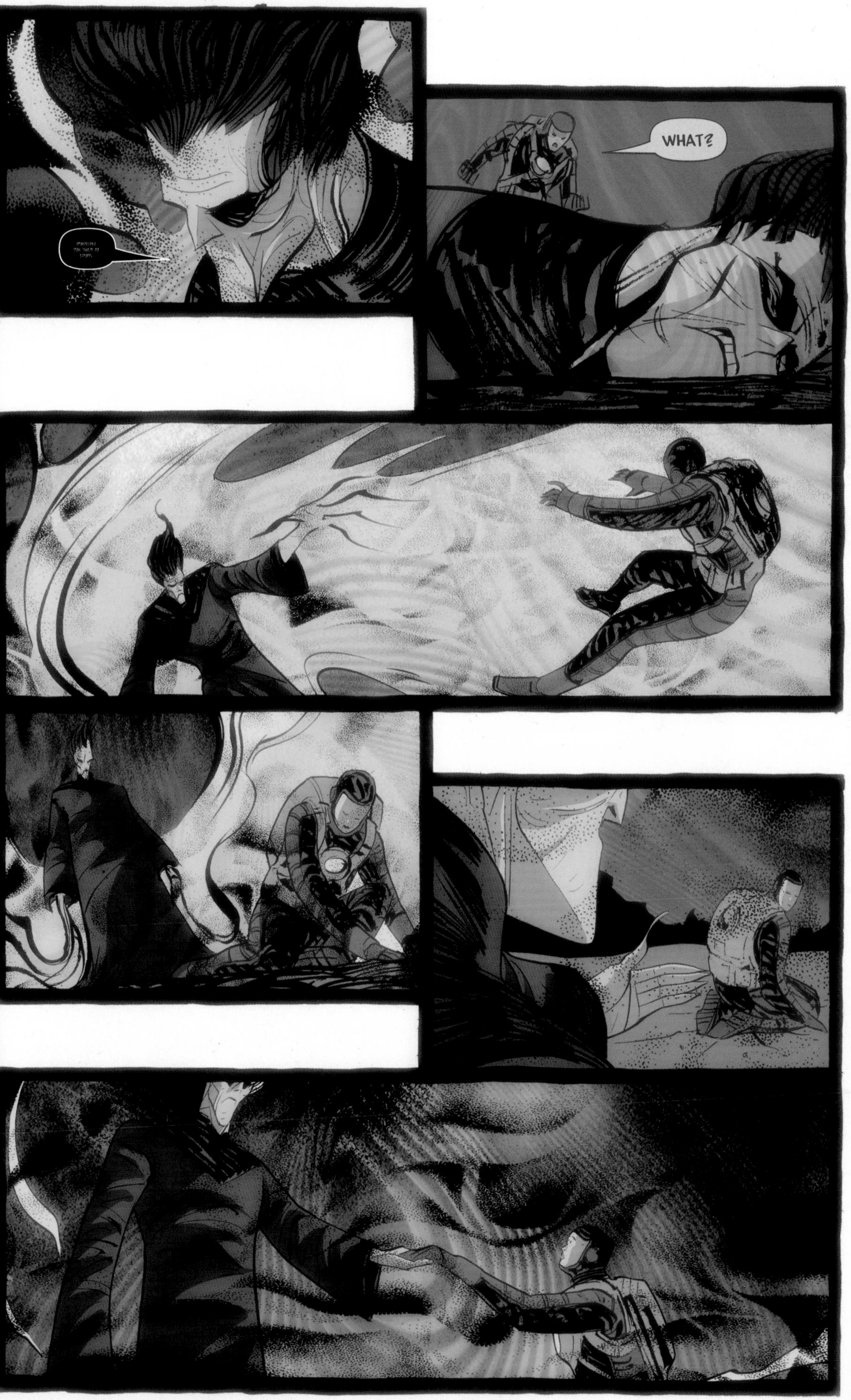
WHAT?

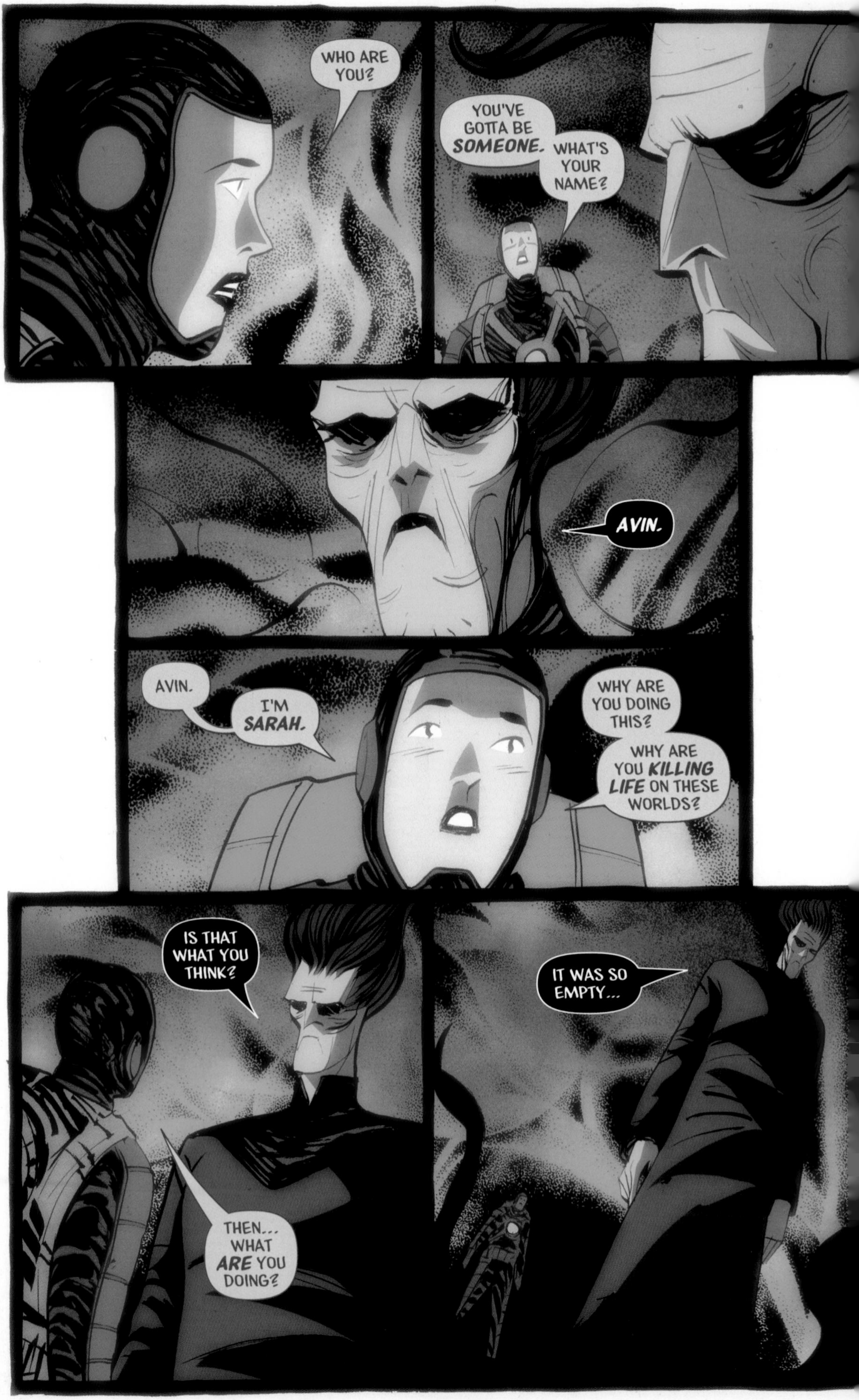
WHO ARE YOU?
YOU'VE GOTTA BE SOMEONE.
WHAT'S YOUR NAME?
AVIN.
AVIN.
I'M SARAH.
WHY ARE YOU DOING THIS?
WHY ARE YOU KILLING LIFE ON THESE WORLDS?
IS THAT WHAT YOU THINK?
THEN... WHAT ARE YOU DOING?
IT WAS SO EMPTY...

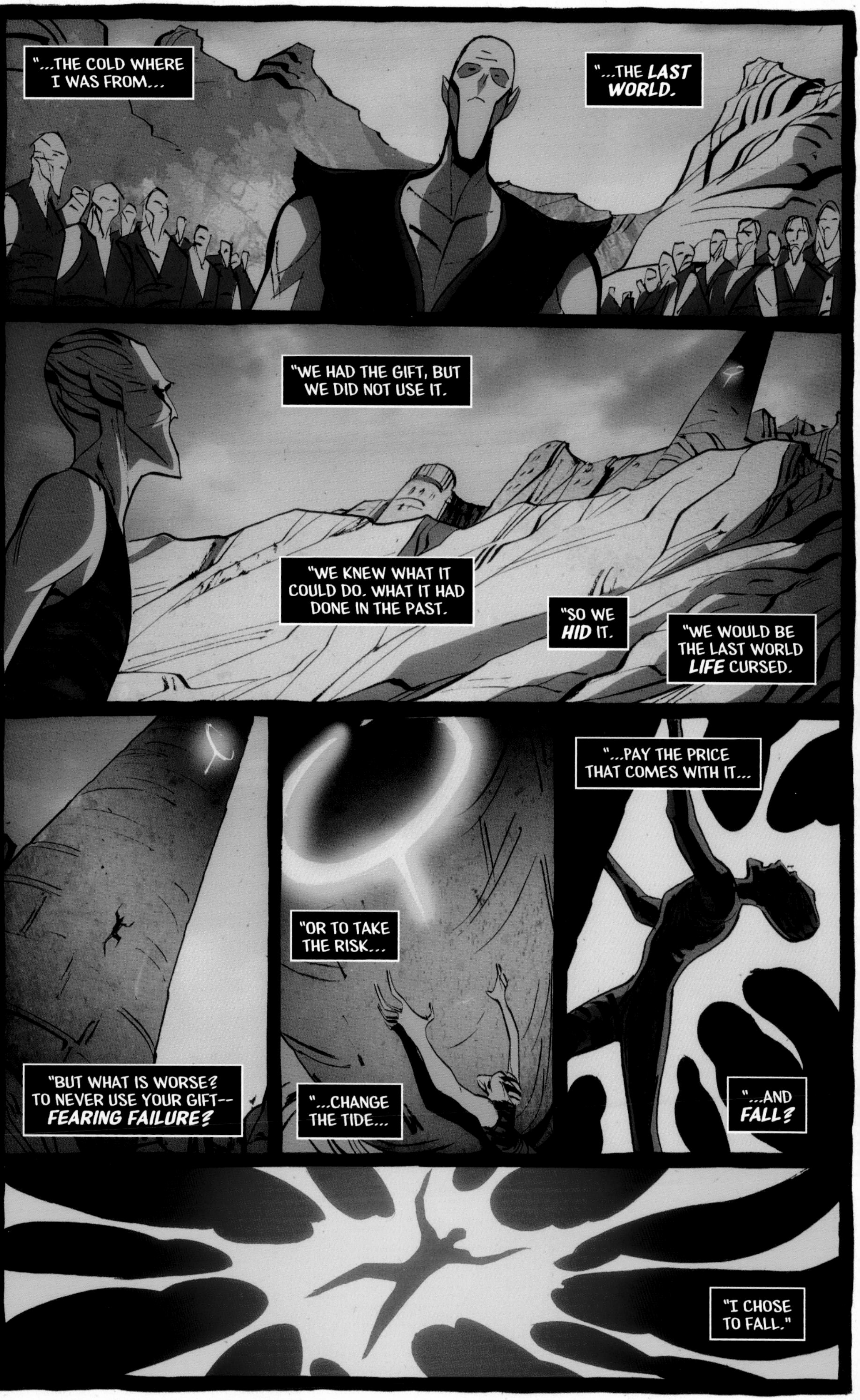

"...THE COLD WHERE I WAS FROM...
"...THE LAST WORLD.
"WE HAD THE GIFT, BUT WE DID NOT USE IT.
"WE KNEW WHAT IT COULD DO. WHAT IT HAD DONE IN THE PAST.
"SO WE HID IT.
"WE WOULD BE THE LAST WORLD LIFE CURSED.
"BUT WHAT IS WORSE? TO NEVER USE YOUR GIFT-- FEARING FAILURE?
"OR TO TAKE THE RISK...
"...CHANGE THE TIDE...
"...PAY THE PRICE THAT COMES WITH IT...
"...AND FALL?
"I CHOSE TO FALL."

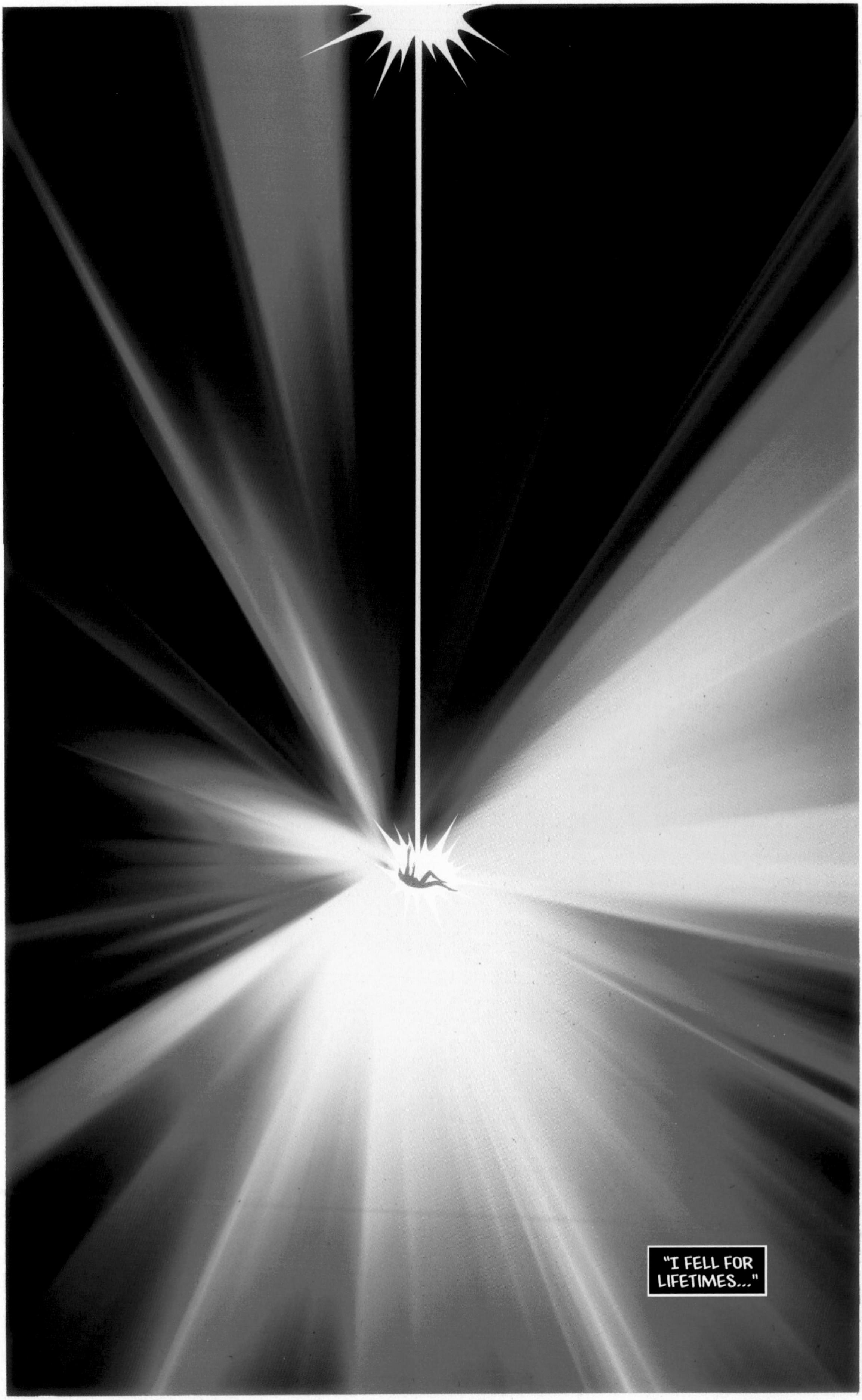
"I FELL FOR LIFETIMES..."

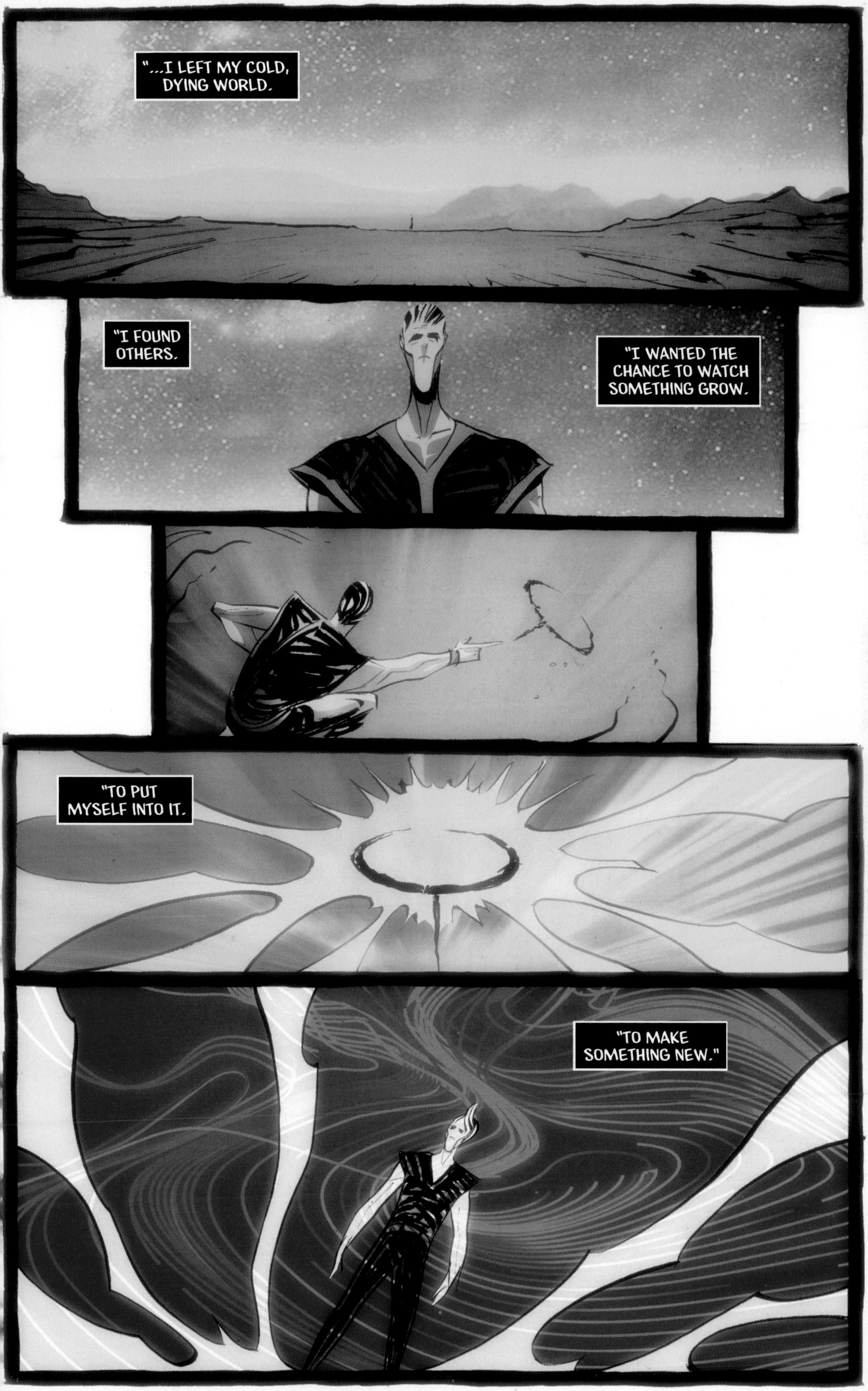
"...I LEFT MY COLD, DYING WORLD.
"I FOUND OTHERS.
"I WANTED THE CHANCE TO WATCH SOMETHING GROW.
"TO PUT MYSELF INTO IT.
"TO MAKE SOMETHING NEW."

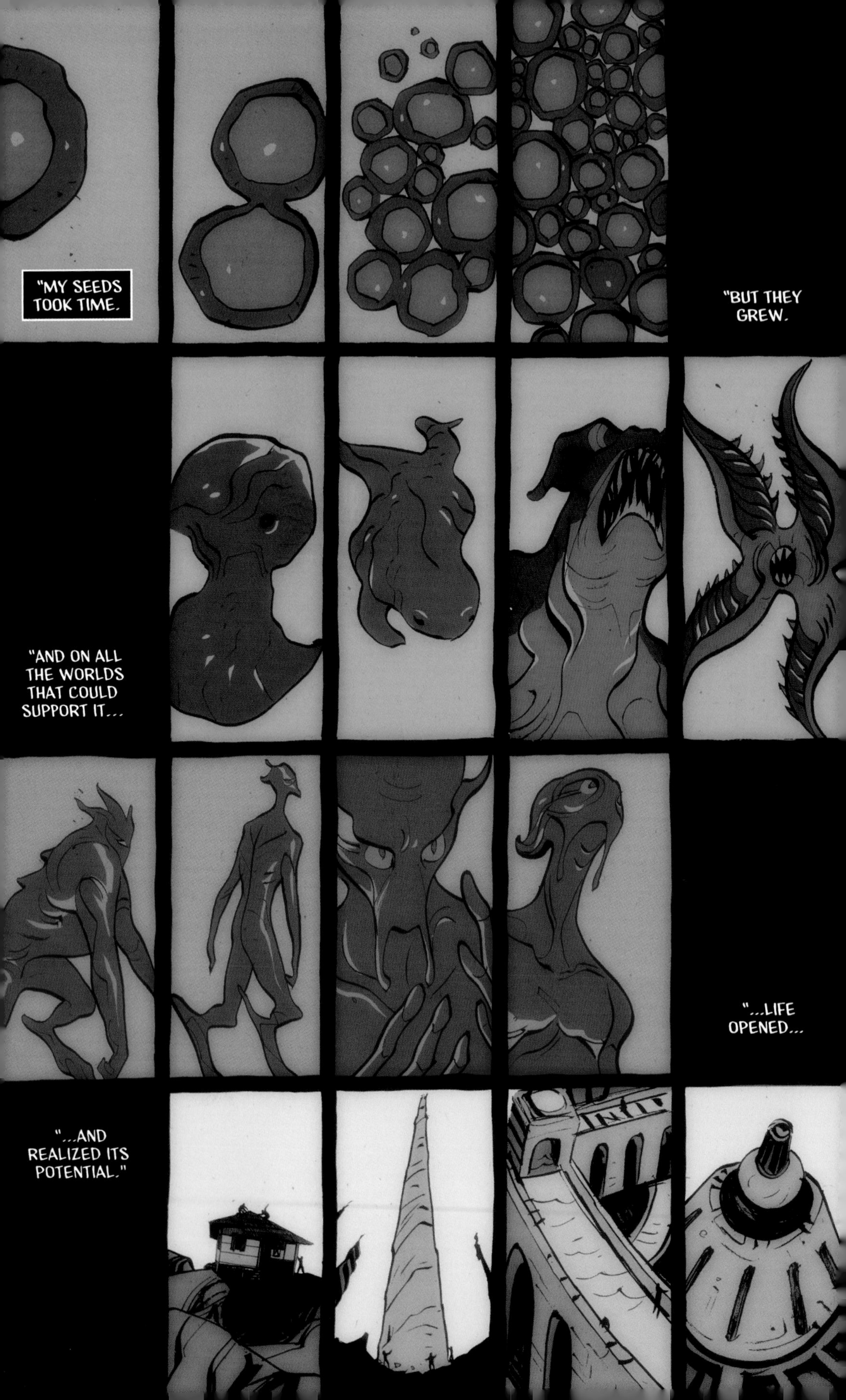
"MY SEEDS TOOK TIME.
"BUT THEY GREW.
"AND ON ALL THE WORLDS THAT COULD SUPPORT IT...
"...LIFE OPENED...
"...AND REALIZED ITS POTENTIAL."

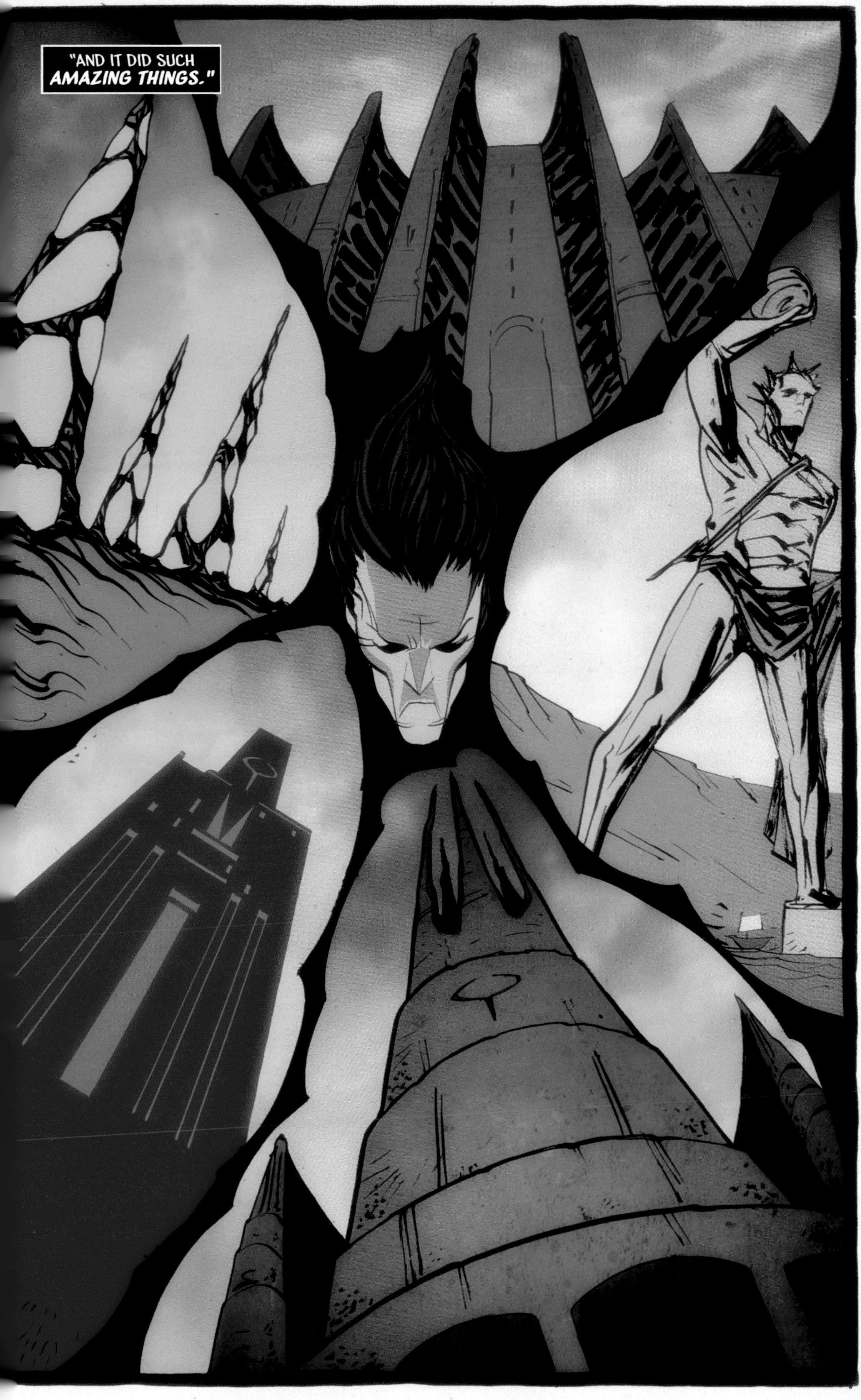
"AND IT DID SUCH AMAZING THINGS."

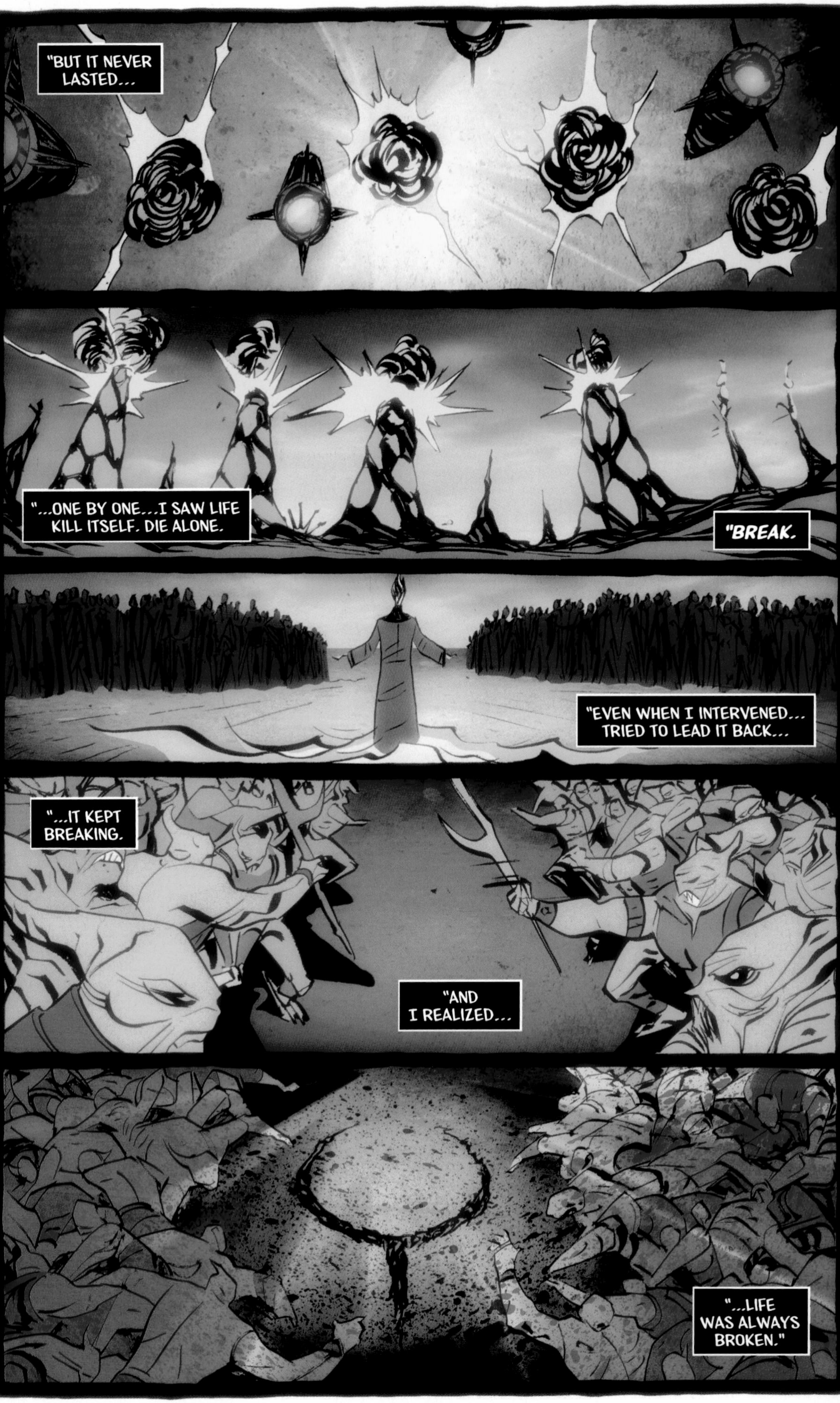
"BUT IT NEVER LASTED...
"...ONE BY ONE...I SAW LIFE KILL ITSELF. DIE ALONE.
"BREAK.
"EVEN WHEN I INTERVENED... TRIED TO LEAD IT BACK...
"...IT KEPT BREAKING.
"AND I REALIZED...
"...LIFE WAS ALWAYS BROKEN."

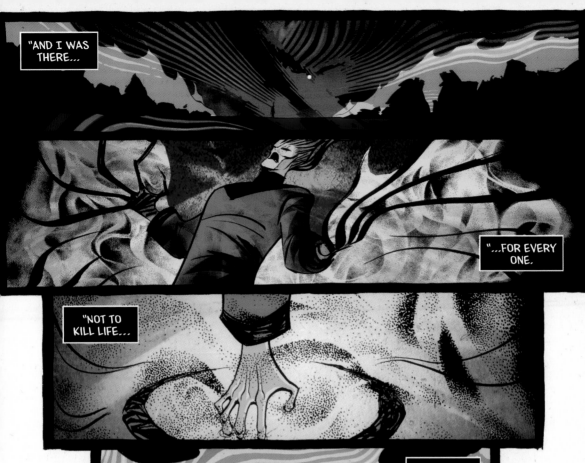

"AND I WAS THERE...

"...FOR EVERY ONE.

"NOT TO KILL LIFE...

"...BUT TO *BURY IT.*"

YOU... YOU WERE BURYING YOUR CHILDREN.

AND MAYBE SEEING IF LIFE GOT IT RIGHT SOME- WHERE...

...BUT IT NEVER DID.

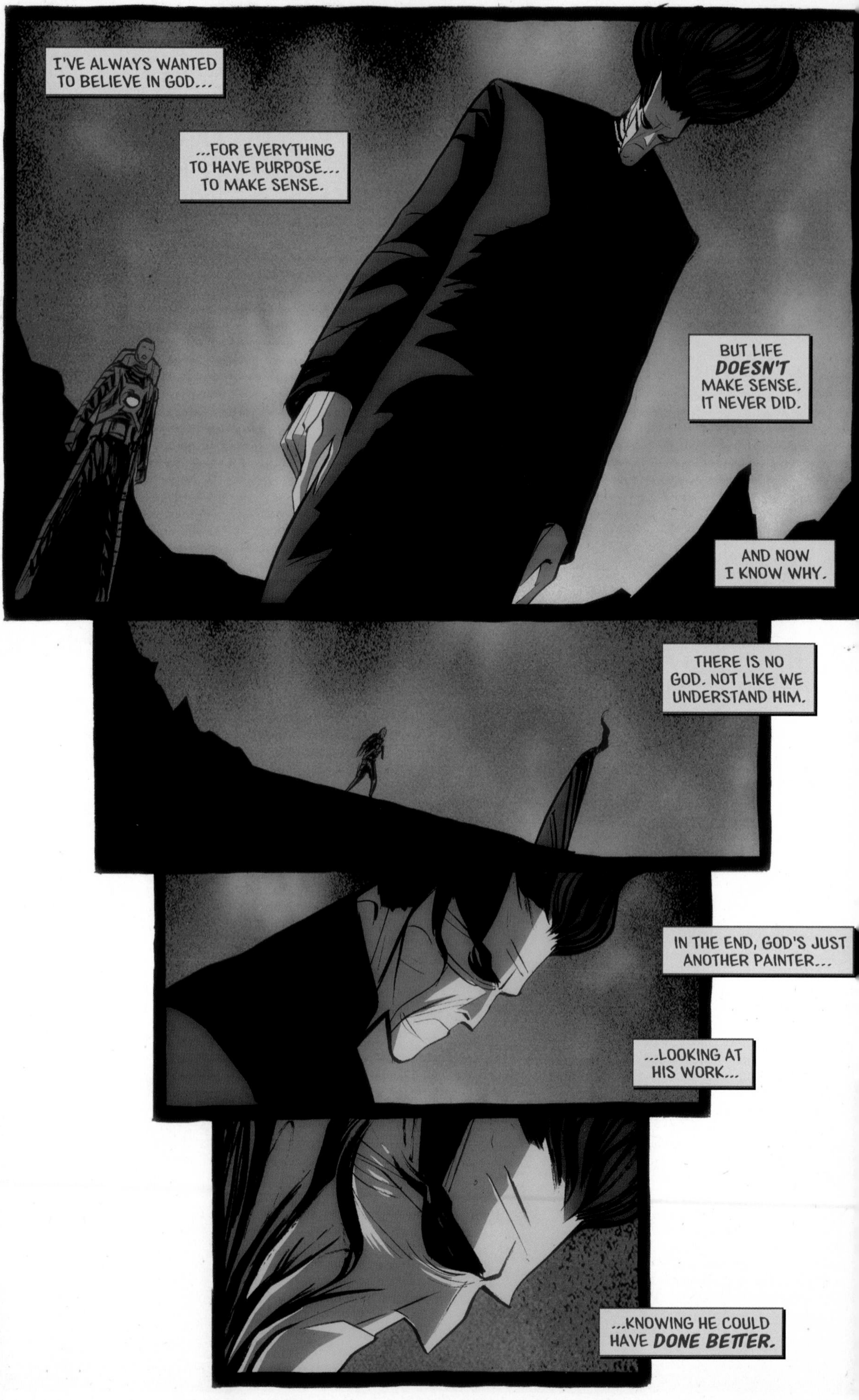
I'VE ALWAYS WANTED TO BELIEVE IN GOD...
...FOR EVERYTHING TO HAVE PURPOSE... TO MAKE SENSE.
BUT LIFE DOESN'T MAKE SENSE. IT NEVER DID.
AND NOW I KNOW WHY.
THERE IS NO GOD. NOT LIKE WE UNDERSTAND HIM.
IN THE END, GOD'S JUST ANOTHER PAINTER...
...LOOKING AT HIS WORK...
...KNOWING HE COULD HAVE DONE BETTER.

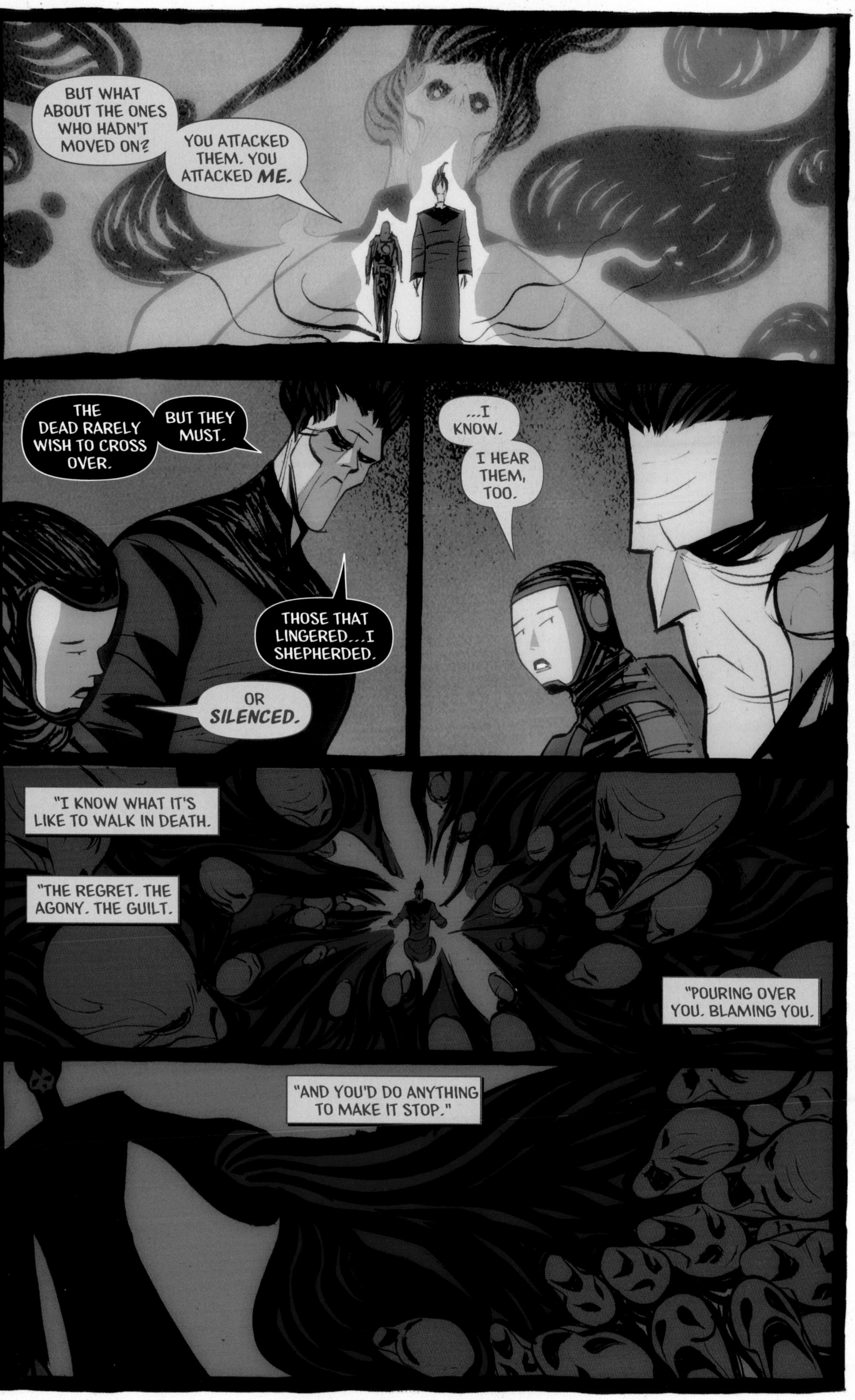
BUT WHAT ABOUT THE ONES WHO HADN'T MOVED ON?
YOU ATTACKED THEM. YOU ATTACKED ME.
THE DEAD RARELY WISH TO CROSS OVER.
BUT THEY MUST.
THOSE THAT LINGERED...I SHEPHERDED.
OR SILENCED.
...I KNOW.
I HEAR THEM, TOO.
"I KNOW WHAT IT'S LIKE TO WALK IN DEATH.
"THE REGRET. THE AGONY. THE GUILT.
"POURING OVER YOU. BLAMING YOU.
"AND YOU'D DO ANYTHING TO MAKE IT STOP."

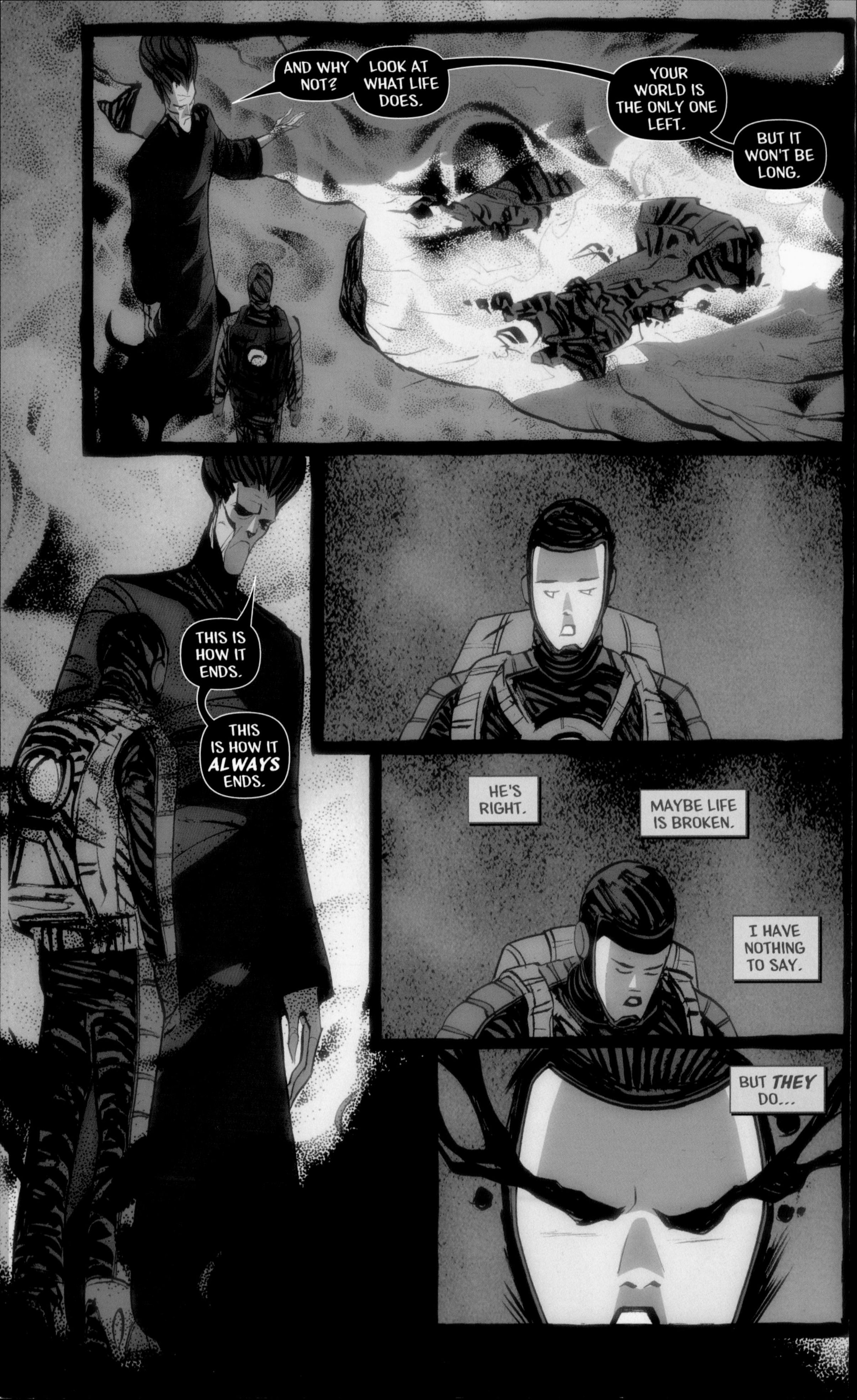
AND WHY NOT?
LOOK AT WHAT LIFE DOES.
YOUR WORLD IS THE ONLY ONE LEFT.
BUT IT WON'T BE LONG.
THIS IS HOW IT ENDS.
THIS IS HOW IT *ALWAYS* ENDS.
HE'S RIGHT.
MAYBE LIFE IS BROKEN.
I HAVE NOTHING TO SAY.
BUT *THEY* DO...

...SO I LET THEM SPEAK.
I AM A LIBRARY. FOR EVERYTHING THEY FELT.
FOR THE PAIN AND LOSS, YES.
BUT THERE WAS *SO MUCH MORE.*
I THINK HE *FORGOT* THAT.

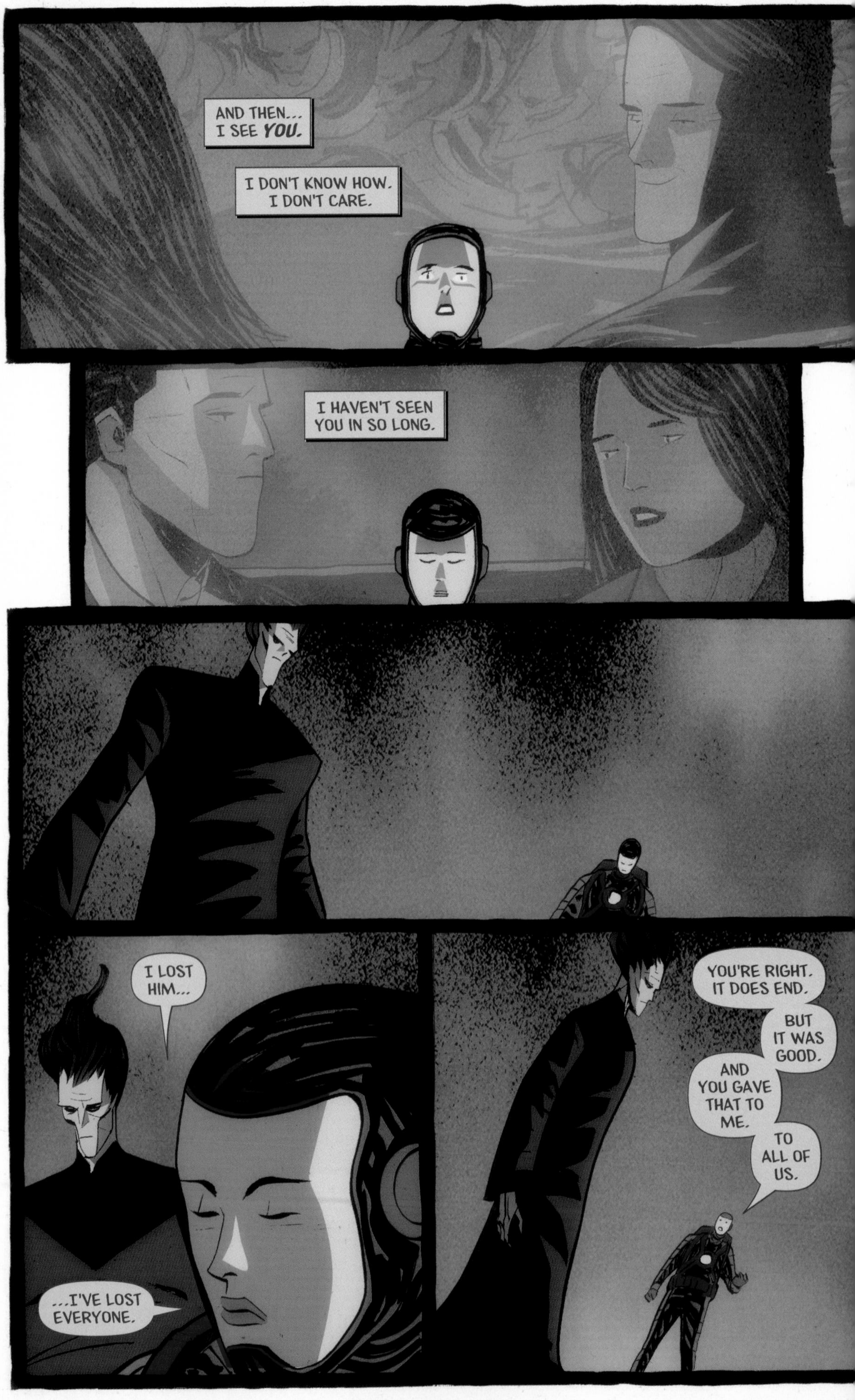
AND THEN... I SEE *YOU*.
I DON'T KNOW HOW. I DON'T CARE.
I HAVEN'T SEEN YOU IN SO LONG.
I LOST HIM...
...I'VE LOST EVERYONE.
YOU'RE RIGHT. IT DOES END.
BUT IT WAS GOOD.
AND YOU GAVE THAT TO ME.
TO ALL OF US.

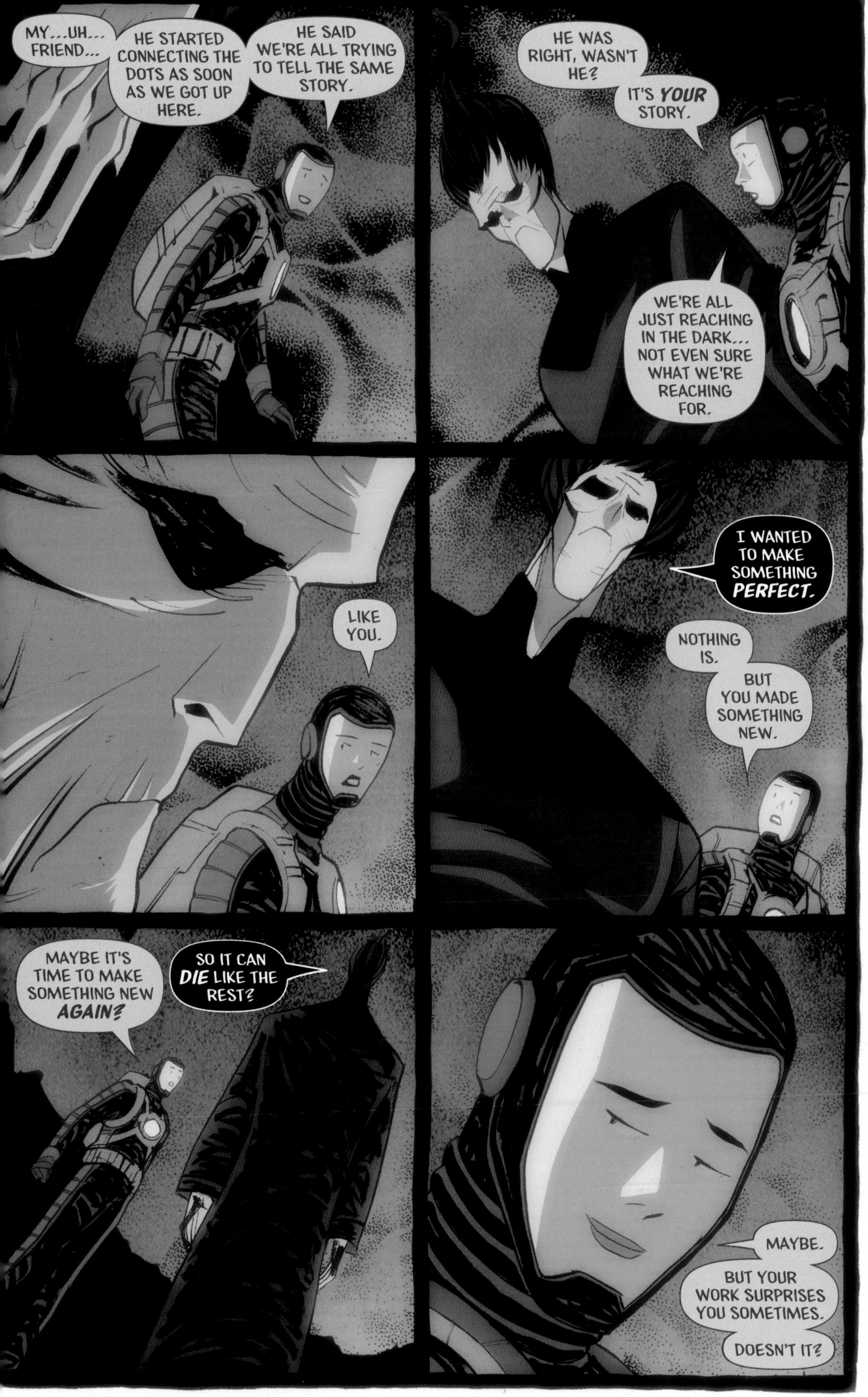
MY... UH... FRIEND...
HE STARTED CONNECTING THE DOTS AS SOON AS WE GOT UP HERE.
HE SAID WE'RE ALL TRYING TO TELL THE SAME STORY.
HE WAS RIGHT, WASN'T HE?
IT'S YOUR STORY.
WE'RE ALL JUST REACHING IN THE DARK... NOT EVEN SURE WHAT WE'RE REACHING FOR.
LIKE YOU.
I WANTED TO MAKE SOMETHING PERFECT.
NOTHING IS.
BUT YOU MADE SOMETHING NEW.
MAYBE IT'S TIME TO MAKE SOMETHING NEW AGAIN?
SO IT CAN DIE LIKE THE REST?
MAYBE.
BUT YOUR WORK SURPRISES YOU SOMETIMES.
DOESN'T IT?

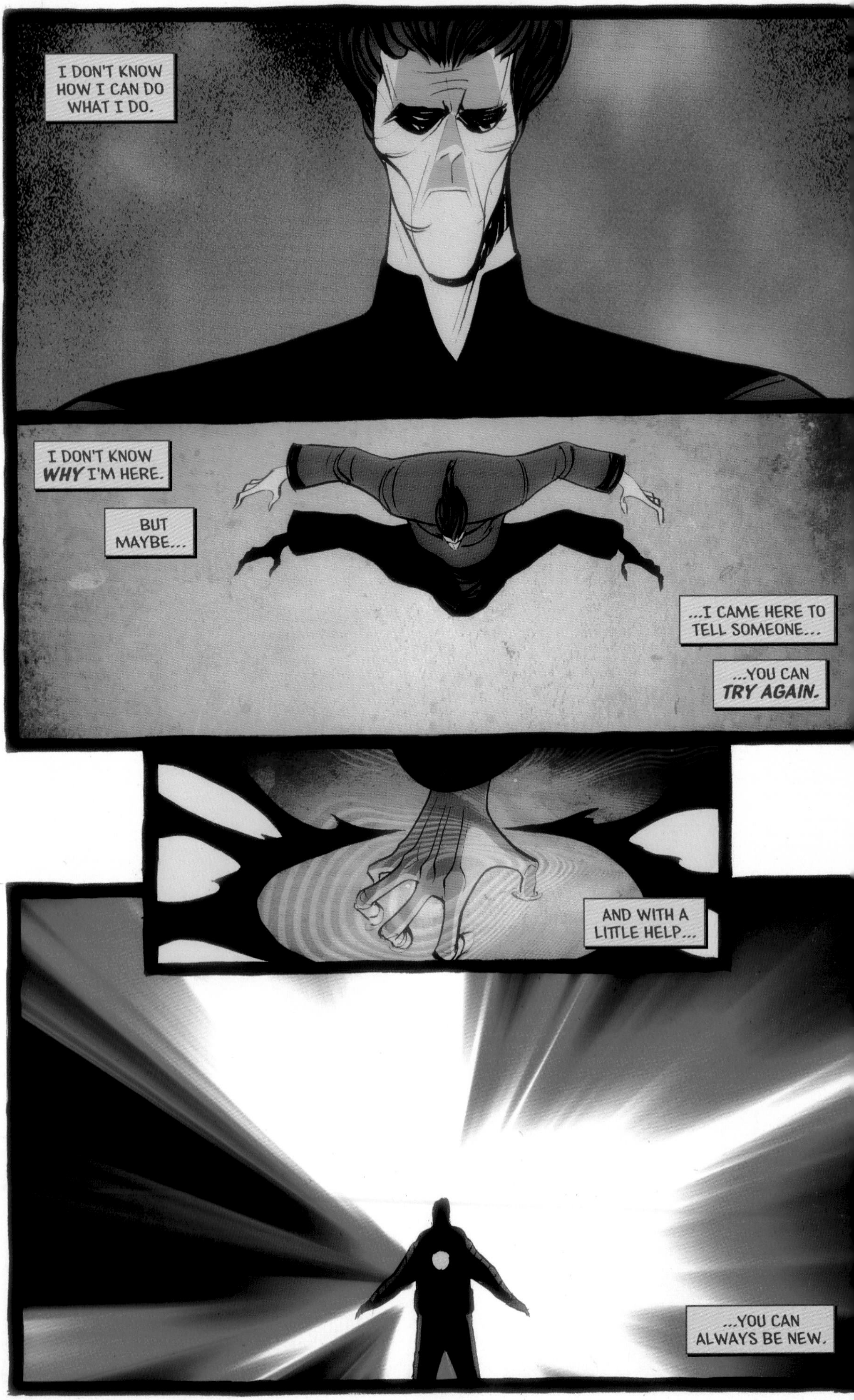
I DON'T KNOW HOW I CAN DO WHAT I DO.
I DON'T KNOW *WHY* I'M HERE.
BUT MAYBE...
...I CAME HERE TO TELL SOMEONE...
...YOU CAN *TRY AGAIN.*
AND WITH A LITTLE HELP...
...YOU CAN ALWAYS BE NEW.

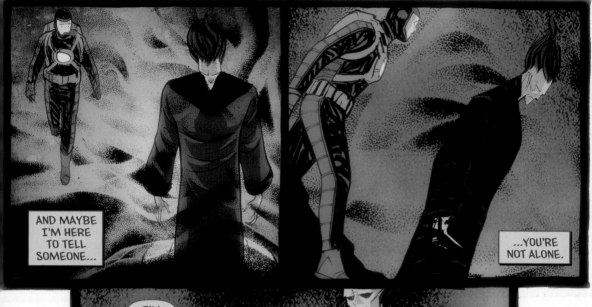

AND MAYBE I'M HERE TO TELL SOMEONE...

...YOU'RE NOT ALONE.

I'M SCARED, TOO.

BUT WHAT'S NEXT?

SOMETHING *NEW.*

WE STEP THROUGH THE ETHER TOGETHER...

...DEEPER THAN I'VE EVER GONE BEFORE.

WE REACH THE END...AND IT'S...

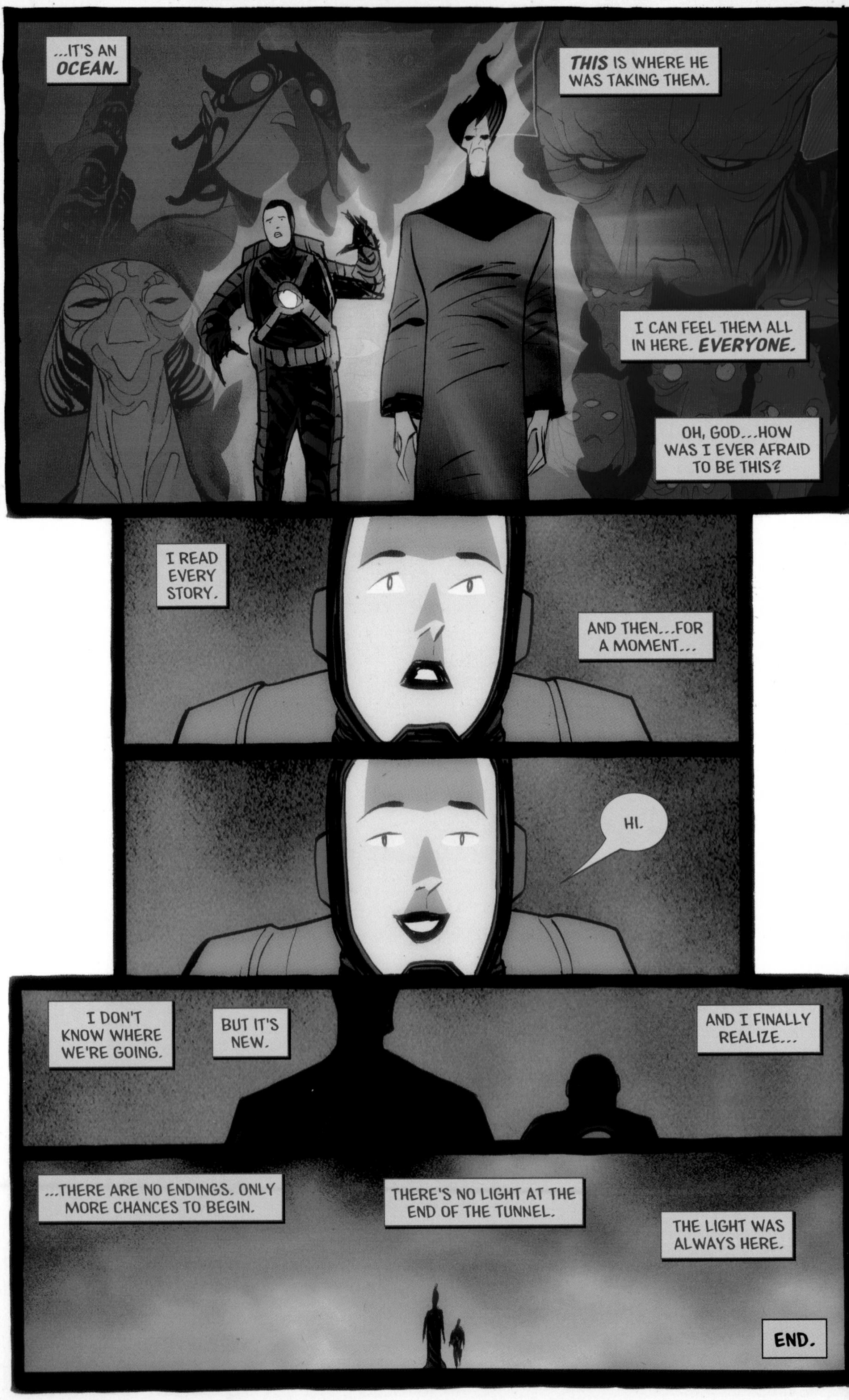

...IT'S AN *OCEAN.*
THIS IS WHERE HE WAS TAKING THEM.
I CAN FEEL THEM ALL IN HERE. *EVERYONE.*
OH, GOD...HOW WAS I EVER AFRAID TO BE THIS?
I READ EVERY STORY.
AND THEN...FOR A MOMENT...
HI.
I DON'T KNOW WHERE WE'RE GOING.
BUT IT'S NEW.
AND I FINALLY REALIZE...
...THERE ARE NO ENDINGS. ONLY MORE CHANCES TO BEGIN.
THERE'S NO LIGHT AT THE END OF THE TUNNEL.
THE LIGHT WAS ALWAYS HERE.
END.

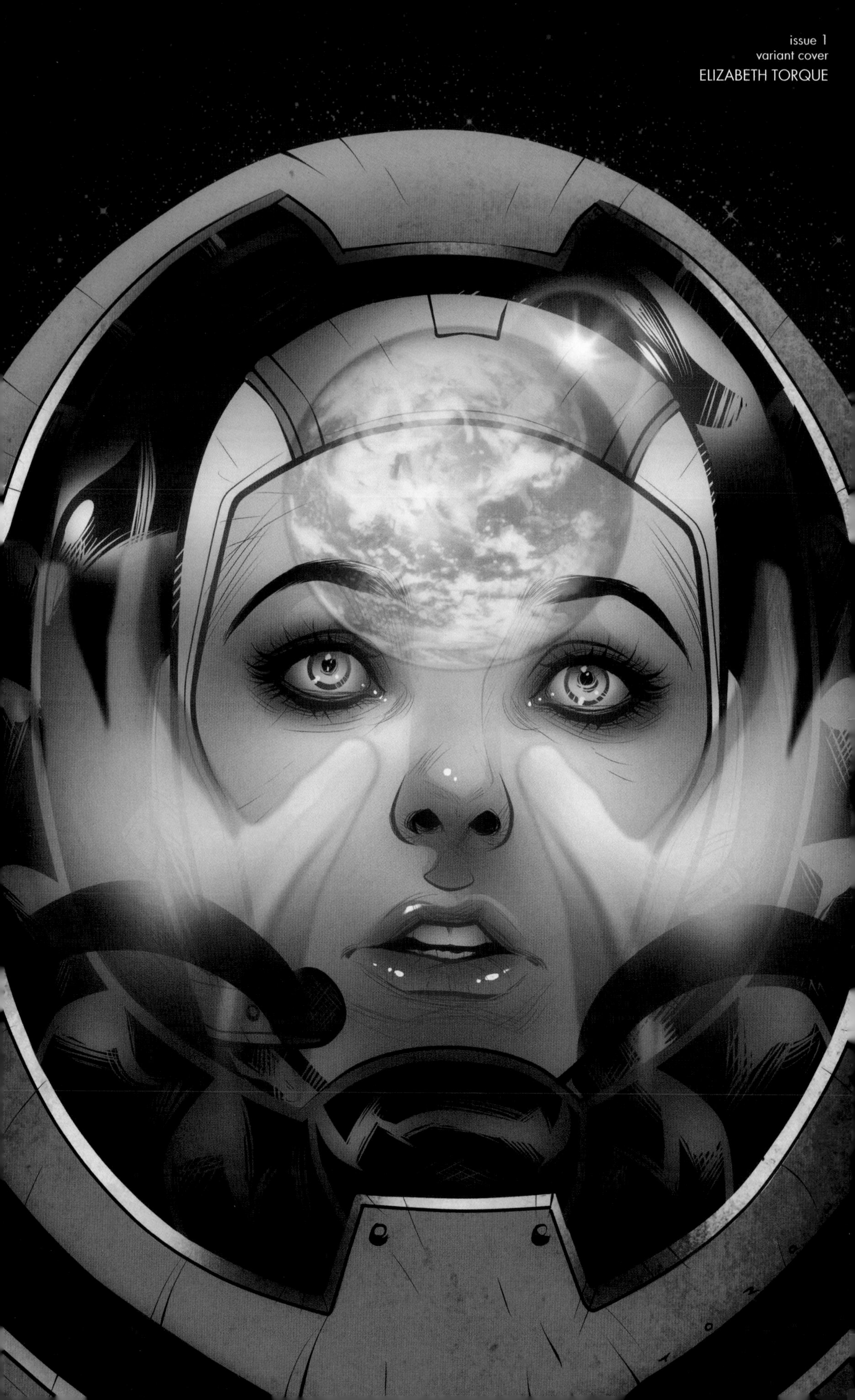

issue 1
variant cover
ELIZABETH TORQUE

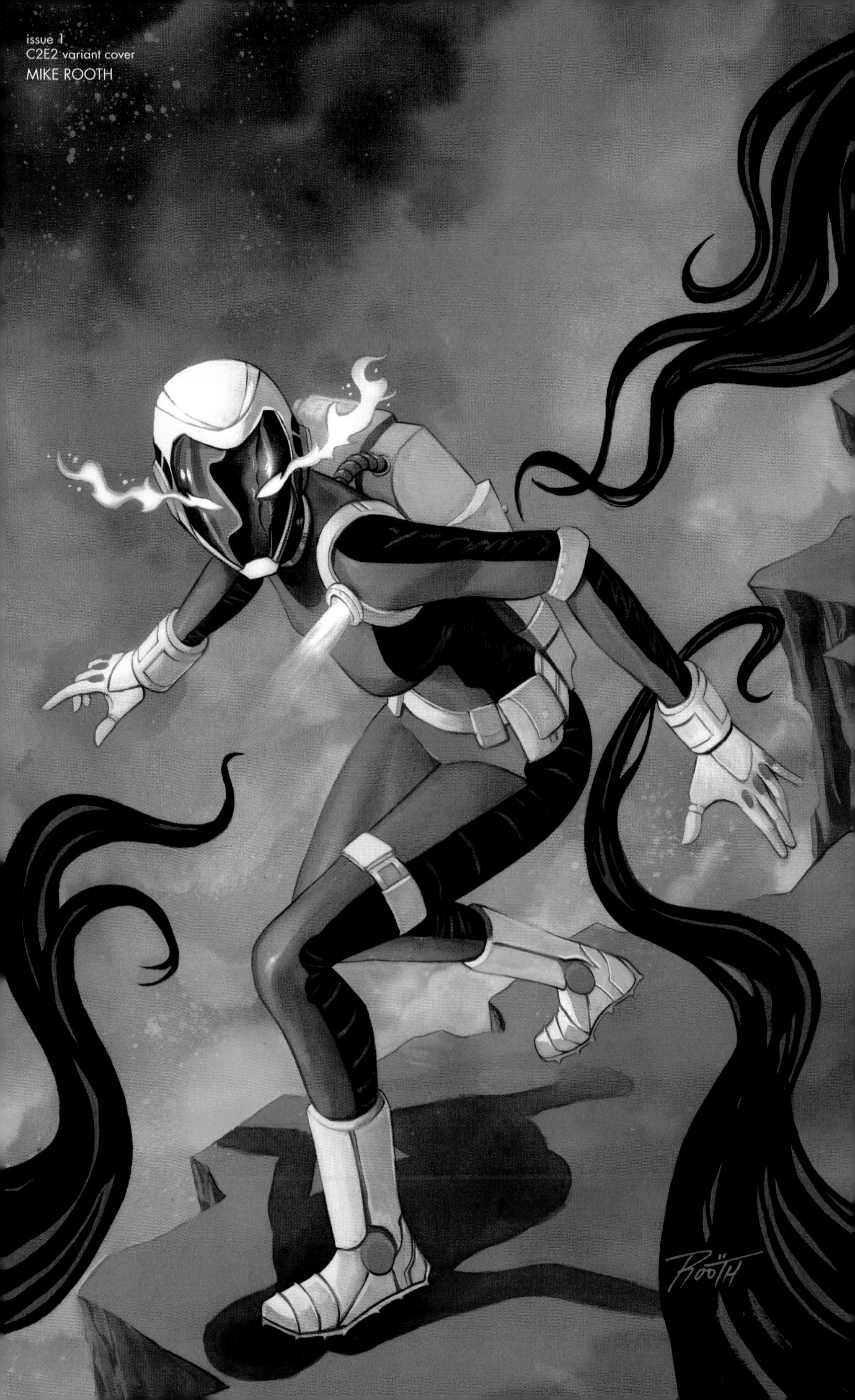
ROOTH

issue 1
C2E2 variant cover
MIKE ROOTH

CHECK OUT THESE GREAT AFTERSHOCK
COLLECTIONS!

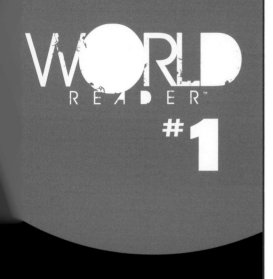

WORLD READER

#1

PAGES 2&3 PROCESS

script by
JEFF LOVENESS

PAGES 2-3: DOUBLE SPLASH PAGE

PANEL 1:
It's a dead world. A shattered alien civilization. A husk of itself. The rubble is all that remains of life here. Down below, among the weathered destruction, we see other astronauts on Sarah's team, surveying the damage... taking it all in. There's about 7-8 of them on the team total, but you don't have to show them all here. Sarah and the massive planetary devastation should be the focus. Design-wise, let your imagination run wild here. Ever read 'Invisible Cities' by Italo Calvino? It's a wonderful book about Marco Polo recounting the bizarre, foreign places he saw in his travels. Might be a good influence for what we'll be doing here. Our hero will be journeying from dead world to dead world, trying to figure out what happened. Each world has its own unique style. Perhaps this one can look similar to something of a heightened, sci-fi Nineveh. Beautiful gates. Remnants of Hanging Garden Architecture... but bombed out. Scorched. Dead.

CAPTION: But we are now...

(I found some Babylonian architecture references for you online- but absolutely make this world your own. These are just thought starters. Heighten the architecture to sci-fi levels.)

WORLD READER #01   PGS.2-3

layouts by
JUAN DOE

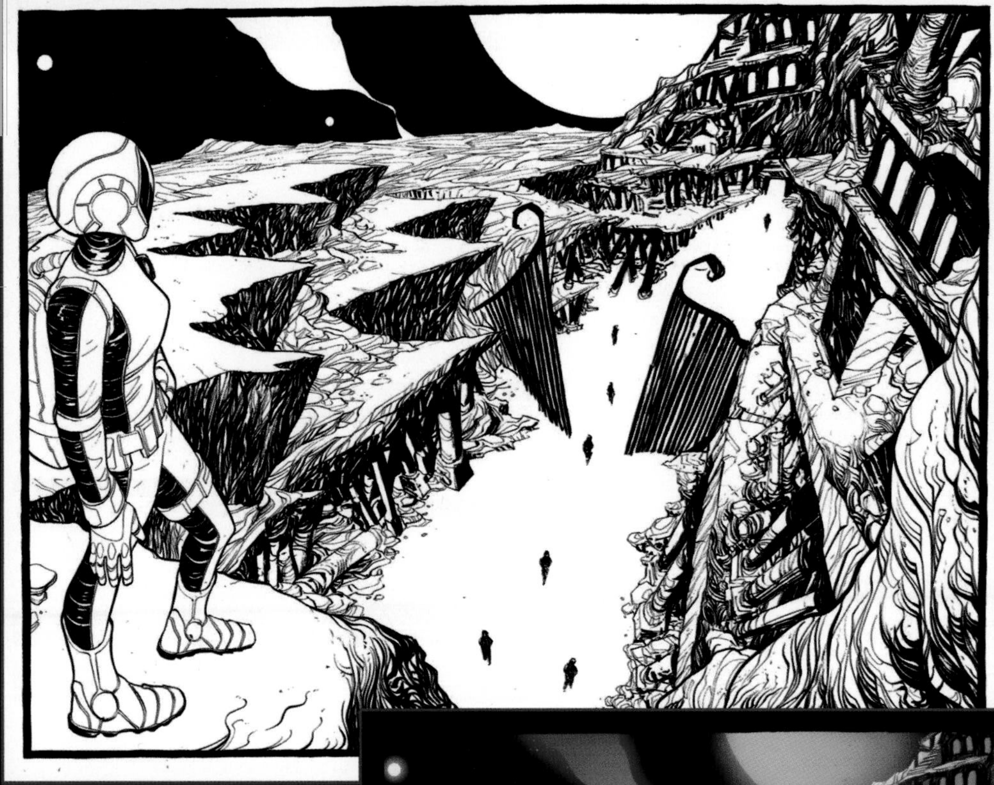

inks by
JUAN DOE

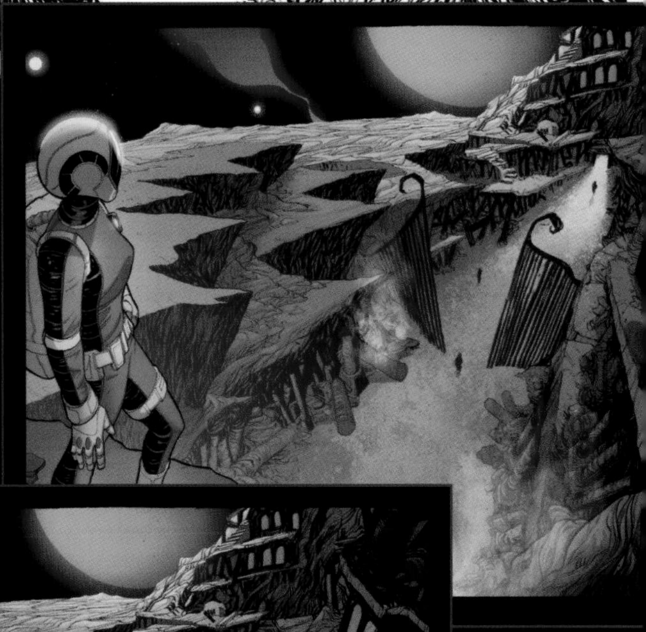

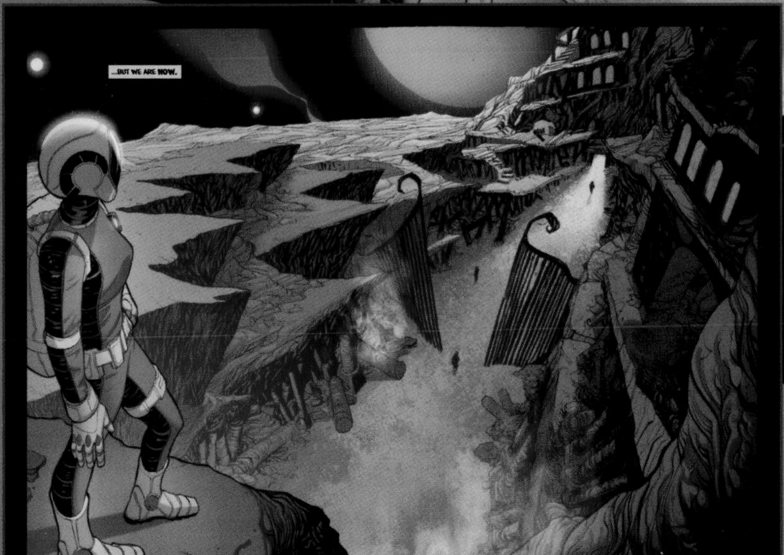
...BUT WE ARE NOW.

lettering by
RACHEL DEERING

PAGE 4:FIVE PANELS

PANEL 1:
Sarah descends from the ridge and moves her way towards the structures.

CAPTION: I never get used to it.
CAPTION: Another dead world.
CAPTION: Just like all the others.

PANEL 2:
She walks among the beautiful, empty gateways - broken and full of vast, empty masonry. Its crafters long dead.

CAPTION: Are we really the last ones left?

PANEL 3
She seems so small and insignificant amidst the ruins. Her helmet emits a small light that's dwarfed by the emptiness. (Her space-suit is sleeker than contemporary astronaut suits. This is humanity in the near-future. We have space travel locked down a bit more... but not by much.)

CAPTION: And if so... what happened?
CAPTION: Who lived here?

PANEL 4:
She finds herself lost in thought as she walks through a broken colonnade.

CAPTION: What did they believe?
CAPTION: Who did they love?

PANEL 5:
Sarah's eyes start to glow with ethereal ability. We get a glimpse of her special ability.

CAPTION: ...Guess that's where I come in.

PAGE 5:FOUR PANELS

PANEL 1:
Profile shot. She kneels down in concentration.

PANEL 2:
Her spirit leaves her physical body.

PANEL 3
Her essence looks around, and the world is different

SARAH: Hey there.

PANEL 4:
She's entered [redacted]

[redacted] Sarah enters to [redacted] of those that remain. In short, let's just say this is "Ghost Whisperer in Space."

While in this mode, she sees [redacted] before. Some are potent, some are ebbing away. Right now... there's not a lot.

Make the hazy, ethereal presences of the "Aliens" of this world human in nature. In general, all [redacted] accouterments as you see fit... but probably nothing [redacted] more or less... like we're all from the same blueprint.

That'll come into play in later issues.

SARAH: What'd I miss?

cript by
EFF LOVENESS

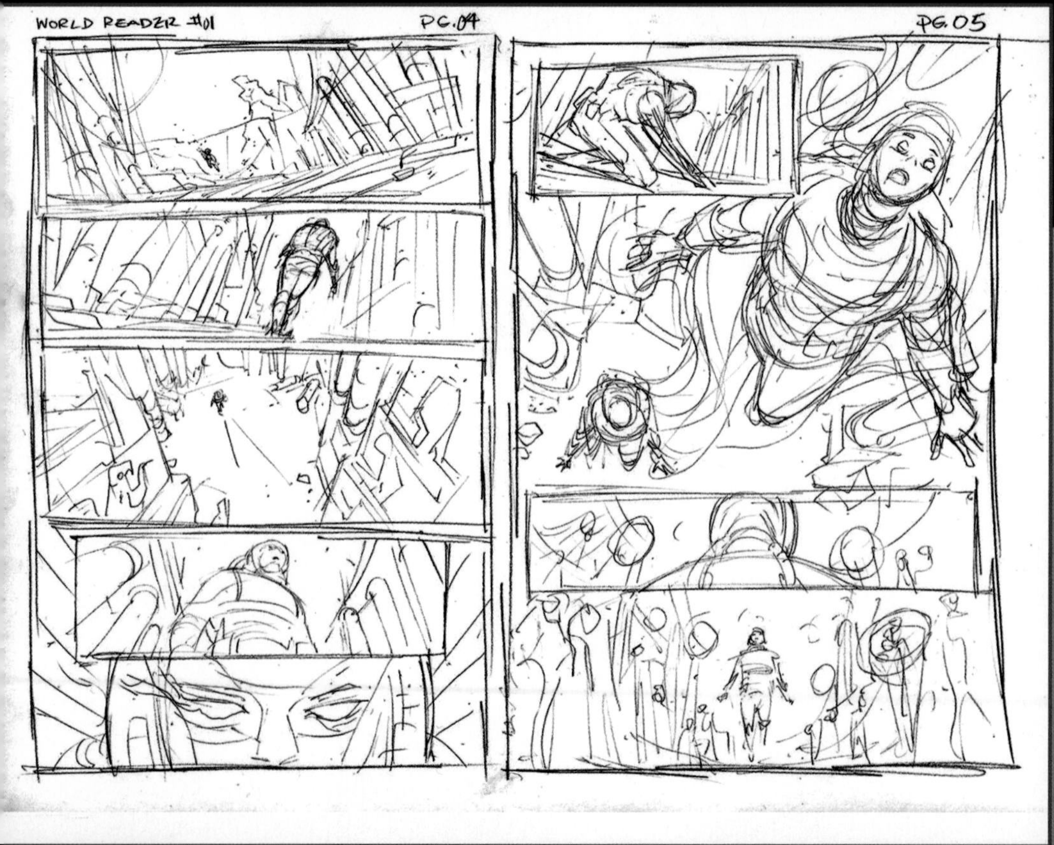

WORLD READER #01
PG.04
PG.05

layouts by
JUAN DOE

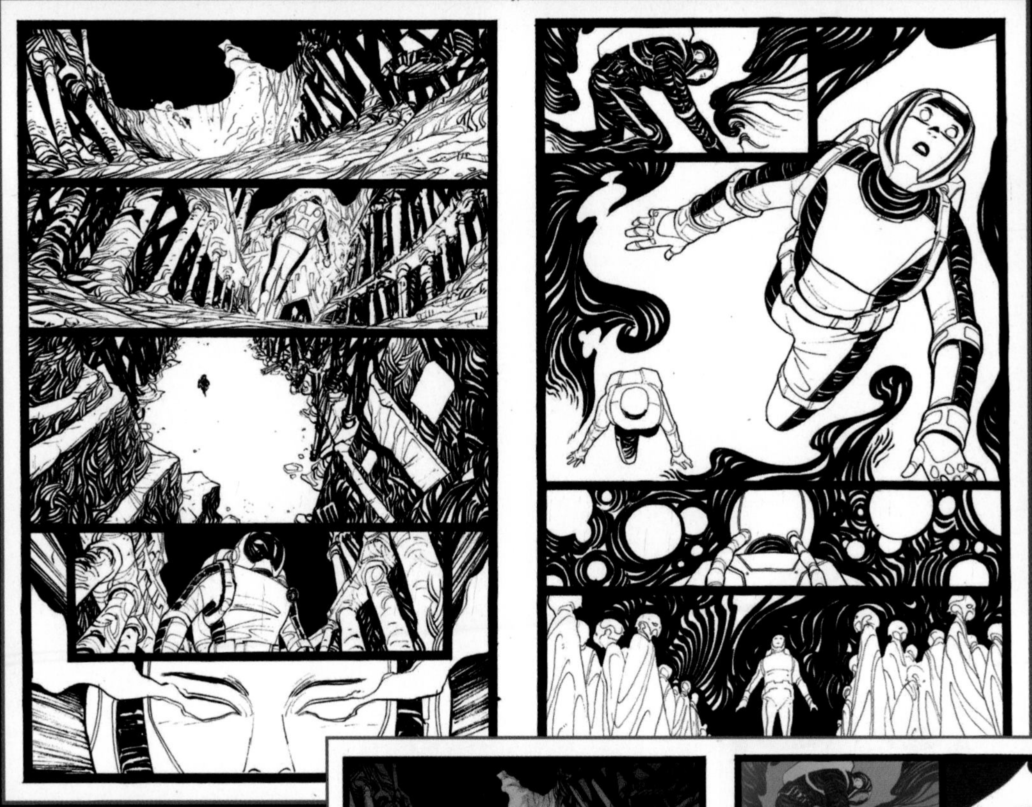

inks by
JUAN DOE

PAGES 4&5 PROCESS

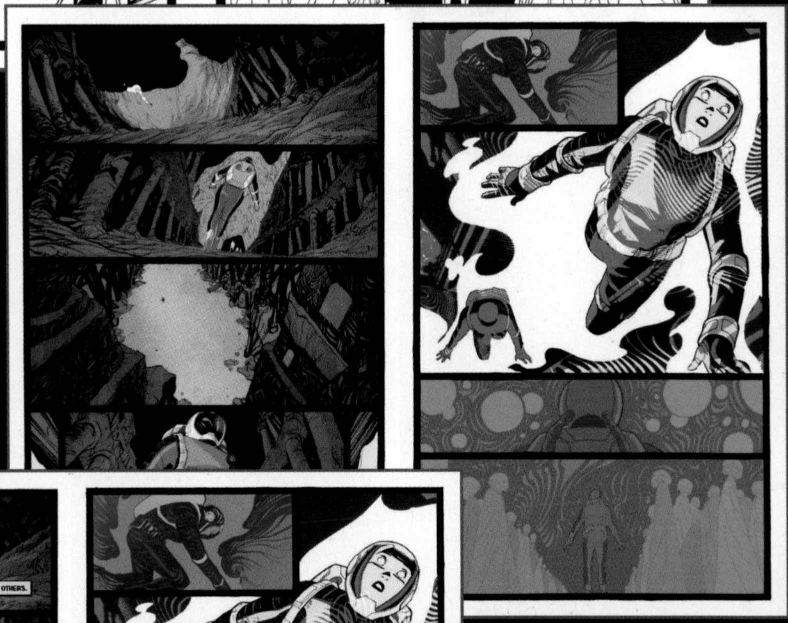

colors by
JUAN DOE

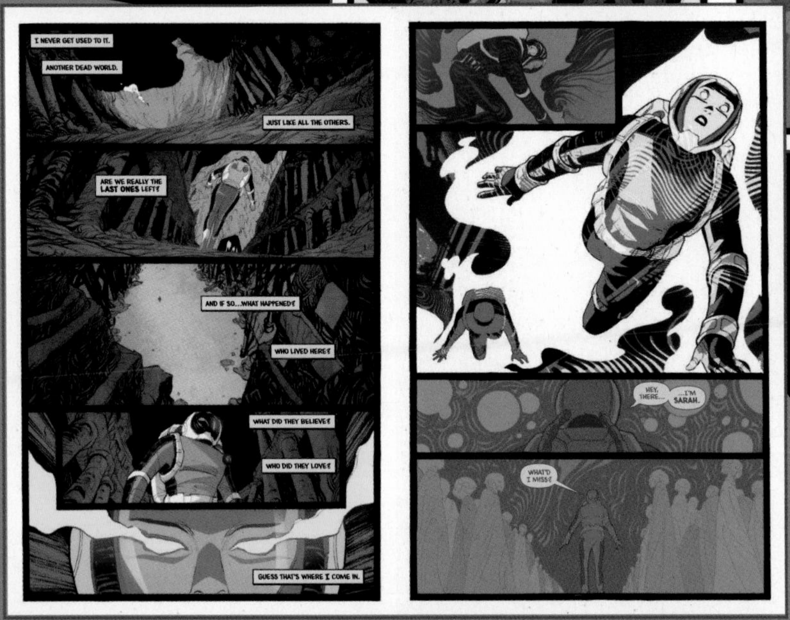
I NEVER GET USED TO IT.
ANOTHER DEAD WORLD.
JUST LIKE ALL THE OTHERS.
ARE WE REALLY THE LAST ONES LEFT?
AND IF SO...WHAT HAPPENED?
WHO LIVED HERE?
WHAT DID THEY BELIEVE?
WHO DID THEY LOVE?
GUESS THAT'S WHERE I COME IN.
HEY, THERE...
...I'M SARAH.
WHAT'D I MISS?

lettering by
RACHEL DEERING

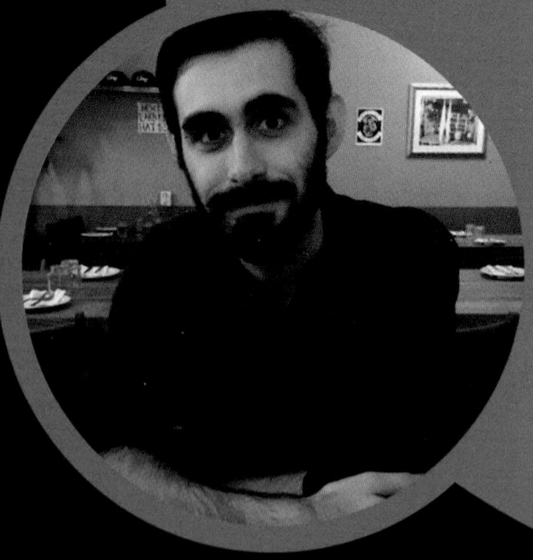

JEFF LOVENESS writer

@JeffLoveness

Jeff Loveness is an Emmy-nominated writer for *Jimmy Kimmel Live!, The Oscars, The Emmys,* The Onion News Network, and Marvel Comics. His Marvel work featured critically acclaimed runs on *Groot* and *Nova*. WORLD READER is his first original, creator-owned series. He lives in Los Angeles, but is from Montgomery Creek—a town you've definitely never heard of.

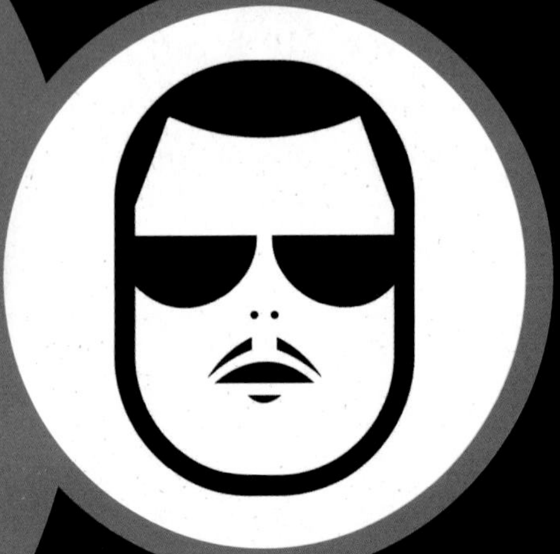

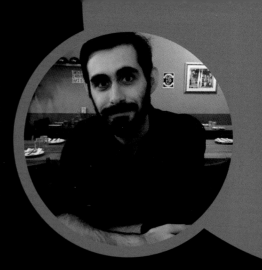

JUAN DOE artist

@JuanDoe

Juan Doe is a professional illustrator with over ten years experience in the comic book industry. He has produced over 100 covers and his sequential highlights include the *Fantastic Four in Puerto Rico* trilogy, *The Legion of Monsters* mini-series for Marvel and *Joker's Asylum: Scarecrow* for DC. He is currently the artist for ANIMOSITY: THE RISE with writer Marguerite Bennett.

RACHEL DEERING letterer

Rachel Deering is an Eisner and Harvey award-nominated writer, editor and letterer. She has worked in some capacity for nearly every publisher in the industry, but is perhaps best known for her efforts on the massive horror anthology *In the Dark* and her writing in *Creepy*. She enjoys collecting arcade cabinets, monster masks and vinyl records in her spare time.

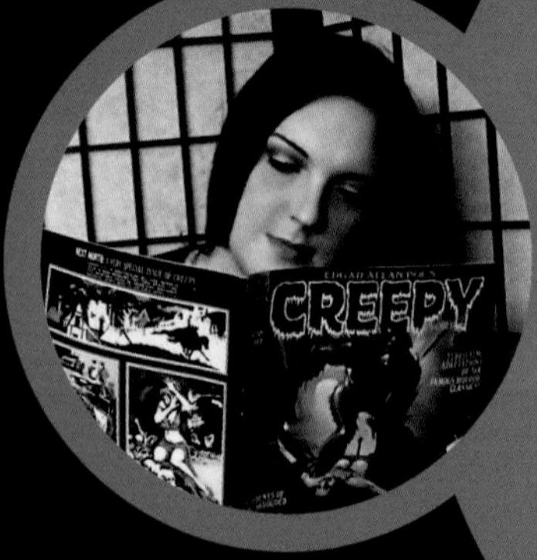
CREEPY

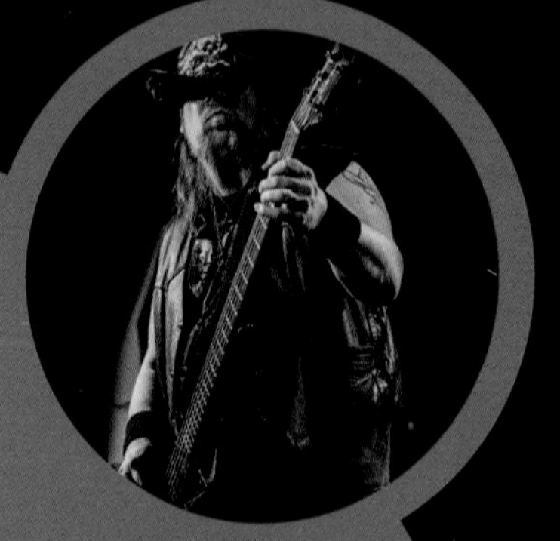

DAVE SHARPE letterer

@DaveLSharpe

Dave grew up a HUGE metalhead, living on Long Island, NY while spending summers in Tallahassee, FL. After reading *Micronauts* (and many other comics), Dave knew he had to have a career in the business. Upon graduating from the Joe Kubert School in 1990, he went on to work at Marvel Comics as an in-house letterer, eventually running their lettering department in the late 90s and early 00s. Over the years, Dave has lettered hundreds of comics, such as *Spider-Girl, Exiles, She-Hulk* and *The Defenders* for Marvel, and *Green Lantern, Harley Quinn, Sinestro* and *Batgirl* for DC Comics. Dave now works on both X-O *Manowar* and *Faith* for Valiant Comics in addition to his lettering duties on AfterShock's BLOOD BLISTER and WORLD READER. Dave also plays bass and is way more approachable than he looks.

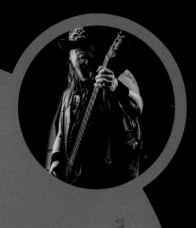